THE UNDERWORLD

By

Alfred T. Overstreet

————————————

Printed in the United States of America
By Evangel Books Publishing Company
863 Monarch Drive
Corona, CA 92879

THE UNDERWORLD

Chapter I
Pulled Down By The Buffer

John Frank was angry! He yanked and swung and guided the heavy floor buffer from side to side as it spun and whirred over the brilliantly polished surface of the dining room floor. Back and forth and faster and faster he yanked and pushed and pursued the buffer like a wild man. He brought the buffer bumping up against the wall in one swing, and then swung the buffer back in a wide arc to come bumping up against a dining table piled high with chairs. Back and forth, faster and faster, he yanked and swung and pursued the buffer.

This was not like John. Everyone at Lynwood Christian Elementary School knew John as a helpful, friendly, easygoing man—never upset, never angry, and never destructive in his work.

John was maintenance man at Lynwood Christian Elementary School. And on his job as maintenance man he worked everywhere around the school, and was loved and appreciated by teachers and students alike for his friendliness and helpful attitude.

But at the close of this particular workday he had finished some ten minutes before clock-out time and stood waiting in front of the clock to punch out. The Pastor saw him standing idle, and said, "John, you shouldn't be here before quitting time. Get back to work until it's quitting time."

"But, Pastor," said John, "I just now finished the last job I was on. And if I were to set up now for a new job it would take me until way past clock-out time with nothing accomplished."

"Get back to work," the Pastor said. "It's not time to clock-out yet." John looked at the clock. It was now five minutes to clock-out time. Then John looked at his Pastor. But his Pastor showed no mercy.

John turned away from the clock, grabbed his utility belt, and tromped down the stairs to the basement. He jerked the buffer out of the storage closet, plugged the cord into the receptacle, moved three tables to one side and piled chairs high on each one; and then continued once again the job he had finished just a few minutes earlier.

Back and forth, over and over again, the buffer flew over the polished surface of the dining room floor. Ten minutes passed. But John was now oblivious to time and continued to pursue the whirring buffer over the luminous surface of the floor.

The floor suddenly began to shimmer and ripple with bright waves of light. And as John pursued the buffer he saw that bright waves of luminous water were rippling away from the floor where the buffer was spinning, and he saw that he was now standing in shimmering waves of translucent water.

A familiar voice cried out from the foot of the stairs, "Brother John, what are you doing working so late?" It was the Becker twins, Bob and Bill Becker, with their little sister, Alice. They ran a few steps toward him, then stopped, and watched in wonder.

The buffer was now swimming in its path through the luminous water. And as John hung on to its handles they saw him sink almost to his knees in shimmering waves of translucent water.

Alice screamed and ran back up the stairs.

"We're coming," yelled Bob. "We'll help get you out."

"No. Stay where you are," yelled John. "You might get stuck too."

But Bob and Bill were already running into the rippling waves of water.

Back down the stairs rushed Alice, followed by Jed Truly, Science and Bible Teacher for Lynwood Christian Elementary School.

Jed stopped at the foot of the stairs, and surveyed the scene before him. He saw that John was now up to his waist in water, with a twin on each side of him struggling to lift him out. And as they struggled, they too sank deep into the waters. "Oh, no!" he cried; and ran past Alice toward the three.

Alice followed right behind him.

Jed now struggled to lift the three before him out of the waters—but instead, sank deep down into the waters with them. Little Alice climbed onto Jed's back and wrapped her arms around his neck.

John's hands held onto the handles of the buffer as if glued there. The buffer gave a high-pitched whirring scream as it dove deep into the bright shimmering waters, pulling John down with it.

John felt the shimmering waters close over his head.

Next, were Bob and Bill—they felt the shimmering waters close over their heads as they held tightly to John.

Next was Jed Truly, Bible and Science teacher for Lynwood Christian Elementary School; he was pulled down and felt the shimmering waters close over his head.

And clutched tightly to Jed Truly was poor little Alice. She too was carried down and felt the bright shimmering waters close over her head.

Chapter II
Into A Dark Tunnel

Down through the translucent waters they sank, pulled down by the still screaming buffer. Then suddenly they broke through and fell to the ground some six feet below them. From there they rolled down some ten feet more before they came up against a pile of freshly dug earth. Above them hung the buffer, swinging gently back and forth, suspended from its cord.

They stood up and began to brush the dirt from their clothes. They were standing in a newly dug tunnel. There was a light far off in the distance. But where they stood it was so dark they could not make out each other's form.

"Everybody OK?" spoke Jed into the darkness.

"I'm scared," whimpered Alice. She heard two voices that sounded like her brothers and asked, "Bob, Bill, is that you?"

Bob and Bill moved toward her. "Yes, it's us," said Bob. "Don't be afraid. We won't let anything happen to you."

Alice moved closer to her brothers, and speaking to no one in particular, said, "It's dark in here. Where are we?"

"I don't know," said Jed. "John, what do you think?"

"I don't know. I really don't know. But there's a light there in the distance. Let's head in that direction and see if that's a way out of here"

John led the way as they felt their way through the darkness. They had advanced only a few feet when John stopped suddenly. "Hey, I forgot!" He cried out. "We don't need to stumble around here in the dark…" He fumbled at his utility belt, and pulled out his flashlight.

"Ssssh! Did you hear something?" asked Jed.

They all stared into the darkness. Yes, they did hear something. Something that seemed to get closer, something moving! Chills ran up and down their backs, making the hair stand up and prickle on the top of their heads.

They waited tensely, staring nervously into the darkness, as the noise got closer and closer. Then finally a large band of men burst out of nowhere into the tunnel they were in. Although far away, the men were clearly visible, for a torchbearer followed close behind them, with his torch held high.

The men were marching at a quick pace, and singing a shameful song. As they drew closer, the five Christians observed that many of the men held shovels. Others held buckets with ropes. One held nothing, and was dancing with shameless abandon to the lewd song they sang.

Then, when the band of men had drawn quite close they suddenly realized they were not alone—and were being watched—and they came to an abrupt stop. After a hurried huddle, they gave a loud shout and rushed toward the five Christians.

Some ran toward the five with shovels lifted, ready to strike them. Others ran with buckets lifted, ready to strike them. And as they rushed upon them, they cursed them, and threatened to kill them. And so, in this manner the little men (for they were little men) began to circle their prisoners.

John watched them carefully as he returned the flashlight to his utility belt. Then, without taking his eyes from them, he pulled two screwdrivers, a box cutter, a crescent wrench, and a hammer from his utility belt. He gave screwdrivers to Bob and Bill. He gave the box cutter to Jed. He gave the hammer to little Alice. And he kept the crescent wrench. "I hope they don't try to harm us," he said. "But if they do, use these to protect yourselves."

The torchbearer now stood to one side, with his torch held high, while the little men continued to circle the five prisoners and threaten them with death.

(If these men were not attractive in their character, neither were they attractive in their physique. They were small men, with big heads, and slit, almost closed eyes.)

"Who are you, and what are you doing here?" demanded the smallest man among them.

The prisoners stood there as much in amazement as in fear of these little men. Alice observed that the one who had just spoken was no bigger than she was, and had a huge head, which was way too big to be on such a little man.

The five stood there, not knowing what to say or who should respond to the little man. Then Jed turned to John, with a questioning look. John nodded his head toward Jed, and stepped back.

Jed faced the little man and very slowly began: "Well, sir, I can tell you who we are—but I don't really know if I can tell you what we are doing here." He indicated John, and said, "That's John Frank. He's the maintenance man at our school up above us." Then he nodded toward the Becker children, and said, "Those are the Becker twins, Bob and Bill Becker. And the girl, next to them, is their little sister, Alice Becker. They are students at our school up above us. And my name," he continued, "is Jed Truly. I teach Science and Bible at our school up above us..."

"I know all our teachers," cut in the little man quickly, "but I don't know you! You're an imposter! I will ask you once again, who are you? And what are you doing here in this new tunnel? How did you get here?"

"I told you. I'm Jed Truly. I teach Bible and Science at Lynwood Christian Elementary School. But I don't know what we are doing here, or how we got here—except that we dropped down from above into this tunnel right back there where it begins...uh...I mean right back there where it ends. But I have no idea at all what we are doing here. Or how we can get out of here. Can you please tell us where we are and how we can get out of here?"

"Liar! Liar! You're a liar. Bah! You dropped down from above into our new tunnel! Tell the truth. Who are you? And how did you get here?"

And with these words the little man drew back his fist and drove it into Jed's stomach. Jed doubled over in pain, gasping for breath.

The little man watched in pleasure at Jed's pain. "Tie their hands behind their backs," he commanded. "We'll take them to the Dean of Education to see what he will do with them."

"No!" cried Jed. He reached out, grabbed the little man, wrapped an arm around him, and with his other hand pressed the box cutter to the little man's nose. "If you touch one of these children, I'll cut your nose off! And if I have to, I'll cut out your eyes! Tell your men to leave us alone! Tell them not to touch us! Do it now!"

The little man struggled to free himself from Jed's grasp. But his efforts were vain. For Jed held him in an iron grip. When the little man saw that he could not free himself and that at any moment this big man might cut off his nose and cut out his eyes, he said, "OK, we won't touch you. But we are taking you to the Dean of Education to see what he will do."

"Alright, but I'm going to tie you up so you can't do us any harm." And turning to John he said, "John, take one of their ropes, and tie this man's hands behind his back, and give me the other end of the rope."

8

Chapter III
Human Government Is Ordained Of God

Two groups now advanced very slowly back down the tunnel.

The torch man, who had followed the little men before, now led them, holding his torch high above his head. And the little men followed him, staying as far away from the light of his torch as they possibly could.

John Frank led the second group, walking alongside the little man. And behind them, with the rope held securely in one hand, came Jed Truly with the three children.

Bill walked alongside Jed, deep in thought. He had a question. And he had to have an answer. He had been thinking about the threat of Jed to cut off the little man's nose, and even cut out his two eyes. And he had been thinking about the commandment of Jesus, and how we are to treat those who mistreat us. "Brother Truly," he said, "Jesus said that if someone smites us on the right cheek, we are to turn to him the other cheek also. Wouldn't it be wrong for you to...uh...to cut off the little man's nose and to put out his eyes, like you said you would—when Jesus said to turn the other cheek, and to bless those that curse you?"

"No. It wouldn't be wrong at all. It would be right! You see, Bill, every law, in both God's government and in man's government, *has a penalty* for those who break it.

"But *God's government is probationary*. There is *no penalty now* for breaking God's law. But under *human government*, *all penalties are inflicted now, during this life*. And *can even be inflicted while the criminal is in the act of committing a crime*—such as in the need to kill the enemy during war; and the necessary killing of murderers, who are shooting down innocent people.

"It was my duty to tell him he would suffer a severe penalty if he or his men mistreated us, especially if he mistreated you children. There must be a severe penalty for men who do evil, to restrain them from doing evil."

"But Brother Truly, does that mean we are not to turn the other cheek? Does it mean we are not to bless them that curse us? Does it mean it's OK to hate our enemies and curse them that curse us?"

"No, Bill! We are to live by everything Jesus said. And the Apostle Paul says the same thing that Jesus said. He says, 'Bless them which persecute you: bless, and curse not…Recompense to no man evil for evil…Dearly beloved, avenge not yourselves, but rather give place unto wrath: for it is written, Vengeance is mine; I will repay, sayeth the Lord.'" Romans 12:14, 17, 19

"But didn't you promise you would take vengeance on him when you said you would cut off his nose and put out his eyes?"

"Oh, No, Bill! I did not promise to take vengeance on him. I promised to make him pay a penalty for any harm they might do to you. It would be wicked for me to allow them to harm you. You heard them threaten to kill us when they first rushed upon us. And if I let them tie you up and harm you, when I have the power to keep them from it, it would be wickedness and injustice in me. Do you think that the policeman who kills the man, who is shooting down little children on a school playground—to keep him from killing even more children—has done wrong in the eyes of God?

"How would you like it if there were no policemen to stop wicked men from doing evil? Now I'm not a policeman, but I do have the same authority as a policeman would have under these circumstances. John and I are in the place of policemen now. We have the authority and the power and the solemn duty to use all the force in our power to protect you children from these evil men.

"The Scribes and the Pharisees were very religious men, but many of them were evil men; and they purposely quoted the penalty for breaking the law, as if it were the precept, to justify their acts of violence toward others. They said, 'An eye for an eye, and a tooth for a tooth' to justify their violence toward others.

"And some evil men today go to the other extreme, and purposely quote the precept, as if it were the penalty, in order to make the death penalty and all war wrong. They quote the words of Jesus where he said, 'Do not kill'; and then they say, 'See, the death penalty is wrong, and all war is wrong.'

"But we know that when Jesus said, 'Do not kill,' he was not teaching that the death penalty is wrong; neither was he teaching that it is wrong to go to war and kill the enemy to protect your country.

"For God says in Genesis that the penalty for murder is the death of the murderer: 'Whoso sheddeth man's blood, by man shall his blood be shed.' Genesis 9:6

"So God says we have the duty to put murderers to death!

"That is why I said it would be just and right for me to cut off his nose and put out his eyes. They had no just reason to threaten you with death. And it would have been wicked for me to allow them to tie you up and possibly kill you. So as long as I had the power to prevent them from doing so, it was my duty under God to do it."

*** *** ***

During this conversation they came to the light they had seen at the end of the tunnel. It turned out to be a low burning torch, which they passed just before they made a left turn in the tunnel. They went a hundred feet more, came upon another low burning torch, and made a right turn in the tunnel. And, after this they continued on in the same direction they had been going in before.

Their progress down the tunnel had been very slow even before they made the second turn in the tunnel. But very soon after the second turn they were brought to a complete standstill! For every one of the little men refused to be the closest one to the torchbearer. There was an obstinate and perverse stubbornness in every one of them in refusing to be the closest one to the torchbearer. And this perverse refusal to be the closest one to the torchbearer resulted in all the little men being strung out further and further away from the torchbearer. And this forced the five Christians further and further back into the darkness of the tunnel, where they could not see.

Finally, John, being brought to a halt in the darkness, and seeing the need for more light, switched on his flashlight. Jed and the children welcomed the light with gladness.

But there was an immediate outcry from all the little men. And they fled in terror from the light. In a bunch they forced their way past the torchbearer, knocking him to the ground. Then they continued running down the tunnel until they had penetrated the darkness, where they finally stopped.

At the very same time, the little man with his hands tied behind his back screamed and fell to his knees; and with his eyes tightly closed, threw his head to the ground, moaning as if he were dying.

"What's wrong? What's the matter with you?" John demanded.

When the little man seemed not to hear, but continued to moan, with his head pushing against the ground, John cried out, and demanded again, "What's wrong? Tell me what's wrong with you!"

"The light! It hurts! Turn it off!"

"But we can't turn it off. It's dark in here. And we can't see!"

"Please turn it off. I'll call the torch man to give you light. But please turn that bright light off. It hurts my eyes!"

Chapter IV
The Explosion

Now they continued down the tunnel in a new order: The band of little men led the way, followed by the torchbearer. Behind the torchbearer followed John and the little man with his hands tied behind his back. Then followed Jed and the three children.

Jed now spoke to the little man. "How much further do we have to go before we get out of this tunnel?"

The little man turned to Jed with a puzzled look on his face. "There is no way out of this tunnel. When you leave this tunnel, you will only go into another tunnel. There is no way out."

"But there has to be a way out of here and back to where we live!"

"No, there is no way out! And don't tell me you dropped into this tunnel from up above! You are a liar! I know who you are and where you came from. You came from the Bright Regions. You are one of those religious fanatics from that place. All of our problems come from the religious fanatics in the Bright Regions. And I know you are one of them. Your own mouth testifies that you are one of them, for you said that you teach the Bible; and the Bible is taught only in that place of religious fanaticism. When we come to the Dean of Education, I will testify that you are from the Bright Regions and that you teach the Bible, and you will die for teaching lies out of the Bible."

Jed considered what the little man had said. The little man had said there was no way out of this tunnel. But he had also mentioned the Bright Regions. Could the Bright Regions be a way out of this tunnel and into their world up above? There just had to be a way out of here and back to where they lived! There just had to be a way back home!

Now as they continued their walk up the tunnel Jed could see a dim light up ahead. And he saw that the little men up ahead had quickened their pace, and were drawing quite close to a large opening from which came the dim light. In fact, they also had quickened their pace, and now were quite close to the large opening and its light. "Could that," thought Jed, "be a way out of the tunnel and back home?" Then, even as Jed was wondering about the opening just ahead and a way back home, an explosion roared through the tunnel.

The little men who were closest to the opening were all blown from their feet by the explosion. Some men further back were also blown from their feet by the explosion. And the five prisoners, still further back, were either knocked down by the blast, or quickly fell to the ground in fear of the blast. For the flash and roar of the explosion struck terror to the hearts of everyone there. And added to this was the terrifying sound of bullets striking the shovels and buckets carried by the little men, and bullets thudding into the bodies of the men in the tunnel.

And then, to compound the awful terror, immediately after the flash and blast and roar, and the sound of bullets striking men, there arose in the dark confines of the tunnel the pitiful sounds of men crying out in fear, and pain, and agony. And along with the many cries of fear, and pain, and agony—was the stark cry of a dying man, crying out to God to save his soul from hell.

Chapter V
Professor Blazer, The Mad Scientist

John felt the bullet strike his side as he was thrown off balance by the blast. He sank down onto his back, groaning at the awful pain, and wondering if Jed and the children had been hurt also.

The light from the large opening had gone out with the explosion. So there was total darkness, except for a feeble light from the torch, which lay on the ground ahead of him, and still smoldered with a dying flame.

Out of the darkness, John heard the voice of Jed, "Alice, are you all right? Bob, Bill, are you all right? John, are you all right?"

Alice was the first to respond. She poured out her fears with convulsive sobs: "Are we all going to die? It's so dark in here. I want to go home."

Jed spoke soothingly to Alice. "Alice, we are going home. We all want to go home. God will help us, and we'll soon be home."

"Yes," agreed Bob. "God will help us."

"That's right," came the voice of Bill, "God will help us."

Finally John spoke: "I'm so glad to hear your voices! Because now I know you're all alive. Were any of you hit by the bullets?" When no one answered, John continued: "I was hit on my left side, and it hurts something awful. But I don't know how bad I'm hurt. I'm afraid the little men are hurt real bad. I'm afraid many are dead."

Just then, a light shone again through the large opening just ahead, and the five Christians looked that way. A torch man stepped through the large opening with his torch held high. Then a very little man, with a very big head, and adorned with a goatee, staggered out from the large opening. He surveyed the scene of misery and death, then staggered back to lean against the wall, and slowly shook his head from side to side.

John stood to his feet, and stifled a groan. He yelled to the torch man, "Hey, torch man, come on over here. There are men hurt real bad over here. Bring your torch so we can see what needs to be done for them." Then he stepped forward and picked up the torch lying beside the torch man. Slowly the torch began to catch and burn, until it burned normally. He held the torch over the torch man. He was dead!

Wiping tears from his eyes, he turned away. Then he turned back! Had he seen the torch man move? Yes! The torch man had moved! He was getting up! He was not dead!

"John," the torch man now said, "I heard you say you had been hit, and that it hurt awful—but you are on your feet! You don't look as if you've been hurt bad at all."

John felt for the spot where he had been hit, and felt no blood. Then he examined himself more closely and saw the mark where a large bullet had hit his utility belt, but had not gone through. "Praise the Lord," he said, "I'm not hurt bad at all!"

The torch man smiled, and reaching up took the torch from John's hand. He turned toward the large opening, where the little man with the goatee stood, and went directly to him. John, Jed, and the three children followed him.

The little man with the goatee still stood against the wall with a confused look on his face. He stared vacantly at the scene of destruction before him. When John beheld him up close, the thought came to him that he was looking into the eyes of a madman.

John spoke to him about the urgent need of the suffering and dying: "Sir, can you do something for these men who are wounded, hurting, and dying? Can you get a doctor for them? Some of them are dead already and others are still alive and suffering. Can you do something for them?" The little man hesitated for a long time, deep in thought— thought that seemed painful and difficult for him. And then finally blurted out: "I don't know what to do. I don't know where to get a doctor. Send the torch man. He should know. It's his job to know where everything is in the tunnels." And with these words the little man staggered forward a step and then fell back against the wall.

Then John, directing his words to the torch man, asked, "torch man, do you think you can find a doctor for the wounded here?"

"Sure! But, why not send my friend out there to find a doctor? He's a torch man too, and knows every area of the tunnels. He knows where the Medical Department is." And, having said these words, he looked toward the torch man, who was now standing out among the wounded and dead. And, lifting his voice, he said, "Hey, Lighter Man, you are commanded to go immediately to the Medical Department to bring a doctor and as much help as is needed for the wounded here."

"Who says so?"

"I do. And Professor Blazer the Head Astronomer of the Astronomy Department does. And Big John, the Maintenance Man does. Now get going. You haven't got any time to lose. And remember, go to the Medical Department and ask them to send all the help needed for the wounded and dying here."

After sending Lighter Man on his way, the torch man turned back to John and the man with the goatee. "Big John," he said, "this is Professor Blazer, the Head Astronomer of the Astronomy Department. Professor Blazer, this is Big John, the Maintenance Man at their school. And Big John, If you want to know my name, my name is Head Lighter Man."

And with these words Head Lighter Man stepped back. John shook hands with Professor Blazer, and indicating Jed, he said, "Professor Blazer, this is Jed Truly. He teaches Science and Bible at our school. And these children attend the school where we work. That's Bill, that's Bob, and that's Alice, their little sister."

Then John asked the question that was on everyone's mind: "Professor Blazer, what caused the explosion? And, where did that hail of bullets come from? Please tell us what has happened."

The Professor swayed on his feet; opened his mouth to speak, then closed it, and motioned for them to follow him. He then walked back through the large opening to the center of a great vaulted room, where he waited until everyone stood beside him. When the five Christians stood beside the Professor they observed that there were four tunnels that emptied into the huge vaulted room. And they saw that wreckage was strewn all about the room. The vaulted ceiling and walls were pock marked with holes. Close to the wall on one side of the room still stood the wreckage of a tiny observation room. Near the center of the room was a blackened concrete block on which the explosion had been set off. Burnt matter still smoldered near the observation room. And here and there could be seen various sizes of ball bearings lying on the floor.

"I set off the explosion." said the Professor with pride. "It was a scientific experiment to replicate the Big Bang which took place billions of years ago.

"As you know, the expanding universe as it exists today is the result of a gigantic explosion, the Big Bang, that took place some 12 to 20 billion years ago. Our knowledge of cosmology tells us that the creation of the universe, and the present expansion of the universe, began with that gigantic explosion billions of years ago. My experiment was to simply prove the fact that the Big Bang was the cause of the expanding universe as it exists today."

Jed could contain himself no longer! "Professor Blazer, the Big Bang Theory defies reason, reality, and the immutable laws of physics. Even children know it is foolish and impossible. Your theory is not science. It is speculation and superstition. It is the same kind of speculation and superstition that made some men believe that the earth was flat and that men could sail too far out on the ocean and fall off the edge of the earth. It is the superstitious belief of men who have abandoned their God-given faculty of reason and can no longer think! Professor Blazer, I feel sorry for you! There is not a scintilla of science in the whole Big Bang Theory! How could you be so foolish as to corrupt the true science of astronomy with the foolishness of the Big Bang Theory?"

Jed saw the pained look on the face of the Professor, but continued without stopping: "Professor Blazer, there is a fundamental problem for all true scientists with this Big Bang Theory of yours. It is a problem that even little children can see makes it impossible. Explosions do not throw things into precise orbits and precise and systematic order with other orbiting and systematically moving heavenly bodies. Order, and precision, and system are the work of a Creator, and not the work of an explosion! Explosions only cause destruction, disorder, and chaos! Look around you, man! Look at the destruction, disorder, and chaos in this room! Look outside where men are dead and dying because of the explosion you set off, and then tell me that you think a gigantic explosion created the universe as it exists today!

"But the Big Bang Theory has another problem: It does not explain creation! It is absolutely silent as to the nature and composition of the universe before the Big Bang, and how the creation, that existed before the Big Bang, got here in the first place.

"You do admit, Professor Blazer, that *something existed* before your supposed Big Bang! How do you explain how that *something* got here?"

"Oh, you must be one of those religious fanatics who believe the Bible," said the Professor smugly. "Only the gullible and the simpleton believe the Bible. I am a scientist and I must have real evidence before I can believe."

"Why, you hypocrite! You do have evidence, and you ignore it and close your eyes to it and thrust it away from you! You are an astronomer and you know the order and the system and the precise orbits and systematic movements of the heavenly bodies, and yet you say you must have real evidence before you will believe? You hypocrite! No wonder Jesus said of the hypocritical teachers of his day, 'Woe unto you, scribes and Pharisees, hypocrites! for ye compass sea and land to make one proselyte, and when he is made, ye make him twofold more the child of hell than yourselves...Ye serpents, ye generation of vipers, how can ye escape the damnation of hell?' (Matthew 23:15, 33) Professor Blazer, you are not a scientist! You have irrefutable evidence, and you thrust it from you!"

Head Lighter Man saw the pained look on Professor Blazer's face. He saw the Professor throw up his arms as if he might hold back the words that were pouring from Jed's mouth. And he stepped closer to the Professor to get a better look at him. "Get back, you fool," screamed the Professor. "You know I don't like the light! You know the light hurts my eyes. Take your torch and stand back where you were. And take your friends with you. This man," he indicated Jed, "thinks he knows more about astronomy than I do. Why, I have a Ph.D. in astronomy. I am an expert on the subject, and he thinks he can teach me?"

Obediently, Head Lighter Man backed away from Professor Blazer. But Jed still felt compelled to pour out the truth to Professor Blazer.

"Professor Blazer you stand smugly by and say that only the gullible and only the simpleton believe the Bible.

"But you have it all wrong, Professor Blazer. It is not the Bible believer who is a simpleton, but it is you, who is a simpleton; and it is all atheists like you who are simpletons. For you reject **what you know is the truth**. You reject evidence that is overwhelming. You close your eyes to the undeniable reality of the creation. You do this because you hate the reality that there is a Creator who created you in his own image and likeness with a rational, moral nature that makes you responsible before him for all your actions. Professor Blazer, you **hate the truth**!

"Professor Blazer, it isn't that you don't know the truth. It's just that you hate the truth, and you close your eyes to it, and push it from you.

"Professor Blazer, you are not ignorant—for if you were ignorant and had no light, you would have an excuse. But you do have light, and you hate it and reject it and cast it from you!

"Jesus said, '*This is the condemnation, that light is come into the world*, and *men loved darkness rather than light*, because their deeds were evil.' John 3:19

"Professor Blazer, aren't you a fool and a simpleton when your own rational nature testifies to you that the heavens and the earth are filled with system and order and design; and you reject the testimony of your own reason and say, 'There is no Creator?'

"Professor Blazer, aren't you a fool and a simpleton when you deny what you know is reality? You know the creation exists. You can see its order and system and design. And if you deny that God-given order, system, and design that you see and know exists, aren't you a fool?

"Professor Blazer, the Christian is not a simpleton for believing the Bible. It is the atheist who is a simpleton for not believing the Bible. For his rational nature testifies to him that the Bible is true.

"But Professor Blazer, you don't need the Bible to know that God exists and that he created the heavens and the earth. You don't need the Bible to know right from wrong and good from evil. You don't need the Bible to know you are responsible and accountable for your deeds. Every man knows these things without the Bible. He knows them, and would know them even if the Bible did not exist!

"Professor Blazer, 'The very heavens **speak** and **declare the glory of God.**' (Psalm 19:1) And the very heavens **tell us** that God will pour out his wrath upon atheists for their unbelief."

> 'For the *wrath of God is **revealed from heaven*** against all ungodliness and unrighteousness of men, who hold (hold down, hold back, suppress) the truth in unrighteousness; ***because that which may be known of God is manifest in them; for God hath shewed it unto them.*** For the invisible things of him from the creation of the world are clearly seen, being understood by the things that are made, even his eternal power and Godhead; so that *they are **without excuse.**'* Romans 1:18-20

"Did you hear that, Professor Blazer?   God says the atheist is without excuse, because he knows the truth *without the Bible*!

"If men did not know the truth without the Bible, they would have an excuse for their ungodliness and atheism. But God says that they do know the truth without the Bible, so that they are without excuse!

"Man does not need the Bible to know it is wrong for him to lie, steal, and commit adultery. He does not need the Bible to know that the thief, the murderer, and the rapist are responsible and accountable for their deeds and should be punished for their crimes. Men do not need the Bible to know that they must have human government over themselves. They know it without the Bible! Professor Blazer, where does this idea for human government come from? It certainly does not come from the Bible alone. No, it comes from man's rational, moral nature. For ungodly men, and men who do not believe the Bible, submit themselves to moral government over themselves.

"Professor Blazer, none of the animals have moral government over themselves! But men do, because men are *created in the image and likeness of God.* The law of God *is **written in their hearts**.* They are free moral agents. They know themselves to be free, and accountable for all their deeds. Every waking hour they are painfully conscious of moral accountability. The Bible calls this consciousness of moral accountability the *conscience*. The Bible says:

> 'When the Gentiles which have not the law (the law written in the Bible), *do by nature* the things contained in the law, these, having not the law, are a law unto themselves: which shew the work of the *law written in their hearts*, **THEIR CONSCIENCE** also bearing witness, and their thoughts the mean while *accusing* or else *excusing* one another; In the day when *God shall judge the secrets of men by Jesus Christ according to my gospel.*' Romans 2:14-16

"Professor Blazer, this explains why all nations have human government over themselves. It is because of the *irresistible convictions* of right and wrong, and good and evil, given to all men in their rational, moral nature. Men cannot escape these *irresistible convictions*, whether they live according to them or not. For they march inexorably from the rational, moral nature God has given to every man.

"Professor Blazer, the devil has deceived you with his false doctrine of atheism. He has deceived you, and he will take you down to hell for believing his lies instead of believing the truth of God!

"Professor, you need to repent and ask God to forgive you. You need to humble your proud heart before God, and believe the gospel of Jesus Christ that you might be saved."

No sooner had Jed called on Professor Blazer to repent and believe the gospel of Jesus Christ, than did Professor Blazer break out into a filthy diatribe against God. He cursed God and cursed the five Christians, who stood before him.

He did not spare little Alice, but heaped hatred and vitriol on her as well. Nor did he spare Head Lighter Man, but cursed him and called on God to damn him for bringing the five Christians before him.

So the six began to back away from the Professor, for the Professor was uncontrolled in his rage. And as the six backed away from the Professor, he advanced after them, cursing them as he came.

Then, suddenly a voice rang out in the tunnel directly behind Professor Blazer. And, looking up, they saw the little man, who screamed out as he ran toward them, "Stop them! Hold them there! They teach the Bible! Don't let them get away!"

John turned to Jed and asked: "Isn't that the little man I tied up?"

"Yes it is," replied Jed. "He must have gotten away when the explosion went off. We'd better get out of here, and we'd better get out now."

"Yes," said John. "And look! He's got a group of men with him. And look! He's got a gun! Let's go! Let's go now!"

On hearing this, Head Lighter Man stepped in front of John and said, "Quickly! Follow me! I'll show you where to go."

John and Jed gathered the three children, and the five followed Head Lighter Man as he ran toward the right hand tunnel. Professor Blazer also ran toward the tunnel to block their way.

There was a blast from the little man's gun, and the bullet came perilously close to the five Christians.

Professor Blazer now blocked the entrance, and he threw up both his hands to stop them.

The gun blasted the second time and the bullet that was meant for the five Christians penetrated professor Blazer's enormous head. He fell dead at their feed as they ran past him into the mouth of the tunnel.

Chapter VI
Escape From The Killer Mob

Head Lighter Man ran before the Christians with his torch held high.

John glanced behind, and saw that there was a torch man guiding the little man and his hate-filled killer mob.

The little man fired another round, and again the bullet came dangerously close to them. "Head Lighter Man," cried John, "he's shooting at us. Extinguish your torch so he can't see us."

Head Lighter Man quickly extinguished his torch. But, the Christians were still visible. "Keep moving," urged John. "Keep moving. We've got to get away from them."

Suddenly Head Lighter Man was by their side. "Take my hand," He said. "And follow me. We are about to go into an old tunnel that has not been used for some time."

The opening to the old tunnel was not in a place easily seen. It was off to the right of the tunnel they were in, and farther back in a bend of the tunnel. And even with a light it would remain in shadows, and not be seen, had a person not glanced behind him and seen it as he passed by.

Added to this, the opening was almost closed. A cave-in of dirt and rocks had almost closed the opening, so that only Head Lighter Man and the three children could pass through the opening easily, and then only on hands and knees. As for Jed, and especially for Big John, it was difficult work for them to worm their way through the small opening.

And once they were in the tunnel, and had the torch lit, they could see why the tunnel was no longer in use: there were cave-ins within the tunnel that would require more digging to make it easier to get through the tunnel.

"Head Lighter Man," asked John, "Do you think it's safe to have that torch lit? Won't the little man see the light?"

Then John considered the words he had just used, and apologized. "I beg your pardon, I didn't mean to insult you by using the words, *little man*."

A smile touched Head Lighter Man's face. "You know," he said, "It's funny that you called him, the *little man*. For that's exactly what we've called him. And that's exactly what we call most all the Professors. We call them, the *little men*. For although we lighter men are small, we are not nearly as small as the Professors. And another thing, our heads are not nearly as big as theirs, either. Some of them have such big heads they are unbalanced, and have trouble standing." Head Lighter Man smiled at what he had said. And John could not help but smile also at the image of little men with such big heads that it was hard for them to stand and keep their balance.

Head Lighter Man continued. "As for the little man, we know he is a little man among many other little men. So, to distinguish him from the other little men, I think, henceforth, we should call him by the name, Little Man. He was once a Professor too; in the Psychology Department, until he was dethroned by someone who had more BAs, MAs, and PhDs than he had. And was relegated to be Chief Digger for new tunnel construction. But I don't think we need to fear that he will find us in this tunnel. He's new on his job. He's familiar only with the new tunnels. And I don't think he even knows this tunnel exists. It is only when we leave this tunnel and go into the tunnels that are in current use that we need to worry about seeing him."

"But why," asked John, "do you live in tunnels at all since there is danger from cave-ins; and they are dark all the time and require some light to see by? Why don't you live outside where there is always light and sunshine?"

"Because the light hurts their eyes! A long time ago we lived in the Bright Regions where the sun always shines. Then, as time went by, men began to complain that the light hurt their eyes. Not everyone complained, but a lot of men did.

"They began first by digging caves to get away from the light. Then they dug the complex of tunnels that we have here today, where they can teach without the light that hurts their eyes."

"But, Head Lighter Man, is there something wrong with their eyes that it makes the light hurt their eyes?"

"No, there's nothing wrong with their eyes. It's just that the light hurts them, and they run away if we bring the light up too close to them. As for myself, I have never been afraid of the light. Nor have any of the other Lighter Men. In fact, we are chosen to be Lighter Men precisely because we are not afraid of the light and are willing and able to work with light. But we are despised by those who fear the light, because they are not comfortable around the light as we are."

"Head Lighter Man, will you take us out to the place where there is light and the sun shines bright? Will you take us out to the Bright Regions? We want to go back home where we live."

"I'll take you out if I can. I came here when I was still young. But I think I can take you out. But to get there we must go through the Education Department. There's no way to get to the Bright Regions without going through the Education Department. And we will have to see the Dean of Education when we go through there—and the Little Man knows that, and will probably be waiting for us there."

Then John asked the question that had been on his mind for some time, "Head Lighter Man, why have you befriended us when it seems that all the other men here in the tunnels hate us—all of them except you?"

Head Lighter Man stopped and stood thinking for a few moments before answering. Then he said, "You know Big John, I began thinking well of you—all of you, after we went through that terrible explosion together. There, lying on my back, with my eyes closed in fear of what might happen to me next, I heard the voices of those around me who were suffering and wounded and dying. Not one voice was raised with a concern for his neighbor.

"Then I heard the voice of Professor Truly. He was concerned for others—for you and the children. Next I heard your voice. Although you were wounded and hurting from the explosion, you were not concerned so much for your own welfare, as for the welfare of the little men who were suffering and dying. And you called for a Lighter Man to bring his torch to see what needed to be done for the little men. Then, on top of all that, you asked Professor Blazer to get medical help for those who were still alive. None of us expressed our concern for one another. But when you showed you cared for us, I couldn't help thinking well of you."

After saying this, Head Lighter Man stood lost in thought for a while before continuing. "Another thing, my mother was a Christian and made me memorize verses from the Bible. I know John 3:16, and could quote a few other verses as well. I know something of the Bible. I've just never lived by it. And others here in the tunnels have had Christian instruction as well.

"Some of them I knew personally while I was still a young boy in the Bright Regions. You may find it hard to believe this, but the Little Man who wants to kill you for believing and teaching the Bible—his father was a preacher of the gospel. I knew them both while I was still a young boy in the Bright Regions. The Little Man confessed Christ as his Savior and was baptized in water. He probably knows as much Bible as you do Big John. But like me, he doesn't live by it."

Having said this, Head Lighter Man turned and led off down the tunnel. "If I remember right," he said, "it's not much further to the end of this tunnel." They walked some two hundred yards further without speaking. And then Head Lighter Man cried out in dismay, "Look! The tunnel is walled up! Now, what are we going to do?"

But as they came up to the wall they saw that it had a small door. Head Lighter Man tried the door. "It's locked," he said. "Now, what do we do?"

"What do we do? Jed repeated. "We pray. Let's pray and ask God what we should do."

Jed knelt down on the ground. John and the three Becker children knelt down with him and began praying to God. Head Lighter Man, embarrassed to be standing by himself while the others were all kneeling in prayer, finally fell to his knees to join them in the form of prayer. Thus they continued crying out to God for some time.

After rising from prayer, the twins asked for the torch, and going to the door, they began fiddling with the doorknob. Suddenly they swung the door wide open and gave a shout of victory. The others ran up to them and asked how they had gotten the door open. "It was easy," said Bill. "We just disarmed the doorknob and lock mechanism like Brother John does when he paints the doors at school."

John looked at the doorknob and lock mechanism lying on the ground. He looked at the screwdrivers, which the twins still held in their hands, and began to laugh with a holy laughter that bubbled up from deep within his soul. He leaped up and down and danced all around with the joy that flows from the soul of one who is full of the Holy Ghost. (Ephesians 5:18-19, Acts 2:13-18, 38-39) Finally he stood still, lifted his hands toward heaven, and breathed a quiet thanksgiving to God, "Oh, my Blessed Lord! How great thou art! I'm supposed to be the Maintenance Man! But these eighth graders are quicker and smarter than I am at my own trade. Glory to God! Thank you Lord! Glory to your holy name!"

Chapter VII
Prisoners Again

Head Lighter Man led the way as they stepped out of the old tunnel.

One of the Becker children had struck up the Christian marching song, *Onward Christian Soldiers*, and the three were happily marching and singing, along with John Frank. Ahead of them, Head Lighter Man stopped. He turned, and, facing them, announced that they were very near the Education Department and that there was no way they could escape seeing the Dean of Education. Then he added in a whisper, "I'm afraid of that man. I don't know why, but there's something about the Dean of Education that scares me."

As Head Lighter Man finished these last words a look of fear came across his face. And he stood speechless, staring past the five Christians, his face frozen in terror.

Then they heard the chilling voice of the Little Man: "Raise your hands above your heads! And don't move! If one of you moves I'll shoot the girl. I'm taking you to the Dean of Education. Now keep your hands up, and move forward."

The prisoners moved forward, their hands raised, fearful that the Little Man would shoot little Alice. In less than a minute they were fed into another tunnel, a very long and spacious tunnel. The tunnel was circular, and was populated with buildings on both sides of a walkway. The walkway between the buildings seemed totally dark except for the light given by the torch of Head Lighter Man. But as the prisoners walked along, they soon saw that some of the buildings were dimly lit; for the shadowy figures of students could be seen through the windows as they sat at their desks. And the dim light that was within the buildings came from two or three small candles that had been rationed very stingily among the students.

The tunnel continued in its circle for perhaps a half mile, and then on their left they saw students lined up in a side tunnel, flashing credentials to guards, in order to gain admittance to the same great circular tunnel in which the six were being held prisoners.

The Little Man gave the command to stop. "You can stop now, and take down your hands. But don't make a false move. If you do, just as sure as I'm standing here, I'll shoot the girl." Then, looking around, he added with pride in his voice, "This is One Mile Circle. We have just completed one half of the Circle. It continues on in its circle to complete a full mile. The complete One Mile Circle contains all the buildings and class rooms needed to teach the full curricula of the University of One Mile Circle"

He pointed with his gun to their right, and said, "The Dean of Education is in there. Turn to your right and go up those stairs."

They ascended the stairs. They walked between two towering columns. They approached a great double portal. And looking up, they saw above them, inscribed in large Roman letters: **HALL OF EDUCATION**. Then they passed through the great double portal into a spacious room.

And there they saw the Dean of Education.

Chapter VIII
Dean Allotrope

The Dean was seated in a great chair, the chair was resting on top of a dais, and from this elevated position the Dean looked down upon his audience as if he were looking down from a great throne.

But, the five prisoners were surprised at the diminutive figure of the Dean. For he was a very small man. And after all the talk the prisoners had heard about the Dean of Education they expected him to be someone of great stature, with an imposing figure. But he was only a small man, and of no great stature at all. In fact he was another copy of the Little Man and Professor Blazer, except that he had an even bigger head.

"What have we here?" The Dean asked, as he inspected the Little Man approaching him with the gun still held in his hand. The Little Man, under such close scrutiny from the Dean, was now somewhat embarrassed by the gun, and held it awkwardly in his hand as if it were an accusing witness that he would like to make disappear.

Nevertheless the Little Man lifted his eyes to the Dean and said, "Dean Allotrope, Sir, I have brought these two men, with the three children. The men most certainly must die. For they teach the Bible. Also, Head Lighter Man must die. For he is a traitor, and has been helping these men to hide and escape the death they deserve."

Dean Allotrope threw up both hands, and spoke impatiently to the Little Man. "Professor Judas, that's enough of that! Put away your gun. No one is going to die." And then, casting his eyes on Head Lighter Man, he cried out, "As for you, Head Lighter Man, extinguish your torch. There's more than enough light from the candles here, without that light from your stupid torch." Then, because Head Lighter Man did not comply within a nanosecond, he stood to his feet, clenched his fists, and cried out in a rage: "Put it out! Put it out! Don't you hear? Put it out, right now! You know that too much light hurts my eyes! Put it out! Put it out, right now!"

Head Lighter Man quickly extinguished his torch. Then he stood where he was; trembling, hurt, and humiliated because of the cruel urgency of the Dean, and the terrible rage and fury poured upon him.

Now that Head Lighter Man's torch was extinguished there was light only from two candles, and each candle stood some ten feet away on either side of the Dean.

And directly behind each candle there was a tree, with its corresponding chart. To Dean Allotrope's right, and behind the first candle was the tree of life with images of different animals, which were supposed to show how one animal evolved into another. Near the top of the tree there were monkeys and apes. And, finally, at the very top, there was what was supposed to be an ape-man, with the stooped shoulders and the two long arms of an ape, and with half-ape and half-man-like features.

And, along with the tree of life, was a chart, which showed images of the same animals as the tree of life, but only in chart form. And behind the tree of life and the evolution chart stood two huge dinosaurs, along with a collection of dinosaur bones and the casts of several huge dinosaur footprints.

Then to the left side of Dean Allotrope was another tree, the tree of knowledge, which was supposed to show man's evolution and growth from a brute beast into an intelligent and knowledgeable, civilized man. And at the very bottom of the tree of knowledge, below the tree trunk, was the picture of a body of water, with lightning striking the water, showing that the first life was created by spontaneous generation. (Most evolutionary scientists believe that the first life was created by spontaneous generation from a pre-biotic soup or slime. Other evolutionary scientists believe the first life came to the earth from outer space! They seem to have no trouble with the superstitious belief that life could come from outer space, or that life could create itself out of pre-biotic soup!)

Above the body of water, where lightning was striking the pre-biotic soup, were pictures of fishes, snakes, birds, and animals (ferns, grasses, plants, and trees were missing for some unexplained reason) that were supposed to have evolved from that first, self-created life. Then, just above the fishes, snakes, birds, and animals were the pictures of monkeys and apes, followed by the images and profiles of missing link ape-men.

Then, above the missing link ape-men, on the top two branches of the tree of knowledge were placed notations, with pictures illustrating the progressive knowledge and discoveries of prehistoric man.

This progressive knowledge began with the Stone Age, and went through the Bronze Age, the Iron Age, and on up to the Modern Age. And so in ascending order were shown stone axes, stone knives, and other stone tools. Then followed the bow and arrow with flint arrowheads. Then followed the discovery of fire; the discovery of iron and other nonferrous metals; the invention of the wheel; the beginning of farming, pottery, and weaving; the domestication of animals, and the beginning of village living. After this, came the invention of an alphabet, and writing. (The invention of talking, speaking, thinking, and reasoning were not mentioned for some unexplained reason.) And then followed the great knowledge, and science of the Modern Age.

And, on the left side of Dean Allotrope, there was also a chart, outlining in chart form, prehistoric man's advances in learning and knowledge, from the time of his appearance on earth up to the present.

But now, Dean Allotrope had begun to speak, and he was speaking directly to the five prisoners. And they stared up in astonishment as they watched an amazing transformation take place. For Dean Allotrope was transformed into a different person right before their eyes!

Chapter IX
Dean Allotrope, The Devil's Messenger

His small body and large head slowly faded away and morphed into the body of a normal sized, well-proportioned man. His short, black hair was transformed into a full head of wavy hair, bright and golden; and both his face and hair shone with a radiance that dazzled his onlookers. His clothes turned bright white, and shone with such brilliance that the six who gazed up at him were bathed in light.

"My friends," he began. "Welcome to the University of One Mile Circle, and our Hall of Education. I am so glad that you are here. I want to extol, and I must extol wisdom and knowledge and education. It is knowledge and education that separate us from, and elevate us above, the brute beasts.

"Knowledge and education are the great need of man today. Education cures the blight of war. Education begets peace and unity in a world where there is misunderstanding and division. Education delivers us from ignorance, superstition, and bigotry. Education delivers us from hatred and war and all the evils that beset us in this world."

Dean Allotrope paused, and repeated his last words again: "Education delivers us from hatred and war and all the evils that beset us in this world! Notice," the Dean continued, "that all the evils that are in our world today are here because of ignorance. We have silly superstitions because of ignorance. We have prejudice, bigotry, and divisions because of ignorance. We have hatred, killing, and war— because of ignorance. Education will do away with all these evils, and bring unity and peace to our world.

"Your own Bible says, 'Get wisdom, and get understanding. Wisdom is the principal thing; therefore get wisdom: and with all thy getting get understanding.' (Proverbs 4:5, 7) So, according to the Bible, the principal thing for man is to get wisdom and understanding.

"Think what it would have been like if early prehistoric men had never advanced in knowledge and learning—why men would still be living like cave men! Still living in caves today!"

A great big laugh erupted from Big John. His laughter was entirely spontaneous and involuntary. He had instantly perceived how ludicrous the Dean's words were, and he had burst into laughter. "Indeed?" he had thought. "The Dean himself was still living in a cave—like a cave man! What was this tunnel, but a long, extended cave? And all the other little men were still living in caves—like cave men. They were all cave men, living in the Dark Ages, in endless dark tunnels, where they never saw the light of day!"

(But Big John was embarrassed by his involuntary outburst and apologized immediately: "I'm sorry. I didn't mean to laugh at you.")

But Dean Allotrope continued as if he had neither heard John's laughter nor his apology: "But, because of great advances in knowledge, man no longer lives in caves! And as man continues to advance in knowledge he will finally be saved from all the barbarism and savagery of his ignorance.

"But some men are prone to cling desperately to their ignorance and superstition in the midst of great learning! The rejection, by the Church, of Copernicus and Galileo, are good examples of this.

"Galileo taught the truth that the sun does not go around the earth, but that the earth goes around the sun, and that the earth spins on its axis, giving the illusion that the sun is going around the earth. But even though he taught the truth, the Church resisted it and persecuted him, because they believed the false teaching of Ptolemy that the earth was the unmoving center of the universe, and that the sun moved around the earth.

"Copernicus had already shown that the theory of Ptolemy was false, but the Church had rejected his arguments as heresy. So, Galileo constructed a telescope and was able to demonstrate that Copernicus was right and that Ptolemy had been wrong all along. Instead of saying, 'Thank you for correcting our wrong beliefs,' the Church instead put Copernicus' work on its index of prohibited books and warned Galileo to abandon his opinions and to abstain from teaching, defending, or discussing them anymore.

"Galileo invited some members of the Church clergy to look into his telescope and prove for themselves that what he had said was the truth; but they refused, because they were afraid that if they looked, their beliefs would be proven false.

"Galileo was persistent and wrote a book proving the falseness of the views which the Church had held for 1400 years. This brought the wrath of the Church upon him. He was tried and found guilty by the Church Inquisition, was compelled to recant all his Copernican doctrines, and spent the last eight years of his life under house arrest. It was 200 years later, in 1835, that the works of Copernicus and Galileo were finally removed from the Church's index of prohibited books."

In part, Dean Allotrope's words were convincing and persuasive to his listeners. This was because much of what he said was known to be historical fact. And, again, because his words appeared to be coming from the mouth of an angel or some supernatural being. And so his words fell as words of knowledge and wisdom. They fell as words of reason and truth. They fell as words of one who could utter neither falsehood nor deceit. But someone has said, "The devil speaks an ocean of truth in order to gain entrance with one lie."

"The history of the Church," continued Dean Allotrope, "is one of error and superstition—and clinging fanatically to that error and superstition.

"This is shown by the fact that the Church instituted many Crusades, in the name of their God and their religion, to march on other nations and make war with them. They instituted some eight Crusades over a period of some 200 years, in which they killed others in the name of their God and their religion. The Christian religion is a religion of blind ignorance, fanaticism, and superstition. They reject science, because science shows that the Christian religion is a religion of myth and superstition.

"The belief in God and the devil, and the belief in heaven and hell are myths and superstitions. The belief in sin, and the belief that the sinner will go to hell for his sins, where he will be punished forever— are also superstitions. The belief that man has an everlasting soul that will never die and the belief in an eternal existence after death, with a heavenly reward for the righteous and punishment in hell for the wicked, are also superstitions.

"There is no God!   Have you ever seen God? I haven't. The only god you will ever see is man himself. For man himself is a god, if he knows who and what he is.   For what makes man a god, is the knowledge that he has by himself, alone—by his own efforts and learning—ascended to the most exalted position of all the other animals.

"But, although we occupy the most exalted position among all the other animals, we know we are only animals. And animals are not responsible for their deeds. We do not punish animals for what they do. We do not speak of animals as sinners! So the idea that we are sinners, and that we are responsible and accountable to God, and deserve punishment for sin, is only a superstition of the Church.

"Now we want you to attend some of our classes. It will do you good. Broaden your mind. Too often we are narrow-minded in our beliefs because we have had a limited education. I would especially recommend our biology class. In the biology class you will be given scientific evidence that shows life has evolved from a single-celled organism into all the complex, multi-celled organisms that exist today."

Jed could restrain himself no longer! The truth of God was like a fire shut up in his bones that compelled him to speak out against this messenger of Satan. And, now, as he gazed up at the angelic form that was speaking lies against the God of truth, he opened his mouth and cried out with a loud voice:

"The Lord rebuke you, Satan! Get behind me, you child of the devil and messenger of Satan! Your message is a lie. It comes directly from your father the devil, the father of lies. And your doctrine of evolution is one of the blackest lies ever inspired by the devil."

And it was here that Jed addressed the Dean by his name:

"Dean Allotrope! For Allotrope is your name! And you are true to your name! For you have transformed yourself into another form. But your transformation is only a lie of the devil. You are not an angel of light! No! You are an angel of the devil. And your father the devil has sent you as an angel of light to lie and deceive God's people. The Apostle Paul warned Christians of your kind:

'And no marvel; for *Satan himself is transformed into an*

angel of light. Therefore it is no great thing if *his ministers also be transformed as the ministers of righteousness*; whose end shall be according to their works.'" II Corinthians 11:14-15

Jed was not finished. In fact he had just begun. He opened his mouth to continue—but was arrested by loud hissing sounds, and convulsive, jerking movements in the angelic form above him.

And all those who were there heard the loud hissing sounds and saw the convulsive, jerking movements of the angelic form. And, as they watched, they saw three serpents rise up out of his head, busily writhing in his hair, and raising their heads, and hissing and striving with one another for space in his wavy hair.

And then those present saw arise yet another serpent, a huge serpent, directly behind the apparition that was now Dean Allotrope. The serpent continually moved its huge head and massive body back and forth, around and over the head and shoulders of Dean Allotrope.

And then, coming from somewhere very high above the huge serpent that was weaving back and forth and over and around the head and shoulders of Dean Allotrope—they all heard the mighty voice of God, THUNDER:

THE DEVIL IS THE FATHER OF LIES.

THE DEVIL DECEIVES THE WHOLE WORLD.

RESIST THE DEVIL, AND HE WILL FLEE FROM YOU.

(John 8:44, Rev. 12:9, James 4:7)

When the mighty voice of God had thundered—Dean Allotrope exploded with a loud popping sound, he uttered one short, anguished shriek and was swallowed up in deep, dark blackness. And out of that deep, dark blackness could be heard great blasphemies from the dragon, that old serpent, and Satan, and the devil—who is the enemy of God and man, who is a liar and the father of lies, and who deceives the whole world. Matthew 13:24-30, 39-43; John 8:44; Revelation 13:5-8, Revelation 12:9, and James 4:7

Chapter X
Forced To Study Evolution

Deep, dark blackness engulfed them all.

Hurriedly, John switched on his flashlight to see where Jed and the children were. The light picked up little Alice, over to his right, clinging desperately to her two brothers, with Jed Truly standing next to them.

Then he moved the beam behind him, till it picked up Head Lighter Man, who was manifestly relieved to see the light.

Then John moved the beam until it caught Professor Judas and Dean Allotrope standing together in front of the dais. (For Dean Allotrope had come down off the dais to speak privately with Professor Judas.)

When the beam of light fell upon them, they cried out with a pitiable wail and doubled over in agony. Then they ran here and there, shrieking and screaming, trying to escape the light. The screaming and wailing of Dean Allotrope and the Little Man continued until the Little Man, finally exhausted, fell to the floor, and with hands covering his eyes, pleaded, "Please! Please turn off your light! We'll light the candles if you'll only turn off that bright light. And," he added, "Head Lighter Man can even light his torch, if he moves all the way back to the doors, and dampens it."

Immediately John switched off his flashlight, and the Dean lit the two candles.

The five Christians went back with Head Lighter Man, all the way back to the doors. Head Lighter Man lit his torch, and from there they watched the Dean and the Little Man in what appeared to be a heated argument. For even though the two spoke in hushed tones, it was easy to see that what they had to say was tense and emotionally charged:

"Get them out of here! Especially the one who does the preaching! Get them out of here!

"I don't believe he heard a word I said! Did you hear him rebuke me, and tell me to get behind him? Did you hear him say the devil was my father, and that I was a child of the devil?

"Oh! And he called me a liar! And said I was teaching lies! I hate him! I hate him! I hate them all! Get them out of here! Get rid of them!"

"Do you want me to get rid of them permanently—I still have my gun?"

"No, not yet! I don't believe in the death penalty! See if they can be educated first. Take them to the Biology Department for classes on evolution. If they don't learn, do as you wish with them. But, I prefer imprisonment.

"And when you have discharged your duty of overseeing their education, I am sending you back to fill your former position as Head Psychologist of the Psychology Department."

"But what will happen to Professor C. More Light? He was eminently qualified in psychology, and had degrees in other fields as well, and in addition was continuing his studies."

"I haven't time to explain it all right now, except to say that he is now an advocate for intelligent design. And he has just published a book giving the evidences for intelligent design. And among the evidences for intelligent design given by Professor C. More Light—is the information code in deoxyribonucleic acid, the DNA that exists in the cells of every living organism on earth. Whether a frog or a monkey or a tree, whether a worm or a tomato plant or a man, each species has its own unique information code with specific information and precise directions on how to replicate itself. According to Professor C. More Light, this information code is present in the cell of every living organism on earth, and could only have been put there by an Intelligent Designer. Oh, Professor Judas! Can't you see what his book will do to our belief in biological evolution? We must get rid of him, before he destroys our teaching on biological evolution. Biological evolution is fundamental to what we teach here at the University of One Mile Circle! Without it, we hardly have reason to exist!"

"But Dean Allotrope, have you notified him of his termination yet? Have you informed him that I will be filling his position as Head Psychologist of the Psychology Department?"

"No. But I will do so immediately. Now take the prisoners to their classes in biological evolution."

And having said this, the Dean lifted his eyes to the prisoners, and spoke to them in a strong, reassuring voice, "I have enjoyed visiting with you, and talking with you. Professor Judas will be taking you to sit in on a few classes in biology. I wish you well in your studies."

Chapter XI
Death—Or Life Imprisonment

Head Lighter Man followed behind the Little Man and the five Christians, holding his torch up high. Eerie shadows played upon the buildings as they hurried forward.

John looked down at the Little Man, who still held the gun in his hand. "How many classes must we sit in on, before we are free to go?"

"Only a few classes, if you learn well. If you don't, you will die."

"No! That's not true." Said John. "Dean Allotrope said he does not want any of us to die!"

The Little Man (thinking that Big John had overheard his conversation with Dean Allotrope) cried out angrily: "You were eavesdropping! You heard Dean Allotrope say that he doesn't believe in the death penalty. But, he also said that if you are not rehabilitated by these classes and do not renounce your belief in God, you will be imprisoned for life, or put to death. And he left that up to me!"

"Professor Judas, I did not eavesdrop. I did not overhear your conversation with Dean Allotrope. But I distinctly remember his words when you first brought us to him. You called for us to be put to death. And he stopped you, and said, 'Professor Judas, that's enough of that. Put away your gun. Nobody is going to die.' Now does the word of Dean Allotrope mean anything or not? When he says, 'nobody is going to die,' does it mean that, or not?"

"Yes." The Little Man conceded. "The word of Dean Allotrope means something. But he has left your case in my hands. And I am warning you now, if you are not rehabilitated after these classes, and do not renounce your belief in God and the Bible; you will never be released! But you will either be imprisoned for life, or put to death. And Dean Allotrope has left that matter in my hands!"

Chapter XII
Abundant Light In Some Classrooms

They continued on down the path from one classroom to another. Some were vacant and as dark as the pathway itself. Some were dimly lit, so dimly lit that the teacher and students could hardly be seen through the windows.

But then they passed classrooms where electronics, physics, and computer science were taught. They passed classrooms where algebra, geometry, trigonometry, and calculus were taught. And they passed classrooms where law, government, and the science of logic were taught. Most of these classrooms were so well lit up that some light even shone through the windows and out onto the pathway.

John Frank spoke to Professor Judas about this remarkable fact: "That's strange! Why is it so dark in most classrooms, but these last classrooms we passed seem to have abundant light?"

The Little Man was nervous with the question, but felt obliged to say something: "Oh, I don't know why some classrooms have more light than others. But they do. But it is only a few classes like math that give us any real problem with the light..."

The Little Man was embarrassed by his halting and incomplete response to John's observation on the abundant light in some classrooms.

But now they had arrived at the door of a classroom with the words '**BIOLOGICAL EVOLUTION**' printed on the outside. And the Little Man, thoroughly angry with Big John for his searching question on the abundant light in some classrooms, now glared up at him, and commanded; "You, John! Open the door, go in, find a seat, and sit down!"

John opened the door and entered into a room that was almost totally dark. The only light in the room came from two candles that were burned down so low that they were almost out. And they were way in the back of the classroom, so that the teacher, who was at the front of the classroom, could hardly be seen. John walked forward very carefully, and the other prisoners followed him; each one reaching out to touch the one before him, in order not to stumble in the darkness.

After the five prisoners had gone in, the Little Man went in; and finally, Head Lighter Man came in with his low burning torch.

The Professor, even though he had just cause to be angered by the interruption, had quietly endured the whole disturbance—until the light from Head Lighter Man's torch filled his classroom. Then he screamed, "Stop! Take it out! Take it out right now!"

He took one step toward the torch, then stopped, and backing away, he covered his eyes, and screamed hysterically: "Take it out! Take it out! Take it out! Oh, it hurts my eyes! Take it out! Take it out!"

By now Big John had reached the Professor, and laying a hand upon his head, he asked, "Why? What's wrong? Tell me why the light hurts your eyes!"

The little man trembled and replied in a plaintive voice. "Just take that light out. It hurts my eyes. Please take it out."

"But we need some light in here," said John. "We can't see. It's so dark we're running into each other." Then John turned, and, looking back at Head Lighter Man, was about to ask him to extinguish his torch—

But Head Lighter Man did not wait for Big John to tell him to extinguish his torch—he extinguished it immediately without being told to.

After this, Professor U. R. Matter (for that was his name) calmed down enough to ask a student to put two new candles far enough back in the classroom so as not to hurt his eyes.

Professor Judas now spoke: "Professor U. R. Matter, I am sorry to interrupt your class in this way. But I have brought these students to your class for teaching and training on the subject of biological evolution. They have foolish beliefs in God, Creation, and the Bible. We hope to reform and rehabilitate them so that they will renounce their belief in God and the Bible. I will be here to oversee them. So, will you continue your teaching as usual?"

"Professor Judas," said Professor U. R. Matter, "I will teach these new students biological evolution, because I have room for them, and that is my subject. But, remember, this is not a reform school! It is not an institution for the rehabilitation of anyone! So if you want to reform them in some way, do it on your own time, and not on mine! Just remember that I am the Professor here, and don't interrupt my teaching to reform them!"

And, with these words, the Professor continued his teaching.

Chapter XIII
The Big Bang Theory

"I suppose, that for the sake of our new students I should give a brief overview of the material we have covered so far. So let's go back to the beginning. Let's go back to the Big Bang.

"We believe that the universe in which we live began with a gigantic explosion, the Big Bang, some 12 to 20 billion years ago.

"I will quote again, as I quoted at the beginning of this course, from the Webster's New World College Dictionary, fourth edition, 1999, which gives a concise definition of what the Big Bang, or Big Bang Theory is."

Professor U. R. Matter then asked the Reader, a student back near one of the candles, to read once again the definition of the **Big Bang Theory**, taken from the Webster's New World College Dictionary, and contained on the first page of the course syllabus:

> **big-bang theory** a theory of cosmology holding that the expansion of the universe began with a gigantic explosion (**big bang**) between 12 and 20 billion years ago. Webster's New World College Dictionary, fourth edition, p. 142

When the Reader had finished reading the definition of the **Big Bang Theory**, Professor U. R. Matter continued speaking:

"I will have to confess at the very beginning that there are differences of opinion among Astronomers/Cosmologists over the when, where, how, and what of the Big Bang.

"These differences of opinion are only natural because our knowledge of the Big Bang, and the universe that has evolved from the Big Bang, is limited. And, in addition, we have to admit the sad fact that the universe we are able to see is filled with many mysteries and enigmas that at the present time we cannot explain. So then, some Astronomers/Cosmologists estimate that the universe came into existence between 12 and 20 billion years ago. Others estimate that the universe came into existence between 15 and 18 billion years ago. And others have narrowed their estimate down to 13.7 billion years ago.

"But, although divided opinion exists over when the Big Bang took place, there is still universal agreement that the universe came into existence with the Big Bang, and that the Big Bang happened somewhere between 12 and 20 billion years ago.

"I am not an Astronomer." continued Professor U. R. Matter. "So I have no expertise in astronomy. But I wanted you to know what the Astronomers themselves believe about the Big Bang, that created the present universe.

"I have told you in former lectures that they candidly admit that there are mysteries about the present universe that they do not understand, and cannot explain. They admit that there are things they know to be true about the Big Bang and our present universe that contradict some of our known laws of physics.

"So when and how the Big Bang took place, and what the Big Bang was, will continue to be a matter of some speculation as long as there are so many unanswered questions about the present universe.

"We just have to admit that there are some things about the Big Bang, and the present universe, that we do not now know, and probably never will know.

"But we know that the Big Bang gave birth to the present universe. And we know that in time the universe evolved into galaxies, stars, and planets. And that, along with these, our own solar system and our own planet earth evolved and came into existence.

"We also now know with a high degree of certainty that the moon was formed when some heavenly body struck the earth. We are quite sure of this, because the same materials that were thrown into space by that impact are the same materials that are found in the crust of the earth.

"We also now know with certainty that the earth is not the center of the universe and without movement—as was the theory of Claudius Ptolemaeus. For both Copernicus, and Galileo proved conclusively that the earth does have movement, and that it circles the sun.

"So, now we know that both the earth and the sun are only common, ordinary, relatively unimportant heavenly bodies. For they are but two similar heavenly bodies in a vast universe of like heavenly bodies."

Having shown to his own satisfaction that the earth and the sun were only common, ordinary heavenly bodies, and relatively unimportant; Professor U. R. Matter next began a monologue on the earth, and the origin of life on the earth:

"Earth was formed about 4.5 billion years ago. It took several hundred million years more for it to cool enough for the first life to form. The first life, we believe, was a simple one-celled organism, the prokaryote.

"The Eukaryote, a multi-celled organism, made up of cells with true nuclei that divide by mitosis, evolved from the prokaryote hundreds of millions of years later, sometime during or after the Precambrian era.

"Again, I must say with all frankness, that we cannot be certain how the first life came into existence, because the time was billions of years ago; and there is no fossil record available for what took place then. So, we have to resort to some conjecture on how the first life began.

"There are three main theories on how life came into existence on the young earth.

"The first theory is the theory of self creation. This is the theory that the first life sprang from non-living matter, a lifeless soup or slime, somewhere out in a shallow body of water. Most Biologists, I among them, believe this theory.

"I know that *self creation* is another way of saying *spontaneous generation*. But many of us Biologists believe that conditions were so different 4.0 billion years ago, that, although spontaneous generation is impossible now, it was not impossible then.

"A second theory is that life came from outer space. This theory is called '*panspermia.*' And it holds that a countless number of comets and meteorites fell from outer space to the early earth, and brought with them the *seeds of life* from outer space.

"Yet a third theory is that the first life arose from very hot, deep-sea vents. Deep-sea vents were discovered in the 1970s and raised the possibility that life might have arisen in the area of these very early, very hot, deep-sea vents. The reasoning of those who believe this theory, is, that the ancestors of today's modern prokaryotes could have thrived in these very hot conditions, and could have lived on the inorganic sulfur compounds that are sometimes found in these deep-sea vent areas.

"Also, debate goes on among scientists over whether or not the rock compositions that resemble fossil prokaryotes in a Martian meteorite found in Antarctica are evidence of early life on Mars.

"In fact, debate continues to abound among Biologists over the origin of life on earth, and over whether there may be life on other planets.

"So, we are left with only one certainty on the matter of the origin of life on the earth—that we just *cannot be certain how life came to exist on the earth*. Can I tell you then, with certainty, how life came to exist on the earth? No, I cannot. I just know that it does exist, but I cannot tell with certainty how it came to exist."

Little Alice shot up out of her seat! Her right arm shot up and she waved it wildly about as she spoke out with a loud voice!

"I can." She said. "I can tell how life got on the earth. I can tell how the animals got here. And I can tell how we got here. God created us. He created the sun and the moon and the stars and the earth, and all the things that are on the earth. We learned that in kindergarten. But I'm in the first grade now. It's in Genesis, the first book of the Bible. The Bible tells how God created everything."

Chapter XIV
Jed Asks For Permission To Speak

There was total silence while Alice stood there. Then cheers erupted, and loud applause arose from every corner of the classroom.

The Little Man simmered with rage!

He had been about to stand up before the whole class and criticize Professor U. R. Matter for making evolution sound like it was only a quack theory. Or worse yet, a choice among several quack theories. And this little upstart of a girl had stood up and said that God created everything!

Why did Professor U. R. Matter have to do such a poor job of teaching evolution! And now the girl had stolen the hearts of the students, and he could not speak out against her either. And Professor U. R. Matter had already warned him not to interrupt his teaching.

But he would interrupt him! The little girl had interrupted him, and had gotten away with it!

He stood slowly to his feet. He stood there nervously, wondering exactly what he could say about Professor U. R. Matter. The eyes of the whole class were on him as he stood there.

Now he wished he had not stood up, for it suddenly dawned on him that there would certainly be dire results if he complained of the professor's teaching. Especially before his whole class! So he stood there, before the whole class, embarrassed, head downcast, not able to lift his eyes and complain of Professor U. R. Matter's teaching.

Professor U. R. Matter looked at him, and asked, "Professor Judas, do you have something to say?"

"No." Whispered the Little Man in a tiny voice. And the Little Man sank slowly down into his chair.

"Then I will resume my teaching: We are matter. The whole universe is matter. The first life arose from matter. The right combination of chemical elements came together and somehow a living organism came into existence out of that matter. Matter is what I am, and matter is what you are. And matter is all that we are!

"So when we die, our body decomposes and we go back to matter. And that's the end of us. There is no soul that lives on after we die. There are no 'happy hunting grounds' that our souls can go to after we die. So if you want to be happy, now is the time. Like the Bible says, 'let us eat, drink, and be merry; for tomorrow we die.' (quoted erroneously and out of context) I Corinthians 15:32

"I will not detail the evolution of plants and animals. For I have covered the evolution of plants and animals fully in past lectures. Except to say that all the plants and animals, including man, evolved from that first prokaryotic life form born in the shallow waters of the young earth.

"Now I will continue with the subject of the last lecture—the evolution of man.

"Man is of the order Primate. Other Primates are monkeys, the great apes, the chimpanzees, and the lemurs.

"The first Primates descended from insectivores in the Cretaceous period. These early Primates were probably small tree dwelling mammals.

"Although we humans no longer live in trees, we still retain some of the traits of our early ancestors who did live there. And this brings us to prehistoric man and how he has evolved from the monkeys and the apes."

When Professor U. R. Matter spoke the words '*prehistoric man*...has evolved from the monkeys and the apes,' Jed Truly stood to his feet. "Professor U. R. Matter," he said. "I would like very much to say a few words. And what I have to say is contrary to what you are teaching. Do I have permission to speak?"

Chapter XV
No Such Thing As Prehistoric Man

Professor U. R. Matter hesitated a few moments. Then, expelling his breath, said, "I guess so; go ahead and speak."

Jed began. "Professor, there is no such thing as a 'prehistoric man.' There is no such thing as a 'prehistoric animal.' There is no such thing as 'prehistoric fishes or birds or plants or any other living thing upon the earth.' There is not even such a thing as a 'prehistoric sun, moon, earth, or universe of stars. Nothing in God's creation is prehistoric. God has written the history of the whole creation and of every living thing in his book, the Bible.

"He has described in detail how he created the sun, the moon, the stars, and the earth. But especially does he go into detail about the earth. For he created the earth specifically to put man on it, along with all the other forms of life he created—grasses, and trees, and plants, and birds, and fishes, and animals of all kinds.

"So the earth is the most important body in the entire universe; and it is the very center of the universe in God's purposes and plans!

"The earth (on which God created man) and the sun (which was created to make life possible on the earth) are the most important and significant heavenly bodies in the entire universe! Professor, I repeat, the earth on which you live and breathe is the most important and significant planet in the entire universe!

"God created the earth to populate it with life. With trees and plants and grasses on every hill and valley. With fishes to swim the rivers, the lakes and the seas. With birds to fly in the heaven above. With animals to populate the mountains and the valleys. And then God created man in his own image and likeness to have dominion over all of God's creation on the earth.

"The earth is unique. It is the only planet in the entire universe where life can and does exist. I do not mean that God could not have created many other planets throughout the universe where life could exist like it does on the earth, but he did not. God created only one earth in the entire universe. And he created the earth to be hospitable to all the forms of life that he created.

"Did you know, Professor U. R. Matter, that the earth's very size, rotation, and orbit, that the earth's very location in the Milky Way galaxy, and that the earth's very location in our solar system were all established by God so that the earth could harbor life? Did you know further, that there are many other factors, such as the actual mass of the sun and moon and planets, in relation to the earth and its mass, that all work together to make the earth a hospitable place where life can and does exist?

"Just recently astronomers have discovered planets orbiting other stars (1995). But most of their orbits are elliptical, And their elliptical orbits alone make them completely unable to sustain life.

"But the earth's orbit around the sun is more circular than elliptical. If the earth's orbit around the sun were elliptical instead of circular it would cause extreme heat parts of the year and extreme cold other parts of the year—and life would be unsustainable.

"The earth's very distance from the sun is just right. This is no accident! If the earth were just a little closer or further from the sun, life could not exist on the earth. We would either burn up or freeze to death! And that is, once again, why a circular orbit of the earth around the sun is absolutely necessary for life on the earth.

"Professor U. R. Matter, the earth is not ordinary, common, or unimportant. It is the only planet in the entire universe created by God to be the habitation of all the species of life that he has created upon it—and especially of man, his master creation, created in his very own image and likeness.

"And God created the sun *specifically for the earth*, and for every living creature upon the earth—to provide light and heat and energy.

"And let's not forget the moon! For it, too, was created by God. And it was created for the good of the earth and for the good of all its inhabitants.

"Professor U. R. Matter, the moon was not formed when the earth was hit by another celestial body. There is no evidence at all to support such a supposition. But there is overwhelming evidence that God created the moon and placed it in the heavens for the good of the earth and the earth's inhabitants.

"Professor, you know, and everybody else knows, that the universe is a universe of system and order and design. The universe is not a universe of chaos and disorder. And the design and order and system of the universe annihilate the Big Bang theory. For the explosion of the Big Bang could only throw things out of systematic order, and into utter chaos, disorder, and destruction.

"And we do not see chaos, disorder, and destruction in our universe. What we do see, in fact, is a wonderful system, order, and precision. What we see is that all the heavenly bodies have precise orbits—precise orbits that are in perfect harmony with the orbits of all their neighboring heavenly bodies. There is wonderful order, system, and precision in God's universe!

"But the work of any explosion, including the Big Bang explosion, (and I speak of the Big Bang explosion as the astronomers themselves have defined it), could only be a work of destruction, disorder, and chaos. *The Big Bang could not possibly create even one orbiting heavenly body, or move any heavenly body into any semblance of order or system*! Precise orbits, and order, and system, are the work of a Creator and not the work of an explosion! You know that, professor U. R. Matter, and every other man knows that! And to deny it is to deny reality!

"There is a fundamental problem for every sober and reasonable man—for every man who is a true scientists and thinking man—with the Big Bang Theory. Explosions do not throw things into precise orbits and precise and systematic order with other orbiting, and systematically moving heavenly bodies—order and precision and system are the work of a Creator. They are not the work of an explosion!"

Chapter XVI

No Evidence For The 'Big Bang'

"Professor U. R. Matter, you are an atheist and an evolutionist. You believe that you are matter and nothing more. You do not believe in the miracles recorded in the Bible.

"I am sure that you claim to be a scientist. And that you would say you cannot believe in miracles because you are a scientist.

"You would probably say you must have hard evidence before you can believe. Yet you readily believe in the incredible miracle of the Big Bang without hard evidence. And you readily believe in the incredible miracle of the spontaneous generation of life without hard evidence.

"Yes, you are credulous enough to believe the fabulous story that a whole universe just miraculously popped into existence out of absolute nothingness, *without any evidence at all*! And, you are credulous enough to believe the fantastic fiction that life one day suddenly just popped into existence out of the slime somewhere out in the water!

"O, my dear friend, there's a lot of 'popping into existence' with you 'scientists' who just can't believe in miracles! Of course you don't want to call it 'popping into existence' although you know that 'popping into existence' is a true description of what you say happened in the Big Bang, and in the spontaneous generation of life on earth.

"At least the life on earth 'pops into existence' *out of something*! But with the Big Bang, the whole universe, and all of existence, and space and time, and everything that didn't exist before, just pops into existence *out of nothing*! *Absolute nothing*!

"Why, I wouldn't be a bit surprised if a whole troop of horses just popped into existence out of nothing right here inside your classroom!

"And, Professor, why not? Is it any harder for horses to pop into existence, than it is for existence itself, and space and time, and a vast young universe to just *pop into existence out of nothing*?"

Chapter XVII
You Believe The Devil's Lies

"Professor U. R. Matter, the teaching that man evolved and descended from the apes is a lie of the devil. It is a lie of the devil meant to make men believe that there is no God and no Creator.

"So the lie that man evolved and descended from the apes did not begin with you, Professor U. R. Matter. It did not even begin with Darwin. It began with the devil. And you are teaching what your father the devil has taught you!

"Listen to what the Bible says about the devil, his children, and his lies.

'Ye are of your father the devil, and the lusts of your father ye will do. He was a murderer from the beginning, and abode not in the truth, because there is no truth in him. When he speaketh a lie, he speaketh of his own: for *he is a liar, and the father of it.*' John 8:44

'He that *committeth sin is of the devil*; for the devil sinneth from the beginning. For this purpose the Son of God was manifested, that he might destroy the works of the devil. Whosoever is born of God doth not commit sin; for his seed remaineth in him: and he cannot sin, because he is born of God. In this the *children of God are manifest*, and the *children of the devil.*' I John 3:8-10

"The devil is a sinner. (I John 3:8) The devil is a liar. (John 8:44) The devil is a murderer. (John 8:44) And the devil hates God, and slanders his righteous character!

"God had warned Adam and Eve that they would surely die if they ate of the tree in the midst of the garden. But the devil hates both God and man; and he came to Adam and Eve, and slandered God! He said that God had lied to them when he told them they would die if they ate of the forbidden tree. He slandered God, with these words: 'Ye **shall not surely die**: for **God doth know** that in the day ye eat thereof, then your eyes shall be opened, and *ye shall be as gods*, knowing good and evil.' Genesis 3:4-5

"And now, Professor U. R. Matter, you have slandered God! You have lied about God and called God a liar! God says he created everything that exists. But you deny what God has said, and say that God lies! Professor, you are doing the works of your father the devil!

"Professor, I do not want to say what I am about to say. But I must say it, because it is true.

"*You are a murderer*! Your father the devil is a murderer, and you do the works of your father the devil! With your godless doctrine of evolution you murder all your students who believe you! You send them down to a devil's hell without faith in their Creator and the Merciful God who would forgive their sins, and save them, if they would only believe in him.

"Professor, do you realize *the enormity of your sin against God and man* in preaching the godless doctrine of evolution?"

Chapter XVIII
You Cherish The Doctrine Of Evolution

"Professor U. R. Matter, you cherish the doctrine of evolution!

"You cherish the doctrine of evolution, because it calms your gnawing fears of God and his judgment—For there is no God to fear if you evolved from an animal. But everyone knows he did not evolve from an animal!

"He knows he is completely different from the animals! He knows his is a rational, moral being, and completely different from any of the animals.

"Professor U. R. Matter, we are not like the dumb beasts of the field at all. The gulf between the non-rational, non-moral, brute beasts and rational, moral man is so vast, it could never be bridged by a silly thing called evolution.

"The very fact that men are free moral agents, and have moral government over themselves—and the beasts of the field do not—is irrefutable proof of the fact that there exists a vast gulf between man and the animals.

"The theory that man evolved from a non-rational, non-moral, non-free, non-responsible, brute beast into a free and responsible, rational, moral man, is so obviously impossible that it is ridiculous and laughable on the face of it.

"First God created the animals! And then God created man! And man was created in the very image and likeness of God—a rational, responsible, free moral agent.

> 'And God said, Let us make man *in our image, after our like-ness*...so God created man in his own image, in the image of God created he him; male and female created he them.' Genesis 1:26-27

"Professor U. R. Matter, you have slandered God and called him a liar again and again! You have said that man is matter, and that he is nothing more than matter. You have said that man has no soul. That when he dies, he ceases to exist, and that that is the end of him.

"But God says that when he created man, 'man *became a living soul!*' (Genesis 2:7) Man is not an animal that dies, and then ceases to exist. Man is both soul and body. His body will die, but his soul will exist forever! And when he dies he will be judged in the next life, according to his deeds in this life. God has made a decree. And he has declared it in these words:

'It is appointed unto men once to die, but after this the judgment.' Hebrews 9:27

"Man is created in the **image and likeness of God** with a **rational, moral nature**. Man's own nature **reveals** to him that he is rational, and completely different from the animals; his nature **reveals** to him that he is a free moral agent, and accountable before God for all his deeds. These revelations are *irresistible*. All men have *irresistible convictions* of truth and error, right and wrong, good and evil, and justice and injustice. All men have them, and no man can free himself from them—they **flow inexorably from the** *rational, moral nature God has created us with.*

'For when the Gentiles, which *have not the law*, **DO BY NATURE** *the things contained in the law*, these, having not the law, are a law unto themselves: which show the work of the **law written in their hearts**, their **conscience** also bearing witness, and their *thoughts the meanwhile accusing or else excusing one another*, in the day when God shall judge the secrets of men by Jesus Christ according to my gospel.' Romans 2:14-16

"Man has a *conscience*! None of the animals have a *conscience*! If they did, they would be like man, and be responsible and accountable for their deeds!

"Man's **conscience** is an *ever present consciousness*, in his mind, of his responsibility for his deeds. It is a *consciousness of right and wrong, of good and evil, and of justice and injustice.* Man's **conscience** *urges him to do right and not do wrong*; it convicts him of his *responsibility* to submit himself to both God's moral government and man's moral government over him. If man **had no conscience**, if he **had no knowledge of right and wrong**, he would be like the animals, and he would have *an excuse for his sins*. But man does **have**

a conscience. And he knows he will be judged by God, in the world to come for his sins—he knows that God will *judge the secrets of his heart by Jesus Christ according to the gospel.* Romans 2:15-16

"Professor, you know you are a sinner, and will be punished by God for your sins. The Scripture in Romans 1:32 says that *'all men know* this! They know that all men who commit the sins listed in Romans 1:26-31 are worthy of God's judgment for their sins! They know this intuitively! They know this **without having read the Bible**!

"Professor, if someone robs you of all your possessions, if someone burns down your home, and murders your wife and children—you don't say that the one who did all these evil deeds is blameless. You don't say that he deserves no punishment for murdering your wife and children. No! You say that the murderer deserves to die for killing your wife and children!

"But any animal in the wild can kill another animal, and no one says, 'Look at that wicked animal. He's a murderer! He should suffer the death penalty for the murder he has committed.'

"No! For animals are only animals, and do not have a rational, moral nature. They do not have the **law of God written in their hearts**—They do not have a **conscience** that tells them what is right, and what is wrong.

"But we do! For we are not animals. And we did not come from animals. We are completely different from the animals!

"Professor U. R. Matter, when God made us, he made us *in his own image and likeness*: rational, moral beings. He made us free moral agents, with freedom to choose between good and evil. We are responsible, rational, moral beings, with free will, and accountable before God for all our actions.

"Professor U. R. Matter, how do you explain the *image of God that is in* all *men*, but *in none of the animals*? You know you cannot explain it with evolution! This should show you that evolution is a lie of the devil, and that **God created man completely different from the animals—in his own image and likeness**!

"My dear friend, I want to quote a little more of what the Bible says about the devil and his work to **lie** to you, to **deceive** you, and to **take you down into hell with him** at the final judgment:

'Ye are of your father the devil, and the lusts of your father ye will do. He was a *murderer* from the beginning, and **abode not the truth**, because there is **no truth in him**. When he speaketh a lie, he speaketh of his own: **for *he is a liar*, and the *father of it*.**' John 8:44

'And the great dragon was cast out, that old serpent, called the Devil, and Satan, which *deceiveth the whole world.*' Revelation 12:9

'Then **cometh the devil**, and **taketh away the word** out of their hearts, *lest they should believe and be saved.*' Luke 8:12

'And the beast was taken, and with him the false prophet that wrought miracles before him, with which he *deceived them* that had received the mark of the beast, and them that worshipped his image. These both were cast alive into the lake of fire burning with brimstone.' Revelation 19:20

'And *the devil that deceived them* was cast into the lake of fire and brimstone, where the *beast* and the *false prophet* are, and shall be tormented day and night for ever and ever.' Revelation 20:10

'Then shall he say also unto them on the left hand, Depart from me, ye cursed, into everlasting fire, *prepared for the devil and his angels*...And these shall go away into everlasting punishment: but the righteous into life eternal.' Matthew 25:41, 46

"Professor, you are preaching *the devil's lie of evolution* to your students. Do you realize that God will punish you forever and ever in hell for preaching that lie?

"Listen to what the Bible says about the final destiny of those who **tell lies, love lies,** and **make lies.**

'*All liars* shall have their part in the lake which burneth with fire and brimstone.' Revelation 21:8

'And there shall in no wise enter into it (heaven) any thing that defileth, neither whatsoever worketh abomination, or *maketh a lie.*' Revelation 21:27

'For without (outside of heaven) are dogs, and sorcerers, and whoremongers, and murderers, and idolaters, and *whosoever loveth and maketh a lie.*' Revelation 22:15

'But the fearful, and unbelieving, and the abominable, and murderers, and whoremongers, and sorcerers, and idolaters, *and all liars,* shall have *their part in the lake which burneth with fire and brimstone:* which is the second death.' Revelation 21:8

"Professor U. R. Matter, God is speaking *to you* in these Scriptures. Your entire life is a lie. You cherish the blackest lie in the entire universe. You have built your whole life upon the lie that there is no God who created the heavens and the earth.

"Professor, you must **repent** and **believe** the gospel of Jesus Christ if you would be saved:

'**Except ye repent**, ye shall all likewise perish.' Luke 13:3

'For God so loved the world, that he gave his only begotten Son, that whosoever **believeth** in him should not perish, but have everlasting life.' John 3:16

"Professor, *do not harden your heart* against the truth. But repent, and be saved. If you reject God's truth and the gospel of salvation in Jesus Christ, you will suffer **everlasting punishment** in hell.

'But unto them that are contentious, and **do not obey the truth** but obey unrighteousness, *indignation and wrath, tribulation and anguish, upon every soul of man that doeth evil.*' Romans 2:8-9

'For if we sin willfully after we have received the knowledge of the truth, there remaineth no more sacrifice for sins, but a *certain fearful looking for of judgment and fiery indignation, which shall devour the adversaries*....For we know him that hath said, Vengeance belongeth unto me, I will recompense, saith the Lord. And again, The Lord shall judge his people. It is a fearful thing to fall into the hands of the living God.' Hebrews 10:26-31

'But the fearful, and unbelieving, and the abominable, and murderers, and whoremongers, and sorcerers, and idolaters, and all liars, *shall have their part in the lake which burneth with fire and brimstone: which is the second death.*'" Revelation 21:8

Chapter XIX
Judas Calls His Colleague A Bumbling Idiot

Jed Truly, Bible and Science Teacher for Lynwood Christian Elementary School, sat down.

Silence filled the room, but only for brief moments.

Professor U. R. Matter had listened nervously throughout the long discourse given by Jed Truly. It was his class. He was the teacher. And the man had taken so long. He had already gone well over the class time.

But the man was knowledgeable. He spoke with authority and clarity. It was manifest that he was a master of the subject matter under discussion. And what he had to say was persuasive and even compelling. So compelling, that Professor U. R. Matter found himself more and more interested in hearing him as he continued. Why he would even like to sit down and talk with the man. But he would not like his students and colleagues to know the way he felt.

But the man had finally finished and had taken his seat. And he was relieved, for the man had taken so long! But he must stand now and dismiss the class. He leaned forward on the balls of his feet, and was poised to rise…

Then suddenly Professor Judas shot to his feet and began to rant and scream at Professor U. R. Matter: "Professor U. R. Matter! You are a bumbling idiot! You have allowed this crazy preacher to take up all your class time to preach a hell-fire and brimstone sermon to you from the Bible! He has gone on and on with his preaching, and you did not once sit him down and silence him!

"And this little girl," and he turned to Alice, and pointed to her with his finger, "stood and talked about God and the Bible, and you did not sit her down. You have demonstrated, with this girl, and especially with this fanatical preacher, that you have no control over your class.

"Furthermore you are incompetent! You don't know how to teach! You make evolution sound like it is nothing more than the theory, the guesswork, and the conjecture of men who cannot think!"

The Little Man tried to continue his wild rant, but was suddenly overcome by a violent paroxysm of coughing and gasping for breath.

And now, Professor U. R. Matter rose up in anger! He had been shamed! Not just privately, but openly and publicly, before his entire class—and before these strangers in his class!

Professor U. R. Matter glared at the Little Man (who had now collapsed into his chair), and spoke with measured contempt. "Professor Judas, this is my class! And I will conduct it as I wish. You do not belong here. I did not invite you. Nor did I ask you to speak. In fact I warned you not to interrupt my class and not to speak.

"As for the man who just spoke, I will admit he spoke longer than I expected, but he asked for permission to speak. And I gave permission. And by the way, although I do not believe all that he has said, I must admit it would be difficult or impossible for me to answer much of what he has said.

"But you have interrupted my class two times. And both times without permission. And, I have not agreed with what you have had to say either time. You are a lout and a contemptible boor. Now get out! You do not belong in my class!"

Then Professor U. R. Matter spoke to the whole class and said, "I am sorry, but we have run way over time. Even though it is late, you may go to your next class. I am late, but I am still going to my next class. Class is dismissed!"

But Professor Judas did not get up or move. And he directed his words once again to Professor U. R. Matter. "Go on and leave for your next class if you must. But I am staying here with these prisoners. They are going on trial right now to see if they have learned anything, and are ready to renounce their belief in God and the Bible. And if not, they will die today." And as Judas finished these last words he waved his gun in the air so that everyone could see it.

Some of the students had stood, and were about to leave the classroom. But, now, curiosity compelled them to stay, and they sat back down in their seats.

And now Professor U. R. Matter spoke out angrily to Judas, "You do not threaten me with a gun and tell me when I will come and go from my class. I have told you to leave, and you are defying my authority as long as you stay!" And with these words he sat back down.

Then, as an afterthought, he said, "bring out two more candles, I want more light!"

Chapter XX
Head Lighter Man Is Called First

Like his father the devil, Professor Judas was exceedingly cunning. So he called on the weak and inexperienced first.

Head Lighter Man was startled when he heard his name called.

Why had the Little Man called his name? What had he to do with believing in God and the Bible? Did the Little Man think that he, Head Lighter Man, was a Christian? Did he think that he knew God, and that he walked in the light of God's word? He knew he did not.

The Little Man called his name again, insistently: "Head Lighter Man, come immediately! I want to question you concerning your friendship with these Christians. You are a traitor. You have gone over to their side and are helping them. I want to know if you renounce your friendship with them. I want to know if you now renounce them, their God, and their Bible. And if not, you will die today!" And, again, he waved his pistol in the air.

Head Lighter Man was afraid. He lifted himself to his feet and slowly made his way to stand before the Little Man. And there he stood trembling.

The Little Man saw his advantage, and said, "Head Lighter Man, you will surely die today—yes, this very day—if you do not renounce your friendship with them, (he pointed with his gun at each of the five prisoners) their God, and their Bible."

"Is it wrong," responded Head Lighter Man, "to be a friend to those who have shown nothing but friendship and love to me?" Head Lighter Man was surprised that his trembling had disappeared and he had posed his question in a clear strong voice. He saw also that his question had surprised the Little Man.

"You're not asking the questions," said the Little Man. "I am. Now, are you a friend of these five prisoners, or not?"

"Yes, I am," said Head Lighter Man. "I would be a liar if I denied that I was their friend."

68

This was not going the way he had planned! He now asked the question that he thought would turn Head Lighter Man against his Christian friends: "Do you now renounce your friendship with them, and swear that you will never help them again? Your life depends on your answer! Answer, yes or no!"

"No, I will not renounce my friendship with them! And I will help them in any way I can! They only want to get back home. And their home is somewhere out in the Bright Regions. And if I can help them get to the Bright Regions, that is what I will do! They have been friends to me, and I can't help but be their friend."

The Little Man fumed, and spoke with all the rancor and bitterness in his spirit, "You have a chance to redeem yourself from the sentence of death. You can renounce their God and their Bible and you redeem yourself from death. But if you do not renounce their God and their Bible you will die today! Do you understand?"

"Yes, I do understand! But what reason would I have for renouncing God? I have never made a profession of faith in God before. All my life I have been completely neutral when it comes to God. Or have thought I was. But now I remember the words of Jesus. He said, 'He that is not with me is against me; and he that gathereth not with me scattereth abroad.' So I have always been against God!

"But one thing I can say for sure about him. He has never been against me! He has never stood against me or imagined evil against me. He loves me, a miserable sinner. Why should I stand against him now?

"No, I will not stand against God! I will not renounce God or the Bible. I believe with all my heart what my mother taught me from the Bible, in John 3:16, if I can still quote it." And he quoted, slowly and with great feeling, the words of John 3:16:

'For God so loved the world, that he gave his only begotten Son, that whosoever believeth in him should not perish, but have everlasting life.'"

The light from the two new candles revealed tears in the eyes of Christians, and students alike in the classroom that day. John spoke :

softly and reverently in thanksgiving to God: "Amen! Praise the Lord!" And although his words were quietly spoken, they were heard in every corner of the classroom.

The Little Man simmered with rage, and spat out hate filled words: "You stupid fool! You are condemned to die!" And pointing to the front of the classroom, he hissed, "Go sit there, until the trial is over!"

Chapter XXI
Little Alice Is Called Next

"The little girl will come next," said the Little Man.

"Wait!" cried out Jed Truly. "You can't put little Alice on trial. She's only seven years old! She is too young to be put on trial for her beliefs. None of the children, and neither Head Lighter Man nor John Frank have contended for God and the Bible. I am the only one who has spoken out for God. Put me on trial. Nobody else should be tried."

John Frank had also risen to his feet to speak against the Little Man's insane desire to try little Alice. "You are an evil, bloodthirsty child of the devil! You hate God and man, and would murder God if it were possible.

"Why is it that you hate Christians, and desire to murder them? It can only be because the devil is in you, and you are bound and determined to do his works! You know that your desire to try little Alice comes from the hatred and cruelty in your heart, and not from any desire to do justice.

"In fact, you know that you have no just cause to try any of us. There is no just cause to try Jed Truly. There is no just cause to try me. Much less a just cause to try anyone else. Give up your insane war against God, and repent of your desire to murder Christians."

The Little Man cursed Big John, and cried out, "Shut up! I hate you!

"Alice!" the Little Man screamed, "come stand before me!"

Little Alice stepped quickly before the Little Man, and stood serenely, facing him, and looking down upon him. She had to look down on him, for he was seated, and even if he were standing he was no taller than she.

The Little Man looked up at Alice and felt a vague nervousness at the thought that she was as big as he was. "Little Alice," he said, "do you remember, that less than an hour ago, you stood in this classroom and extolled God as the Creator of heaven and earth and all things on the earth? You said that God created everything, even though Professor U. R. Matter had just said that there is no God and no Creator!"

"But I know that God is my Creator, Mr. Little Man! And Professor Matter said *he didn't really know* how the world began, and *he didn't really know* how life began. But *I know*, Mr. Little Man! I learned it when I was in kindergarten, and I learned it in Sunday school, and I learned it at home. My mom and dad told me that God created us. My brothers told me that God created us. Everybody knows that God created us!"

"Stop! Stop! Stop that!" gasped the Little Man. "Don't call me Mr. Little Man! My name is not Mr. Little Man! My name is Judas! When you talk to me you will call me Professor Judas!

"Now listen, little Alice, you have been taught a myth and a lie from the Bible. You have been taught that there is a God, and that God created you. You must give up that myth, and believe what science teaches us—that we descended from monkeys and apes."

"Oh, no!" said little Alice. "I didn't come from a monkey! Listen to the poem I learned in first grade."

I didn't come from soup or slime in far off lake or sea.

I descended not from tomato plants nor evolved from a buzzing bee.

I didn't come from a little leaf, a worm, a snail, or a tree.

I didn't come from a crocodile, a fish, or a dumb monkey.

I'll tell you whence I came dear friend, from God who created me.

And then, just as if she had been performing on stage (and indeed little Alice was on stage, with an audience wholly captivated by her happiness, her simplicity and her unaffected presence) she curtsied before them, then turned to the Little Man for her sentence.

But, even as she curtsied, the room erupted with applause. The applause continued and even increased in volume so that the Little Man was embarrassed and shamed by it. What would they think, and *what would they do* if he told her before them all that she had to die for her belief in God? "Go," he said, "and sit there with Head Lighter Man."

Chapter XXII
The Twins Are Called As One Person

Next, the Little Man called for the twins to stand before him.

John and Jed both jumped to their feet. John spoke out first, "Which twin do you want to try first? Bob, or Bill? Call one at a time. You can't try them together. Who do you want to stand trial first? Bob, or Bill?"

"I want them both. Don't tell me what I can and can't do! I will try them together, and if either one of them is guilty they will both be condemned."

When the students had heard the Little Man's words, they whispered angrily among themselves and then began to chant: "Unjust, unjust, unjust, unjust, unjust." Over and over they continued to chant, and the chant increased in volume as more students stood to their feet and took up the chant.

Again, the Little Man was embarrassed and shamed. His face red with embarrassment, he stood to his feet and motioned for the students attention. When it was quiet enough, he announced that he would try each boy separately, and he called for Bob to come stand before him.

But before the Little Man could begin questioning Bob, Professor U. R. Matter stood to his feet and said, "Professor Judas, I have watched these proceedings closely. And it's clear to me that they are highly irregular—for you continually make unjust decisions. Professor Judas, my class and I will be watching closely what follows, and if you continue to make unjust decisions, we will not tolerate it!" Then he spoke to his students and said, "Bring out more candles. We must have more light!" And with these words the Professor sat back down.

Bob now stood before the Little Man. Bob was much older than his little sister, Alice; and he stood head and shoulders above the Little Man. He did not wait for the Little Man to question him. But, instead, began immediately to fire questions at the Little Man: "Why have you called me to stand here before you? What am I charged with? Inform me now of the charges that are against me, and tell me who brings those charges against me. Who is my accuser? Have him stand here before me, to lay before me his accusations! I have a right to have my accuser appear before me to make his charges known. And I have a right to examine my accuser to determine whether his charges are based in fact or not. Also, I want to know the exact laws or statutes I am charged with breaking, and when and where I was caught breaking those laws. Will you tell me, sir? I am waiting for your answer!"

The Little Man did not know what to do or what to say. For indeed he could not remember having heard Bob utter a single word before. He fussed and fumed and finally blurted out, "Why, I don't have to answer any of your questions. I'm not on trial here. You're the one that's on trial!"

Bob bent down, until his face was only inches away from the Little Man's face, and spoke with measured contempt: "You have broken all the laws of protocol and jurisprudence with Head Lighter Man and my baby sister, Alice. And you want to continue your miscarriage of justice with me. Sir, you are not fit to sit in judgment of others. For you have no knowledge of law and jurisprudence.

"And furthermore you are lacking in the character and judicial demeanor that belong to a judge. For you call me now to stand trial before you, when you refuse to tell me what I have done wrong! Or tell me now, what have you heard me say, or what have you seen me do, that is in violation of any of your laws here in this dark underworld? Tell me! Speak up! What have *you seen me do,* or what have *you heard me say* that breaks any of your laws?"

Silence filled the classroom as the Little Man desperately cast about in his mind for some word Bob had spoken or some deed he had done, and he found none. Finally he blurted out, "Well, you were with this man who does all the preaching."

Bob shot back, "Does being with someone make you blameworthy or praiseworthy for what they do or say? Professor Judas, you certainly have no knowledge of law and jurisprudence. And you seem to have no knowledge of logic either. For in condemning me for being with Jed Truly you condemn yourself also: *for you have been with him also!* And you condemn all of us who are here in Professor U. R. Matter's class; *for we have all been with Jed Truly for over an hour*!

"But let's get to the heart of the matter! It's not for who I've been with that you condemn me—nor for what I've said or done that you condemn me—but for who and what I am.

"But I am not ashamed of who and what I am. I am a Christian. And I gladly confess to you that I am a Christian. I gladly confess my faith in God, and in his Son Jesus Christ.

"I know God. I know God personally. I know God so intimately, that I would be a fool not to confess him as my God and Savior. So, I will make my confession of faith in God:

"I believe in one God, eternally self-existent in three persons. I believe in God the Father, in God the Son, and in God the Holy Ghost; Creator of heaven and earth, and all things in them. John 1:1-3, I John 5:7, Matthew 28:19

"I Believe in Jesus Christ our Lord and Savior, and that 'there is not another name under heaven given among men, whereby we must be saved.' (Acts 4:12) I believe that Jesus was conceived of the Holy Ghost in the womb of the Virgin Mary. He was crucified and died for our sins according to the Scriptures. He was buried, and rose from the dead on the third day. And without faith in the resurrected Savior, all sinners are doomed and lost forever.

"I believe that without holiness no man shall see God. (Matthew 5:8, Hebrews 12:14) I believe that faith without works is a dead faith; the faith of devils; a faith that leaves the sinner yet in his sins; and a faith that cannot save the sinner. James 2:17-20 and James 2:24-26

"I believe that Jesus Christ 'came in the flesh' (I John 4:2-3, II John 7-11), and is both true man and true God. (Gal. 4:4, Philippians 2:5-8, Hebrews 2:7,9; Hebrews 2:11; Hebrews 2:13-14; Hebrews 2:16-17; Hebrews 4:15) I believe that Jesus is the promised Son of man of Psalm 8:4 and Hebrews 2:6-9. Jesus called himself the Son of man over fifty times in the Gospels. I believe that Jesus was made flesh and dwelt among us, and was a man with the same human nature as all other men—yet he never committed sin. (Hebrews 4:15, Genesis 1:27, Hebrews 2:6-9, 2:11, 2:13-14, 2:16-17) If he was not a true man, he could not have shed his blood and died for sinners. And if he was not a true man, he could not have been tempted in all points like other men are tempted, yet without sin. Hebrews 4:15

"I believe that Jesus Christ will save *all those* who come to him in faith, and that *all those* who reject Jesus Christ will be doomed and lost forever. And I believe that all little children, who die before they reach the age of accountability, are innocent; and will be saved by the grace of God in Jesus Christ.

"And now I finish with another poem to go with the poem my sister recited, which tells, just like her poem, that the so-called 'evolution of the species' is absurd and impossible. True scientists have discovered that the DNA in the cell of every species is unique and different from the DNA in the cell of every other species. The DNA is an information code, comparable to the information code that men program into computers to make them work in the different ways they want them to work. And in the same way that it takes intelligence to program computers to run in different ways, it takes intelligence to program different DNA into the cells of each different species to make each species replicate itself and always be the same species it was created to be. So, the DNA, the information code, programmed into the cells of all the different species, was placed there by an intelligent being—and that intelligent being is God, our Creator!"

A single cell prokaryote

Aspired to be eukaryote.

So he fussed and he fumed

'Til he was consumed.

And ended up nothing, you note.

Another cell eukaryote

Cared not to be prokaryote.

He obeyed DNA,

Worked with God every way,

And was blessed by God always, you note.

So, what will you do my dear friend?

The lie, evolution, defend?

The reward of that lie,

Is to die by and by,

And end up in hell at the end.

The Little Man was speechless. In fact, all in the assembly were speechless, and in awe of what they had heard an eighth grade boy say.

Chapter XXIII
Bill Follows His Twin Brother

That is, all were speechless and in awe of what they had heard an eighth grade boy say—except for the other four prisoners who knew the unusual IQ and near photographic memory of Bob.

Especially did Bill, Bob's twin brother, know his exceptional memory and learning abilities. For they were in continual competition in their educational endeavors. And now, Bill knew that he would be called up next, and knew that he would not be able to confound the Little Man with his knowledge of law and judicial procedure, as his brother had. For law and government were a special interest and study of Bob. But he was ready, he thought, to obey the command of the Apostle Paul in I Corinthians 16:13, 'Watch ye, stand fast in the faith, quit you like men, be strong.'

And, now, with a strong voice, the Little Man called his name: "Bill, go forward to join your brother in the front. You are already condemned to die because of your brother's testimony..."

And, then, after a momentary pause, the Little Man added: "unless you are ready to renounce your faith in Jesus Christ; in which case you will be set free, and both Bob and your little sister Alice will be set free also."

Bill took the few steps it took to stand before the Little Man, who had tempted him to deny his Savior. He stood there, looking down at the Little Man. and cried out in anger and frustration. "Get behind me, you tempter, in the name of Jesus Christ! I will never deny my Lord!

"Jesus warned, '*Whosoever will save his life shall lose it*; but whosoever shall lose his life for my sake and the gospel's, the same shall save it. For what shall it profit a man, if he shall gain the whole world, and loose his own soul? Or what shall a man give in exchange for his soul? *Whosoever therefore shall be ashamed of me and of my words* in this adulterous and sinful generation; of him also shall the Son of man be ashamed, when he cometh in the glory of his Father with the holy angels.' Mark 8:35-38

"I am not ashamed of God. And I am not ashamed of his Son Jesus Christ.

"But Professor Judas, you are ashamed of God! And you are ashamed of his Son Jesus Christ! Please tell me, why are you ashamed of him? Why have you betrayed him? For I know your father preached the gospel of Jesus Christ. And I know that you at one time professed faith in Jesus Christ, and were baptized in water, confessing Christ as your Lord and Savior. Why are you now ashamed of him? Why have you betrayed him?"

The Little Man jumped to his feet! He was apoplectic with fear. He could not bear to have his colleagues know that his very own father had been a preacher. He could not bear to have his colleagues know that he had once been a Christian. Above all, he could not bear to have his colleagues know he had concealed his former faith in God, in order to be accepted and advance himself in his career as an educator.

"Liar! Liar! Why do you lie?" He shouted. "You don't know my father! You don't know me! Why do you make up lies about me?

"Go! Go now! Go sit with the others! You will die for your stupid faith in God and the Bible!" And pointing with his gun to the front, he said, "Go now! Go to the front!"

Chapter XXIV
Judas Calls Big John Next

The Little Man fell back into his chair. He was shaking uncontrollably and did not want to call anyone else just now. But he had to! He would call John next, for he did not want to face the preacher, at least not now.

"John Frank! You're next! Come! I want to question you."

The Little Man watched with a sinking feeling and an awful feeling of fear as Big John took the few steps needed to stand before him. Why, thought the Little Man, was Big John such a huge man? Big John towered above him and his big body cut off his view of the entire front of the classroom. Even the smallest Christians seemed to be much bigger than he was! But Big John was enormous! He waved his pistol around, but this did not take away his awful feeling of fear and awe as Big John stood before him.

"Are you ready to confess your belief in God, knowing that you will die if you do?" asked the Little Man in a shaky voice.

"I gladly confess that I believe in God," said Big John with a booming voice that filled every corner of the room. "But I don't just **believe** in God. I **know** God. I walk with him. And he walks with me. I have fellowship with the Father, and with his Son Jesus Christ. I dwell in him. And he dwells in me. He is *my God* and *my Savior*, who has saved me from my sins. I have been *born again* by the power of God's Holy Spirit. He has *changed me and made me a new creature*. I know what I was before, and I know what I am now by the grace of Almighty God. Before, I was a gambler, a drinker, and a slave to filthy cigarettes. And God set me free from the slavery of all those vices. Before, I took the blessed name of God in vain. I cussed and swore at my fellow men. I fought with them, and laughed them to shame when I was able to beat them. I couldn't keep a job, and I couldn't provide for my wife and children because of my drinking and gambling; and when my wife got saved I mistreated her and the children because they were going to church. I swore at my own wife, and mistreated her and the children because they were serving God!

"But somehow God got a hold of me and saved me. And now I am a born again Christian. I have been delivered from my sins, and I am a new creation in Christ Jesus. II Corinthians 5:17

"I am not ashamed to be a Christian! And I gladly confess Jesus Christ as my Savior. And the gun you hold in your hand will not keep me from saying so. Not only am I a born again Christian, I am also a Spirit filled Christian. Jesus has baptized me with the Holy Ghost just like he did the 120 on the day of Pentecost (Acts 2:4-18, 37-39). God is real. He has delivered me from all my sins—sins I desired to be free from, but sins I could not overcome. I tried to stop drinking and I tried to stop smoking before I was saved, but I always failed. But when Jesus came into my life he freed me from the bondage of all my sins.

"Yes, Praise God, he showed me what a rotten sinner I was. He showed me the terrible judgment I faced. And he showed me how desperately I needed a Savior. And then he saved me and delivered me from all my sins. And now I know God and walk with God! The Father dwells in me! Jesus dwells in me! And the Holy Ghost dwells in me! I Corinthians 12:13, II Corinthians 6:16-18, Romans 8:9-16, I John 4:13-16, Ephesians 4:6, Galatians 3:27, John 6:56, John 17:21-23

"And the worst sinner in the world can be freed from all his sins, and have blessed fellowship with God, and continual joy in the Holy Ghost, if he will only repent of his sins and give his heart to God." I John 1:3, John 14:21-23, Acts 1:4-5, Acts 2:1-4, Acts 2:38-39

John had finished his testimony. And he stood waiting for the Little Man to sentence him.

But the Little Man did not speak immediately. For John's testimony had cut to the quick and awakened unwelcome memories—thoughts that were now bitter to his spirit.

He had once known God. He had once had the peace of God and the joy of knowing his sins were forgiven! But when he came to the tunnels, he had been ashamed to confess Jesus Christ as his Savior. And he had denied his Savior and turned his back on God.

And now the words of God to those who deny their Savior came back to haunt and torment him:

'...*how shall we escape*, if *we neglect* so great salvation...?'
Hebrews 2:1-3

'Take heed, brethren, lest there be in any of you an evil heart
of unbelief, in departing from the living God....For we are
made partakers of Christ, if we hold the beginning of our
confidence steadfast unto the end.' Hebrews 3:12-14

'...For if we sin willfully after that we have received the
knowledge of the truth, there remaineth no more sacrifice for
sins, but a certain fearful looking for of judgment and fiery
indignation, which shall devour the adversaries....' Hebrews
10:25-31

The Little Man forced God's Word from his mind, and, with a surly
voice, ordered John "Go up to the front! You will die with the others!"
Then after a short pause, he expelled his breath and called for Jed
Truly.

Chapter XXV
Jed Truly Extols The Miracle Working Creator

Jed Truly stood before the Little Man and began to speak immediately. "Professor Judas," he said, "you need not ask me whether I believe in God or not. Yes, I believe in God. And, yes, I believe the Bible. I believe the Bible because there is an abundance of evidence for the truth of the Bible, and not one particle of evidence for evolution. Evolution is a lie inspired by the devil to turn people away from faith in God; who created the heavens, the earth, and all the things that are in the earth.

"I want you to consider several facts given in the Bible that make this easy to see.

"Genesis, the very first book in the Bible tells us that God finished all of creation in only six days, and then rested from all his work on the seventh day.

"But God spent *a full five of those six days* creating the earth, and all the things that are in the earth; and *only one of those six days* creating the sun, the moon, and the vast universe of stars.

"So let's start with the first day, Genesis 1:1-5. On the first day 'God created the heaven and the earth—And the earth was **without form**, and **void**.' In other words, God's work on the earth was unfinished. He needed *four more days* to finish it. The earth was **without form** and **void**, it was **completely dark** on the earth, and the earth was **completely covered with water**. So God **created light** on the earth on the first day. Then he divided the light from the darkness and made day and night on the earth on the first day. And he *created the light, and day and night*, **three days before** he created the sun, the moon, and the stars! Genesis 1:1-5, II Corinthians 4:6

"Then on the second day God did more work with the earth. He created a firmament in the midst of the waters that covered the earth, to divide the waters which were under the firmament from the waters which were above the firmament. And God called the firmament heaven. Genesis 1:6-8

"Then on the third day God did additional work with the waters that covered the earth. He gathered the waters that were upon the earth together into one place so that the dry land would appear. And he called the dry land Earth, and he called the waters that were gathered together Seas. But God did not stop there. He said, 'Let the earth bring forth grass, and the herb, and the fruit tree.' And the earth was covered with grasses and herbs and fruit trees. These were mature grasses, and herbs, and fruit trees; fully grown and mature, and able to multiply and reproduce after their kind! Genesis 1:9-13

"Then on the fourth day God created the sun, the moon, and the vast universe of stars. But there was already light on the earth on the fourth day—because God had already created light upon the earth three days earlier! Genesis 1:14-19

"Professor Judas," Jed asked suddenly, "don't you believe that 'with God all things are possible'? That God works miracles? Don't you believe that the God who spoke all the worlds into existence can do anything? Don't you believe that he can create any star, at any distance from the earth—and also create light for that star upon the earth at the same time. Or create light upon the earth **three days before he creates the stars**, as the Bible says he did? God is not a puny little man like us! God is the miracle working Creator! Genesis 1:3-5

"But let's go on. On the fifth day God created the great whales, and fishes of every kind to swim the rivers and the seas; and he created every kind of winged foul to fly above the earth in the open heaven. And these fishes and great whales, were not fishes' eggs or tiny minnows that God created; and the fowl were not eggs in a nest that needed to hatch. God created every species fully grown, and mature! And God blessed them and said, 'Be fruitful, and multiply, and fill the waters in the seas, and let fowl multiply in the earth.' Genesis 1:20-23

"And on the sixth day, the last day of creation, God created the cattle and the creeping things and the beasts of the field after their kind. And God created all the animals fully grown and mature. None of the animals were created helpless little babies to die a day or two after they were created. And after God had created all the animals, he created Adam, in his own image and likeness.

"And when God made Adam, he made him a *fully grown man*. He did not have to grow up from a tiny helpless baby to become a man. And God put Adam, a full-grown man to sleep, and took a rib out of Adam; and from that tiny rib made a full-grown woman to be his wife.

"But you evolutionists like to talk about a 'young earth' of molten hot lava that needed to cool for hundreds of millions of years before it could be a place where life could exist. But God did not wait around for hundreds of millions of years before he created life on the earth. God created the earth, 'old' and 'fully mature.' He created an old earth, fully prepared and ready to nourish and foster life. He created a hospitable earth, an earth ready to harbor and sustain life. In fact, on the *sixth day of creation* the Lord God '*formed man of the **dust of the ground*** (not ***molten hot lava*)**, and man became a living soul.' Genesis 2:7

"The earth was never a young earth as you have imagined, made up entirely of molten hot lava. God created an old earth. God created the earth with high mountains and low valleys, and rivers and seas. He created it with dry land and dirt and soil in places everywhere so that grass and trees could live and grow and provide food for animals to graze and live and multiply. The earth was never a place of total molten lava. Nor was it a place of total brittle lava rock. God created the earth old, with soil all ready to grow things and sustain life.

"But you evolutionists are in love with the superstition that the earth is billions of years old. You reach down into your magician's hat and pull out imaginary numbers for the age of the universe, and the age of the earth. For instance you say the earth is four or five billion years old, and you say the universe is anywhere from 12 to 20 billion years old. But, Professor Judas, you don't know what you're talking about! You throw these numbers of billions of years around as if they were settled science—when you know they are not science at all. How many times have you had to adjust and change the date for the so-called Big Bang? First, you estimate that it happened 12 to 20 billion years ago. 12 to 20 billion years ago, is *not very exact science*! Then you give an estimate that it happened 15 to 18 billion years ago. A little more exact! But 15 to 18 billion years ago is an estimate that just happens to exclude the present age given for the Big Bang. For the present age given for the Big Bang is 13.7 billion years ago!

"The fact is God created the heavens and the earth, and everything on the earth only about ten thousand years ago!

"And God created the earth *fully ready to receive and sustain the life he would create upon it*. The earth was created old, and fully mature, and fully ready for the life that God would create upon it. So it naturally appears to be much older than the one day old it was when he began it.

"After all, God did the same when he created each of the animals! He didn't create any of them as helpless little one-day-old babies. Helpless little babies would all have perished, from the very beginning!

"He created some animals a few months old when he created them. He created others two or three years old when he created them. And he created others much, much older.

"He created male and female rabbits only a few months old because they are mature in only a few months.

"He created dogs several years old because they are mature in several years.

"But he created man about 20 or 30 years old because man is mature in about 20 or 30 years. He certainly did not create man a helpless little infant!

"And God created man completely different from all the animals. *He created man in his own image and likeness*. And he created man to rule and reign over all the animals, and over all his creation!

'And God said, Let us make man in our image, after our likeness: and *let them have dominion* over the fish of the sea, and over the fowl of the air, and over the cattle, *and over all the earth, and over every creeping thing that creepeth upon the earth*. So God created man in his own image, in the image of God created he him; male and female created he them. And God blessed them, and God said unto them, Be fruitful, and multiply, and replenish the earth, and *subdue it: and have dominion over the fish of the sea, and over the fowl of the air, and over every living thing that moveth upon the earth*.' Genesis 1:26-28

"Later, the Psalmist David speaks of the dominant role God has given to man over his creation:

> 'When I consider thy heavens, the work of thy fingers, the moon and the stars, which thou hast ordained; what is man, that thou art mindful of him? and the Son of man, that thou visitest him? For thou hast made him a little lower than the angels, and hast crowned him with glory and honor. Thou madest him to have dominion over the works of thy hands; thou hast put all things under his feet....O Lord our Lord, how excellent is thy name in all the earth!' Psalm 8:3-9

"And this passage of Scripture is repeated in Hebrews, Chapter two, verses five through nine, where it tells us that God 'has put all the world to come in subjection under the feet of *Jesus Christ*, who is the promised *Son of man*.

> 'For unto the angels hath he *not put in subjection the world to come*, whereof we speak. But one in a certain place testified, saying, What is man, that thou art mindful of him? or the *Son of man*, that thou visitest him? Thou madest him a little lower than the angels; thou crownest him with glory and honor, and didst set him over the works of thy hands: thou hast put all things in subjection under his feet. For in that he put all in subjection under him, he left nothing that is not put under him. But now we see not yet all things put under him. But we see Jesus...'" Hebrews 2:6-9

At the word 'Jesus,' the Little Man cried out with a horrible scream that cut off the rest of what Jed was about to say. He shot to his feet, lifted his pistol, and with trembling hand took aim at Jed Truly. His rage and fury was so great that his whole body shook violently.

"Don't say his name again!" Screamed the Little Man. "I hate him! I hate him! And I hate you! You won't stop talking about him. And I'm going to kill you. And I'm going to kill you now!"

Jed fell on his knees, and called out to God to save him from the rage of the Little Man.

There was a clatter off to the right of the Little Man, a shrill scream, and the sound of running feet.

The Little Man was distracted by something hurtling toward his right shoulder. He fired his round, but even as he fired, his arm was knocked upward, and he was bowled over by the hurtling object. When he went down his big head hit the floor with a bang, and he lost his grip on the gun. Then the weight that had him pinned to the floor got up off him, and he lay looking up into the eyes of little Alice, who stood over him with menacing visage.

Chapter XXVI
We're Going Home

Big John took the gun, which was handed to him by a student, and tucked it into a compartment in his utility belt. As long as he had the gun, there was little danger from the Little Man.

He looked around the room. Little Alice stood in the middle of the classroom, surrounded by a circle of admirers. She was being celebrated as a heroine for her daring feat of tackling the Little Man with the gun.

The bullet had gone into the ceiling, and nobody was hurt. The students had tied the Little Man up and left him in a bundle at the front of the classroom. Head Lighter Man stood guard over him. The firing of the pistol in the close confines of the classroom had been unnerving, but now that there was no one hurt, a spirit of calm filled the classroom.

Big John stepped to where Jed sat, and where Bob and Bill stood alongside him. "Now," John said to Jed in a low voice, "We are free to go home. The Little Man is tied up, and I have his gun. He can't harm us anymore. Are you OK now?"

"Yes. I'm OK. Let's go home!"

"Alice! Come!" said Big John in his big booming voice, "Head Lighter Man! Come! We're going home!"

Chapter XXVII
The Bright Regions

Head Lighter Man led them around a final turn; and they all saw the light streaming in at the mouth of the tunnel.

Head Lighter Man extinguished his torch and began to run. He burst through the opening into the bright sunshine, and began to dance and whirl about, shouting for joy, as if he had just been let out of prison. He turned to his five friends, who were as happy as he to be out of the dark tunnels, and said, "Were home! We're in the Bright Regions. And I'm telling you right now, I'll never, never, *ever* go back into those black tunnels again!"

Then, with a more sober voice, he said, "But let's find out where you live! Do you see anything that looks familiar to you?"

And, as he turned, he stopped speaking and stood still. For he was now aware that they were not alone. And that they had interrupted the monologue of a venerable old man standing under an old oak tree holding a Bible in his hands. The old man had been directing his speech to several young men who stood at either side of the entrance to the tunnel.

The five Christians with him were also now fully aware of their surroundings. They saw the old man with the Bible, and the young men standing on either side of the tunnel entrance. And they saw, off in the distance, many great buildings, and houses, and streets, with cars and people moving along those streets, just like in the cities where they lived. And nearer to them they saw fields with crops growing. They saw what looked like groves of fruit trees. And they saw fields dotted with cattle.

And they saw, some distance off to the side of the great city; a huge low-lying expanse where nothing could be seen to live or move—for the whole area was covered with fog. And immediately adjacent to the huge foggy area were caves! Dozens upon dozens of them!

Now the man with the Bible had resumed his speaking. "Did you hear that?" He asked. "Did you hear that young man say, 'I'll never

ever go back into those black tunnels again?' And did you hear him shout for joy when he came out of the blackness of that tunnel?

"And I'll warrant you there's a reason, and the best of reasons, why this man is out of the tunnels, and happy to be out today. But young men," he continued, "has it ever occurred to you how silly it is in the first place to go into those dark tunnels to learn? Nay, it is worse than silly! It is absolute madness! Is it not madness to leave the light, and go where it's dark, to examine something? If you want to look at something, you do not leave the light and go where it's dark to look at it! No! If you want to look at something, and examine it well, you go to a place where there is an abundance of light! You shine all the light upon it that's possible!

"But the tunnels are a place of continual darkness. And the men who love that dark place, and are in that dark place, are there, because they hate the light God has given them. They hate the light that God has given them in the Bible. And they hate the light that God has given them in their very own nature.

"But they can never escape the light of their own nature. It is a light within them, that is with them wherever they go, and wherever they are! It is a light that floods their soul with the knowledge of things rational and moral: *For God has created man in his own image and likeness* with a rational, moral nature!

"And you have that light, young men! You have the light of God within you, a light that will never go out! God has put it there, and you can never destroy it or get rid of it! It is the rational mind that God has created you with! It is the law of God written in your heart! And it is the conscience that God has given you—that tells you what is right and wrong, and good and evil, and just and unjust—that urges you to do the good, and urges you not to do the evil!

"If you go to hell, where all impenitent sinners must go, you will still have that **conscience** with you in hell—forever augmenting your torments in hell, as it *accuses you throughout all eternity for your heedless impenitence and reckless perseverance in sin and ungodliness.*

"And if you go to heaven, with all those who are saved, you will, *for all the ages of eternity* have the *approving smile of a good conscience.*

*No longer a conscience **at war with God**, but now, a conscience **at peace with God, and his law written in your heart***!

"Young men, God has created us in his own image and likeness with a **rational, moral mind like his mind**; a mind that forces on us *irresistible convictions* of truth and error, right and wrong, good and evil, and justice and injustice. These truths are self-evident truths. They are direct perceptions of reason. They are truths that do not need to be proved. All men know they are true without proof:

"Some of the truths that all men recognize as self-evident truths, are those that follow:

"Nothing can both exist and not exist. A statement cannot both be true and not be true. Two contradictory statements cannot both be true. Two and two are four. Two and two are not six. A creation implies a Creator. Sin cannot be imputed where it does not exist, without injustice. Perfect justice cannot punish the innocent for the guilt of another. Sin is personal and non-transferable. No man can be held accountable for another man's sin, without injustice. Men cannot be sinners at birth. Newborn babies are not 'by nature the children of wrath,' 'under the wrath and curse of God,' and on their way to hell. If babies die in infancy (before they reach the age of accountability and know right from wrong); they will not go to hell! Necessary actions and non-free actions (actions *without freedom of choice*) cannot be condemned or punished, without injustice.

"Now all of these truths are known intuitively. They are irresistible perceptions of reason, given to us by God in our rational-moral nature—whether we will receive them and live by them or not! Young men, you have within you the blazing light of a rational nature that intuits truth and error, good and evil, and justice and injustice!

"God has *written his law* in the heart of every man. The most primitive and uncivilized of men around the world, whether in the dense jungles of South America, or in the slums of third world nations, have no excuse for their sins. For the *law of God is written in their hearts*, and they have *irresistible convictions of right and wrong, of good and evil, and of justice and injustice.*

'For when the Gentiles, **which have not the law** (the law

given in the Bible), **DO BY NATURE** the things contained in the law, these, having not the law, are a law unto themselves: Which shew the work of the **law written in their hearts**, their **conscience** also bearing witness, and **their thoughts** the meanwhile *accusing* or else *excusing* one another; *in the day when God shall judge the secrets of men by Jesus Christ* according to my gospel.' Romans 2:14-16

"My dear friends, *God has revealed himself to all men* in the nature he has given them. He has *written his law in every man's heart.* And he has *given every man a conscience* so that every man knows what is right and wrong, good and evil, and just and unjust.

"And because all men know the moral character of their deeds *before they do them,* God has appointed a day in the which he will judge the world *in righteousness.*

'He hath *appointed a day,* in the which he will *judge the world in righteousness* by that man (Jesus Christ).' Acts 17:31

'...in the day when God shall judge the secrets of men by Jesus Christ.' Romans 2:16

"Young men, if you are to escape God's judgment you must believe in the Savior Jesus Christ. And you must repent! For repentance is a *vital part of faith*; and without repentance you cannot be saved.

"To repent is to be sorry for your sins and to hate them. It is to turn from your sins. It is to turn to God in complete submission and obedience to all his will. Anything less than total renunciation of all sin is not repentance! You must turn away from every sin in your life. You must be willing to do God's will in everything! If you refuse to obey God in *just one* of his commandments, you are still unrepentant! James says, 'For whosoever shall keep the whole law, and yet offend in *one point,* he is *guilty of all.*' James 2:10

"And James said, 'What doth it profit, my brethren, though a man say he hath faith, and have not works? Can faith save him?....Yea, a man may say, Thou hast faith, and I have works: show me thy faith without thy works, and I will show thee my faith by my works. Thou believest that there is one God; thou doest well: the devils also believe, and tremble. But wilt thou know, O vain man, that faith without works is dead?' James 2:14, 18-20

"Oh, friends, hear me well on this matter of repentance! The great multitudes who are in hell today, are in hell because they would not give up all their sins! They are in hell because they would not obey God in everything! You must repent of all your sins to be saved!

"But a repentance *without faith* in the Savior Jesus Christ cannot save you either. Your repentance is nothing but fleshly works of self-righteousness if you expect to get to heaven without faith in the Savior Jesus Christ.

"The Apostle Peter said concerning salvation in Jesus Christ:

> *'Neither is there salvation in any other for there is none other name under heaven given among men, whereby we must be saved.'* Acts 4:10-12

"Unsaved men sometimes say, 'One religion is just as good as another. They will all take us to heaven.'

"Listen to me, young men, That is a lie from the devil! *Jesus* said, '*I am the way*, the *truth*, and the *life*: no man cometh unto the Father, but by me.'

"So Jesus is the biggest liar who ever lived, if he is not *the only way* to get to heaven. For he declared unequivocally that '***No man cometh unto the Father, but by me.***' John 14:6

"There is no salvation for any man who will not trust in Jesus Christ to save him. He must believe that Jesus Christ is the only Savior of the world and the only way to get to heaven!

"This world is filled with false religions that cannot save you! You can be a Muslim, a Hindu, a Buddhist, or *any other religion in the world*; but if you do not believe in, and confess Jesus Christ as your God and Savior, you are lost in your sins and on your way to hell.

"You can believe in Judaism, the Jewish religion, and still not be saved.

"The Jewish people who reject Jesus Christ as their Lord and Savior will be damned and lost forever. Matthew 23:33, 37-39

"Some Christians say, 'But the Jews are God's chosen people!' Yes, it's true in a sense that the Jews are God's chosen people; but those Jews who reject Jesus Christ as their Lord and Savior will be cast off by God, and will be damned and lost forever! There is no salvation for anyone, Jew or Gentile, who will not come to Jesus Christ and publicly confess him as their Lord and Savior!

"Oh, hear once again what Jesus said about his death on the cross to atone for the sins of *every single soul* in this world:"

'Even so *must* the Son of man be lifted up (crucified): that *whosoever believeth in him should not perish*, but have eternal life. For God so loved the world, that he gave his only begotten Son, that *whosoever believeth in him should not perish*, but have everlasting life. For God sent not his Son into the world to condemn the world; but that the world through him might be saved. *He that believeth on him is not condemned: but he that believeth not is condemned already, because he hath not believed in the name of the only begotten Son of God....He that believeth on the Son hath everlasting life: and he that beleiveth not the Son shall not see life*; but *the wrath of God abideth on him.'"* John 3:14-18, 36

The old man closed his Bible. He bowed his head and prayed for those who had heard him. Then he lifted his head and looked at Head Lighter Man. "Young man," he asked in a voice loud enough for all to hear, "will you come to our church tonight and tell of your experience in the black tunnels? Our service starts at seven o'clock. Will you come tonight and tell these young men about the dark tunnels? Our church is the Philadelphia Christian Church, on the corner of Strait Gate and Narrow Way. It's only about a mile from here. Will you come tonight, if these young men promise to be in the service tonight to hear you?"

Head Lighter Man answered, "Yes, I'll be glad to come to your church tonight. Yes, I'll come, and I'll tell about the tunnels."

The preacher now directed his words to the young men. "You have heard the promise this young man has made. Now will you promise to be in church tonight to hear him?"

Some of the young men said, "Yes," and nodded in the affirmative; but some remained silent, and did not commit themselves.

"Good!" said the preacher. "We'll see you in church then, at seven o'clock."

Then the preacher, a broad smile on his face, began walking toward the six. And they also headed toward the preacher, with big smiles on their faces.

Chapter XXVIII
The Preacher

"I'm glad to see you," said the Preacher, as he began shaking hands all around. And, as he shook hands with the three Becker children, he said, "I am amazed to see you children come out of the tunnels, for it is a place where children are not allowed. At least I've never known of children going in or coming out before. Tell me how you got in. Tell me why you were there. And, tell me why you are back here now. I know my questions are personal, but I am concerned for your spiritual welfare, so I would like to know."

Jed Truly hesitated to answer the Preacher, but had to, because Big John had lingered behind to speak to the young men at the mouth of the tunnel. So Jed began as best he could. "It is very difficult for us to tell you how we came into the tunnels. For, you see, we dropped into the tunnels from up above. Don't ask us to explain how, for we don't understand how ourselves. But here comes John Frank. He can explain it better. John, tell the preacher here where we came from, and how we got into the tunnels, and how we came to be where we are today."

John shook hands with the Preacher, and began by saying, "God bless you, Brother! We're all from Lynwood Christian Elementary School, except for Head Lighter Man, here, who has been in the tunnels for I don't know how many years. But praise the Lord, he has this very day confessed Christ as his Savior, knowing that to do so would cost him his life. But I don't want to put words in his mouth. He can speak for himself.

"But as for us who just came into the tunnels, as I said before, we're all here from Lynwood Christian Elementary School. Jed teaches Bible and Science there. I am Maintenance Man there. And these three children, Bob, Bill, and Alice, are students there.

"And it's awfully hard to explain how we got into the tunnels. But the truth is we just fell into the tunnel from our school up above. We fell right through the floor! Our school is directly over the tunnel we fell into.

"And ever since we fell into the tunnel we have been seeking a way out so we can go back home. So please, Sir, now that we're out, tell us where Lynwood is so we can go back home."

The preacher was pensive for a few moments. Finally he asked, "Is Lynwood the name of a forest where you live and where your school is located?"

"No, it's not the name of a forest," said John. "It's the name of a city. Don't you know where Lynwood is?"

"No, I've never heard of Lynwood. There is a small settlement not too far from here called Oakwood, but no Lynwood. I'm sorry, friends, there is no Lynwood around here."

"But it has to be somewhere close. It can't be over two or three miles from here. Because where we fell into the tunnel can't be over two or three miles from here."

"I'm not arguing with you on this matter," said the Preacher. "I'm just saying that there's no Lynwood around here. How long have you been in the tunnels?"

"I don't know. Maybe a night and part of a day. It must have been a night and part of a day since it's daytime out here now."

"Have you had food and drink?" asked the Preacher.

"No. And I reckon we're all tired and hungry. And we would sure like a drink of water. But most of all, we'd like to go home. Are you sure there's no Lynwood around here?"

"No! There's no Lynwood around here!" Said the preacher with finality

There was silence for some time after he had said this. Then Bill said, "Sir, we live in Long Beach, and our mother drops us off at school in the morning, and picks us up in the evening. Tell us where Long Beach is."

Before the Preacher could respond, little Alice exclaimed, "And our grandma lives in Seal Beach! Tell us where Seal Beach is and we can go to her house!"

"I'm sorry, but I've never heard of any Seal Beach or Long Beach."

Then Jed questioned the Preacher about cities he was sure he would know about. "How about Los Angeles?"

"I've never heard of it," said the Preacher.

"How about San Diego?"

"No."

"How about Bakersfield?"

"No."

"How about Sacramento? How about San Francisco?"

"I'm sorry. I've never heard of them."

Finally, frustrated and on the verge of anger, Jed asked, "Sir, are we in the United States? Is this California? Sir, I don't want to sound brutish, but please tell us where we are. So we can know the way to go back home."

"Yes, we are in the United States, and, yes, this is California. But I have never heard of any of the cities you have named.

"Right over there," the Preacher said, as he turned and pointed to the large city that spread before them, "is the city we live in. It is called Worldly-Way. Next to it is Wayward-Way. Then a little further away is Wicked-Way. It's the largest and most populous city close to us. Also close to us are the Tri-Cities of Sodom, Gomorra, and Gay-Pride-In-Sin.

"Our cities are named for their worldliness and sin. And I hate their names. And I hate the sin and wickedness that is practiced in them! I hate living in Worldly-Way! And I hate living close to all the other wicked cities that surround us. But we are in this world where there is wickedness and sin. And God commands us to live in this world, without loving it and without becoming a part of it. The Apostle John says.

'Love not the world, neither the things that are in the world. *If any man love the world, the love of the Father is not in him.* For all that is in the world, the lust of the flesh, and the lust of the eyes, and the pride of life, is not of the Father, but is of the world. And the world passeth away, and the lust thereof: but he that doeth the will of God abideth for ever.' I John 2:15-17

"But far worse than the fact that worldliness exists in Worldly-Way, and Wayward-Way, and Wicked-Way, is the fact that worldliness exists in many of our churches, and has swept away the love for God that once ruled in the hearts of God's people.

"Look over there," said the Preacher, pointing to a huge, low-lying expanse covered in fog. "That" said he "is the dwelling place of a mixed multitude of sinners. It used to be made up mostly of sinners who had never known God. But now thousands of former Christians have moved in with the unbelievers, because they now love the pleasures of sin more than they love God. (II Tim. 4:10) They still claim to be Christians, and are offended if you tell them they are not! They think you are mad when you tell them that they are not children of God, but are children of the devil. I John 3:8-10, John 8:44, Acts 13:10

"At one time there were seven strong churches in Worldly-Way. But now there are only two that are really strong. (Rev. 2:8-11and Rev. 3:7-13) That is because so many sinners from the other five churches have moved away from the Bright Regions to the Foggy Bottoms, where their sins are excused and accepted as natural and normal. They love the Foggy Bottoms, because, there, they are taught that they cannot live without sin.

"Their teachers dishonor God, by teaching that *God created them sinners*! I'm telling you the truth! The teaching that we are 'Created and born sinners' is the fundamental teaching of all the settlements down there in the Foggy Bottoms!

"My Friends," the Preacher continued, "almost every day I preach to whoever will listen to me down in the Foggy Bottoms.

"And almost every day I visit one or more of the caves to preach there. The caves are filled with the most hardened of sinners. For they are married to their idols, and are so hardened and confirmed in their sins that it is almost impossible to awaken them, and turn them to God.

"But I did not preach in any of those places today! While in prayer this morning God told me to preach here at the entrance to the tunnels. And now I know why. God has brought you here to testify and preach and open the eyes of many sinners who would in no other way believe and be saved. You will be a sign and a wonder to them because of where you came from, and they will receive your words!

"But now I see the forlorn look on your faces. I see that you are disheartened by the news that your home is not here. I see that you are filled with anxiety because you do not know how to find your way back home.

"So I want you to come home with me now. We can talk there about how you are to find your way back home. And more important, we will pray to God about it, and ask God to show you the way back home.

"But now, I know you're tired, and hungry, and thirsty. When we get home you can rest and refresh yourself; and we'll have something to eat before the service tonight. Come now. Follow me. Home is only a mile away."

Chapter XXIX
Alone In The Dark

Judas lay bound on the floor of Professor U. R. Matter's classroom. His hands and feet had been tied, and drawn together behind his back. He had been dumped like a sack of corn at the front of the classroom.

He was alone.

It was pitch-dark.

From his childhood the darkness had terrified him. And, when he had first come to the tunnels, the darkness had been more terrifying than any darkness he had ever known before.

At first he had complained that there was not enough light in the tunnels to see by, to study by, and to learn. The teachers had pooh-poohed his complaints. And he had learned to live with his fear of the darkness and the awful learning conditions. And then there came a time when he welcomed the darkness, and hated the light just like his teachers! That began when he agreed with them that God did not exist.

Something else changed when he denied the existence of God. The unclean spirits began coming to him!

He was terrified when they came. For they came in the darkness, when he was alone.

He could not see them. But he could feel their presence when they came close to him. Sometimes they made unearthly sounds as they approached, and they imposed their thoughts upon his mind—thoughts that he did not want.

He had resisted them, and told them to go away. But they kept coming back. Always when he was alone.

They were unclean! And they wanted to dwell in him and possess him. Matthew 8:16, Matthew 8:28

And now as he lay in the darkness, he could hear them coming again! He trembled as he heard them come close. "Go away!" He screamed. "Don't touch me!"

They surrounded him. "Don't touch me!" He shrieked.

"Don't be afraid," they said. "We will give you anything you want. We will give you power." Luke 4:6

Judas lay there, shaking in terror. He could not move away from them. And they were touching him. "We will give you power," they repeated.

Judas lay there, without any power to move or free himself. Hatred filled his heart as thoughts of revenge began to fill his mind toward those who had left him tied up and alone. He uttered his thoughts out loud, "Head Lighter Man! I hate you! I hate you and your friends! I will kill you all!"

Then the Little Man cursed bitterly, for he was bound and helpless, and could do nothing. "Power!" He thought with a sudden surge of pleasure. "The unclean spirits will give me power!

"But would the unclean spirits come into him—possess him?

"No!" He shrieked. "I don't want your power." Then sucking in a deep breath he screamed again and again at the top of his voice: "Get out! Get out! Get out!" Then he sucked in his breath again and screamed, "Get out, and never come back again!"

And, suddenly the unclean spirits were gone!

Judas lay on his side, breathing rapidly. He cast about in his mind for some way to free himself from his bonds. But he could think of nothing. Again his thoughts returned to revenge. "When I am free," he thought, "I will go to the Bright Regions. I will hunt them down. And I will kill them for leaving me tied up like this."

Then Judas heard a sound at the door! Terror filled his heart! "The unclean spirits are back!" he thought. He cursed them again and again in a shrill voice. Then he screamed, "Go away! Leave me alone! I don't want you near me! Go away and never come back again!"

The door opened partway, and Judas heard a searching voice, "What is going on in there? Who's there? Why are you cursing and screaming?"

Judas was embarrassed. That was not the voice of unclean spirits! It was the voice of a man! And he would rather die than tell him what had been going on—why he had been cursing and screaming! He replied harshly, "It's about time you got here! Come untie me! Some students left me tied up here, and I must be released immediately."

The student (for he was a student, and a former student of the man tied up on the floor) slowly approached the place where Judas lay. He looked down and said, "I can't see to untie you. I need a light to see by, if I'm to untie you."

"No!" said Judas. "You can untie me without a light. Just reach down and feel the ropes, and you can untie me without a light!"

"Aren't there candles in this classroom?" asked the student.

"Of course there are candles, you stupid ox!" Judas roared. "There are candles in every classroom! But I don't like the light. So you must untie me without a light."

The student turned to leave the ungrateful man. And as he moved away, the man on the floor began to rant and rave, "You stupid ox! Why are you leaving me? If I were free I would kill you! But I have other enemies more important than you, and I will kill them! Tomorrow I will go to the Bright Regions! And I will find them and kill them!"

The student stopped and turned back. "Why that's strange," said the student. "I was on my way to the Bright Regions when I heard the cursing and screaming in this classroom. You see, I've decided to give up my major in psychology and go back to the Bright Regions where there is more sanity. I have discovered that the psychology taught here in the tunnels is a pseudo science that is filled with absurdities, inconsistencies, and unreasonable assumptions. Professor C. More Light has opened our eyes—at least he has opened my eyes—to the fact that psychology by its very nature cannot possibly be a science of certainty. For men are free, and the motives of the mind are secret and often different in every single man—so that no man can know with certainty the psychology of any other man.

"In addition Professor C. More Light has said that the Bible gives the only true and complete psychology of man. And that if you want to understand the true psychology of man, you must read the Bible.

"Professor C. More Light has also told us that the true psychology of man is the study of his psyche, that is, the study of the mind of man and the behavior that results directly from his free and responsible choices. Much of today's study in psychology has nothing at all to do with the psyche of man and his free choices.

"And practically all psychology taught today is based on the false assumptions of evolution. It is based on the assumption that man is only an animal, with a larger and more highly developed brain than other animals, but without a living soul, mind, or psyche that is independent of his brain.

"But the Bible is the only true and complete book of psychology! It alone tells us everything about the psyche of man. It tells us that man is created in the image and likeness of God, with a living soul; that he is created a rational, moral agent, and that he is created with a free will, and thus is responsible and accountable before God for all his deeds."

"Oh! You're quite a preacher, aren't you?" said Judas sarcastically. "Why don't you close your mouth for a while, and come untie me? The candles are there on the table if you must have one. And I'll tell you all about Professor C. More Light. For I know all about him."

Within minutes the student had lighted a candle and untied Judas. During the process he saw that the man on the floor was his former Professor of Psychology!

Judas, now freed, stood to his feet. He strode to the table and rifled through the drawer, searching for his gun. When he could not find it, he swore, and glanced quickly around the room.

Then he directed his attention to the student who had freed him. He looked closely at him, and finally exclaimed, "Why, you were my top student in Psychology. Your name's X. M. Plary! But everyone calls you X. M. for short.

"You can't be thinking of leaving your studies in Psychology now! By now you're about to graduate! You can't leave now!

"And your present Professor is a lawbreaker. It is unlawful for him to mention the Bible and God in his classroom, because the Constitution calls for the separation of Church and State."

"But, Professor Judas, there is nothing in the Constitution about a separation of Church and State. The Constitution merely says, 'Congress shall make no law respecting an establishment of religion, or prohibiting the free exercise thereof; or abridging the freedom of speech, or of the press.'"

"Oh, shut your mouth! Professor C. More Light is finished! I'll be replacing him as soon as I return from the Bright Regions. And don't you leave! You stay right here until I get back."

And without further ado, and without saying, "Thank you," Judas turned his back on X. M. Plary, pushed through the door, and made his way through the black darkness toward the Bright Regions.

Chapter XXX
The Great Commission

Head Lighter Man stepped down from the platform. He had just finished telling of his years in the dark tunnels as a Lighter Man. He told of the oppressive darkness in the tunnels, and of the teachers' rabid fear and hatred of the light.

Then he told of the unusual circumstances of his conversion. He told of being put on trial for helping the Christians who were present with him. He told of being given the choice to reject Christ and live, or confess Christ and die. He told of the peace that flooded his soul when he said he could not and would not speak against Christ; and that he believed John 3:16, which his mother had taught him as a child. He said he had quoted it at that time to all those in the classroom. Then he quoted John 3:16 again for his listeners in the church.

Many in the audience were visibly moved by his testimony. And among those who were visibly moved were the young men who had come to the service to hear Head Lighter Man tell of his experiences in the dark tunnels.

Now, as Head Lighter Man stepped down from the platform, the Preacher met him. They conversed for a few moments and then Head Lighter Man shook his head in the affirmative.

The Pastor stepped onto the platform, went to the pulpit, and made the following announcement: "Christ our Lord commanded all who believe in him to be baptized in water when they are saved. This is the Lord's first command to those who repent and believe the gospel of Jesus Christ. Head Lighter Man has agreed to obey the Lord's command and be baptized tonight after the sermon."

The Pastor wasted no time, but immediately opened his Bible and read his text. Then he offered a short prayer for God's blessing as he preached the Word of God. His text was the Great Commission given by Jesus Christ to his disciples:

'And Jesus came and spake unto them, saying, All power is given unto me in heaven and in earth. Go ye therefore, and teach (make disciples of) all nations, baptizing them in the name of the Father, and of the Son, and of the Holy Ghost:

108

teaching them to observe all things whatsoever I have commanded you. And, lo, I am with you always, even unto the end of the world. Amen.' Matthew 28:18-20

"What I have just read is the Lord's Great Commission to his disciples. It was the Commission given to them forty days after his death, burial, and resurrection.

"Jesus, who stood before his disciples at this time, had died for sinners, had been buried, had risen from the dead, and was now alive. He stood before his disciples, victorious over death, hell, and the grave.

"And he prefaced the Commission he gave them with these words: '*All power* is given unto me in heaven and in earth. *Go ye therefore…*'

"So Jesus promised to give his disciples *all the power in heaven and in earth to carry out the Great Commission*! Jesus promised all power in heaven and in earth, because *it is impossible* for man to carry out the Great Commission without the power of God!

"The Great Commission is given again in three other places. And in each one of them Jesus tells his disciples that they must have the power of God to carry out the Great Commission. He even *commands them not to preach his gospel* until they are *endued with power from on high*!

"This is recorded in Luke 24:46-51. Here, the Lord said that he would send the promised Holy Ghost upon them, and that *before they began preaching the gospel* they were to tarry in Jerusalem until they were *endued with power from on high*!

'And that *repentance and remission of sins should be preached in his name among all nations, beginning at Jerusalem.* And ye are witnesses of these things. And, *behold, I send the promise of my Father upon you: but tarry ye in the city of Jerusalem, until ye be endued with power from on high.*'

"The Great Commission is repeated again in Mark 16:15-20:

'And he said unto them, Go into all the world, and preach the gospel to every creature. He that believeth and is baptized shall be saved; but he that believeth not shall be damned.'

"And *the power to carry out the Great Commission* is given in the verses that follow:

'And these *signs shall follow them that believe*; in my name shall they cast out devils; they shall speak with new tongues; they shall take up serpents; and if they drink any deadly thing, it shall not hurt them; they shall lay hands on the sick, and they shall recover. So then after the Lord had spoken unto them, he was received up into heaven, and sat on the right hand of God. And *they went forth, and preached everywhere, THE LORD WORKING WITH THEM, AND CONFIRMING THE WORD WITH SIGNS FOLLOWING. Amen.*' Mark 16:17-20

"Finally, the *promise of the power* to carry out the Great Commission is given again in Acts 1:8.

'***But ye shall receive power, after that the Holy Ghost is come upon you***: and ye shall be witnesses unto me both in Jerusalem, and in all Judea, and in Samaria, and unto the uttermost part of the earth.' Acts 1:8

"Brethren, *we cannot do the work of God without God's power.* And it must grieve the heart of God that many of his children are so *filled with unbelief,* that they will not pray for *the power he has promised them.*

'For *the promise is unto you,* and to your children, and to all that are afar off, *even as many as the Lord our God shall call.*' Acts 2:39

'And it shall come to pass *in the last days,* saith God, *I will pour out my Spirit upon all flesh*: and your sons and your daughters shall prophesy, and your young men shall see visions, and your old men shall dream dreams. And on my servants and on my handmaidens I will pour out in those days of my Spirit; and they shall prophesy.' Acts 2:17-19

"And Jesus said:

'Verily, verily, I say unto you, He that believeth on me, *the works that I do shall he do also; and greater works than these shall he do: **because I go unto my Father**.*' John 14:12

'*It is expedient for you* that *I go away* (unto my Father): for if I go not away, *the Comforter will not come unto you*; but if I depart I will send him unto you.' John 16:7

'And I will pray the Father, and he shall give you *another Comforter, that he may abide with you forever.*' John 14:16

'But *the Comforter, which is the Holy Ghost*, whom the Father will send in my name, he shall teach you all things, and bring all things to your remembrance, whatsoever I have said unto you.' John 14:26

'Nevertheless I tell you the truth; It is *expedient for you* that I go away: for if I go not away, the Comforter will not come unto you; but if I depart, I will send him unto you.' John 16:7

'In the last day, that great *day* of the feast, Jesus stood and cried, saying, If any man thirst, let him come unto me, and drink. He that believeth on me, as the Scripture hath said, out of his belly shall flow rivers of living water. (But this spake he of the Spirit, which they that believe on him should receive: for the Holy Ghost was *not yet given*: because that Jesus was not yet glorified.)' John 7:37-39

"Oh, brethren! We *need the Holy Ghost*! We need him *to do those things that are impossible for us to do. We need him to come to those who are lost in their sins to awaken them, and make real to them their great peril and need. We need him to convict them of sin and of righteousness and of judgment.* John 16:8

"*And we need the Holy Ghost to come to us, to endue us with his power: to lead us, to teach us, and to abide with us forever.*

"Oh, brethren! When will we ever learn, that, *without God we are powerless, and can do nothing*!" Zechariah 4:6

Chapter XXXI
What The Great Commission Requires

"Now, my Brethren, I will tell you what the Great Commission requires preachers to do; and what the Great Commission requires new converts to do.

WHAT IT RQUIRES PREACHERS TO DO

"Stated in one simply sentence, Christ's Great Commission requires preachers to *preach the gospel of the Savior Jesus Christ to the ends of the earth.*

"They are to preach that Jesus suffered and died on the cross to atone for our sins. That he was buried, and rose from the dead on the third day. That he ascended up into heaven, is seated at the right hand of the Father, and will return again for his church. They are to preach that all those who believe in Jesus, are pardoned and born again. They are to preach that *pardon* and the *born again experience* are two distinct works of grace, and that the same grace that pardons and justifies the sinner, also purifies him and frees him from the power of sin! They are to preach that to be born again of God is to be made a holy, righteous, loving, sin free person: *a new creation* in Christ Jesus! And they are to preach that the baptism with the Holy Ghost is yet another work of God's grace—in which God empowers Christians to preach the gospel of Jesus Christ with signs following!

"But the Great Commission requires the preacher to do three more things: It requires him to *make disciples of all new converts*; it requires him to *baptize new converts in the name of the Father, and of the Son, and of the Holy Ghost*; and it requires him to *teach new converts 'to observe and do all things that Christ commanded his first disciples to observe and do.'*

WHAT IT REQUIRES NEW CONVERTS TO DO

"In one simple sentence, the Great Commission requires new converts to *obey* the gospel of Jesus Christ.

"The new Christian must *obey the gospel*. He must *be a disciple of Jesus Christ*. He must *be baptized in water*. And he must *observe and do* all that Christ commanded his first disciples to observe and do.

"The new believer must **repent** *and* **believe** *the gospel of Jesus Christ*! Jesus preached the necessity of faith to be saved, but he did not preach faith without repentance. He said:

'Except ye repent, ye shall all likewise perish.' Luke 13:5

"And Jesus said in the Great Commission itself:

'And that **repentance and remission of sins** *should be preached* **in his name** *among all nations, beginning at Jerusalem. And ye are witnesses of these things.*' Luke 24:47-48

'**Repent ye, and believe** the gospel.' Mark 1:15

"And the Apostle Peter also spoke of the necessity of repentance in order to be saved.

"Then Peter said unto them, 'Repent, and be baptized everyone of you in the name of Jesus Christ *for the remission of sins.*' Acts 2:38

'Repent ye therefore, and be converted, *that your sins may be blotted out*' Acts 3:19

"My Brethren, do you think that the *believer* who continues to *disobey* God's commandments has really *repented*?

"Do you think that the believer who *refuses water baptism* has really repented?

"Do you think that the believer who refuses to *become a disciple of* Jesus *Christ* has really repented?

"Many believers refuse to become disciples of Jesus Christ because it costs so much to follow him. They want an easy religion that costs them nothing. But Jesus requires that we surrender everything we have to him, when we come to him."

WHAT IT MEANS TO BE A DISCIPLE OF CHRIST

"What did Jesus teach about being his disciple? Jesus taught that we must *walk like Jesus walked* if we would be his disciple.

'The **disciple** is not above his **master**, nor the **servant** above his **lord**. It is enough for the **disciple** that he be as his **master**, and the **servant** as his **lord**. If they have called the master of the house Beelzebub, how much more shall they call them of his household?' Matthew 10:24-25

'Think not that I am come to send peace on earth: *I came not to send peace, but a sword.* For I am come to set a man at variance against his father, and the daughter against her mother, and the daughter in law against her mother in law. And a man's foes shall be they of his own household. *He that loveth father or mother more than me is not worthy of me. And he that taketh not his cross, and followeth after me, is not worthy of me. He that findeth his life shall lose it: and he that loseth his life for my sake shall find it.*' Matthew 10:34-39

"Now let's read more of what Jesus told *his disciples* it would cost them to follow him and be his disciples:

'From that time forth began Jesus to show *unto his disciples*, how that he must go unto Jerusalem, and suffer many things of the elders and chief priests and scribes, and be killed, and be raised again the third day.'

'Then Peter took him, and began to rebuke him, saying, Be it far from thee, Lord: this shall not be unto thee.'

'But he turned, and said unto Peter, Get thee behind me, Satan: thou art an offence unto me: for thou savourest not the things that be of God, but those that be of men.'

'Then said Jesus unto his disciples, *If any man will come after me, let him deny himself, and take up his cross, and follow me. For whosoever will save his life shall lose it: and whosoever will lose his life for my sake shall find it. For what is a man profited, if he shall gain the whole world, and lose his own soul? or what shall a man give in exchange for his soul? For the Son of man shall come in the glory of his Father with his angels; and then he shall reward every man according to his works.*' Matthew 16:21-27

"Now let's read this same account in Mark's gospel, where it is given not only to Christ's disciples, but also to **all the people who followed Jesus**:

'And he began to teach them, that the Son of man must suffer many things, and be rejected of the elders, and of the chief priests, and scribes, and be killed, and after three days rise again.'

'And he spake that saying openly. And Peter took him, and began to rebuke him. But when he had turned about and looked on his disciples, he rebuked Peter, saying, Get thee behind me, Satan: for thou savourest not the things that be of God, but the things that be of men.'

'And when he had *CALLED THE PEOPLE UNTO HIM with his disciples also*, he said unto them, *Whosoever will come after me, let him deny himself, and take up his cross, and follow me For whosoever will save his life shall lose it; but whosoever shall lose his life for my sake and the gospel's, the same shall save it. **For what shall it profit a man, if he shall gain the whole world, and lose his own soul?** Or what shall a man give in exchange for his soul? Whosoever therefore shall be ashamed of me and of my words in this adulterous and sinful generation: of him also shall the Son of man be ashamed, when he cometh in the glory of his Father with the holy angels.'* Mark 8:31-38

"Now let's read the words of Jesus in Luke's gospel where the cost of following Jesus is given to all the people again:

'And there went great multitudes with him: and he turned, and said unto them, If *any man come to me, and hate not his father, and mother, and wife, and children, and brethren, and sisters, yea, and his own life also, **he cannot be my disciple**. And whosoever doth not bear his cross, and come after me, **cannot be my disciple**….So likewise, whosoever he be of you that forsaketh not all that he hath, **he cannot be my disciple**.'* Luke 14:25-34

"I will read just one more verse from the gospel of John, where Jesus tells what it costs to follow him:

'He that *loveth his life* shall lose it; and he that *hateth his life* in this world shall keep it unto life eternal.' John 12:25

"Dear Christian, do you think that Christ's requirement that we 'hate our life in this world' is unreasonable and impossible? That he requires that which is unthinkable for the Christian?

"If so, I want to tell you, dear Christian, that *every true Christian does hate his life in this world*; for that is what Jesus requires of all those who follow him.

"**Christ himself,** *hated his life in this world*, and is an example of how we are to *hate our life in this world.*

"Our Declaration of Independence says:

'WE hold these Truths to be self-evident, that all Men are created equal, and that they are endowed by their Creator with certain unalienable Rights, that among these are *Life, Liberty, and the Pursuit of Happiness.*'

"I believe these words from the Declaration of Independence. I believe that every human being has the God-given right to life, liberty, and the pursuit of happiness. I believe I have those rights, and I believe you have those rights.

"But Jesus also had those same rights! Yet he *willingly* gave up his right to life, and died on the cross to save us from sin!

"And now he says that *we must be willing to give up our lives and die* for his sake and the gospel's.

"He says, 'If any man come to me, and *hate not his father, and mother, and wife, and children, and brethren, and sisters, yea, and (hate) **his own life also**, he cannot be my disciple.*' Luke 14:26

"He says, 'He that ***loveth his life*** shall lose it; and he that ***hateth his life*** in this world shall keep it unto life eternal.' John 12:25

"He says, '*Whosoever will **save his life** shall lose it; but whosoever shall **lose his life for my sake and the gospel's**, the same shall save it.*

For what shall it profit a man, if he shall gain the whole world, and lose his own soul?' Mark 8:35-36

"My dear friends, Christ tells you what you must do to be his disciple.

"But he will not do it for you. *You must do it yourself!*

"He will not force you to deny yourself, and take up your cross, and follow him. He will not force you to forsake all that you have. He will not force you to hate your own life in this world.

"It is your choice! **You must do it**!

"*You* must repent. Jesus will not do it for you! You must believe in Jesus and come to him. And when you come to Jesus you must become his disciple.

"You have a choice to make. It is a fundamental, life-changing choice. Your choice (if you choose to obey the gospel of God) will change your whole way of life. You will not be the same man you were before. You will be changed by the mighty power of God. You will be born again of the Spirit of God. You will become a new creation in Christ Jesus. You will be transformed from a sinner into a saint!

"Sinner, there are three things you must do tonight to be saved. I will read them again from our text: '*Make disciples* of all nations, *Baptizing them* in the name of the Father, and of the Son, and of the Holy Ghost, and *Teaching them to observe all things* whatsoever I have commanded you.'

"God wants you to do these three things tonight:

"He wants you to become a disciple of Jesus Christ, tonight.

"He wants you to be baptized in the name of the Father, and of the Son, and of the Holy Ghost, tonight.

"And he wants you to observe and do all that he commanded his first disciples to observe and do, *beginning tonight.*

"Will you obey the words of Jesus, tonight? Will you renounce all your sins, tonight? Will you repent and give your whole life to God, tonight?

"If you will, I want you to stand to your feet, and come and stand around this altar; where I will pray with you who have made your decision to follow the Savior Jesus Christ. Come, now! It is Christ who calls you to follow him. It is Christ who calls you to be saved from your sins. Come, now."

Sinners did come to the altar. The group of young men, who had come to hear Head Lighter Man came to the altar. A young married couple came to the altar. And Head Lighter Man came to the altar!

The Pastor now began speaking to the people who had come forward. He asked them if they believed with all their heart in the Savior Jesus Christ. He asked them if they now truly repented of all their sins. And he asked them if they would now follow Jesus and obey his teachings for the rest of their life. And when he had received a positive response from each one, he asked them all to kneel down before God, and to ask God to forgive them and save them from their sins.

And as they knelt in prayer, he encouraged them, quoting verses from the Bible: "If we confess our sins, he is faithful and just to forgive us our sins, and to cleanse us from all unrighteousness." (I John 1:9) And, "Whosoever shall call upon the name of the Lord shall be saved." Romans 10:13

And he continued to encourage them with a reassuring voice, "Call out to God. Don't be afraid to pray out loud. Call upon the name of the Lord, and he will save you."

Then the Preacher quoted Matthew 7:7-8: "Ask, and it shall be given you; seek, and ye shall find; knock, and it shall be opened unto you: for every one that asketh receiveth; and he that seeketh findeth; and to him that knocketh it shall be opened.

"Cry out to God!" the Preacher exhorted, "He will hear you and answer your prayer. He will save you and fill you with the Holy Ghost."

And as the believers overcame their fear of men, and ventured to pray out loud (many had never prayed before), the Pastor began praying with them.

Then suddenly one at the altar began speaking in tongues. Another was so filled with God's Spirit, he began leaping for joy while still on his knees. Others came to their feet, and began shouting and praising God.

Chapter XXXII
Believers Were Baptized In Water

The believers were shown where the baptismal robes were, so that they could prepare themselves to be baptized.

The Pastor stepped down into the waters of the baptismal tank with his Bible in hand.

He told the Church that the new believers were not being baptized in water to be saved; but that water baptism was necessary because it was the commandment of the Lord Jesus Christ. He said, "Jesus himself was baptized in water; not to be saved, but to fulfill all righteousness." Then he read several texts from the book of Acts to show that believers were always baptized as soon as they were saved. Acts 2:41, Acts 8:36-38, Acts 10:44-48, Acts 16:30-33, and Acts 19:4-5.

Then the Pastor received the believers, one by one. But he did not baptize any believer immediately.

He asked each believer, three questions before he baptized him: "Do you believe that Jesus suffered and died on the cross for your sins, that he was buried, and that he rose from the dead on the third day?

"Do you believe that Christ commanded his disciples to *make disciples* of all nations, *baptizing them* in the name of the Father, the Son, and the Holy Ghost, and teaching them to observe all things that he had taught them?

"And, now, have you come to God with your whole heart, and will you serve him and obey him for the rest of your life?"

Then Pastor Truelove (for Truelove was his name) was ready to baptize each one who had answered his questions with a heartfelt yes. And he baptized each one, saying, "Because of your faith in the Lord Jesus Christ and your commitment to follow him and obey him for the rest of your life: I now baptize you in the name of the Father, and of the Son, and of the Holy Ghost. Amen."

Chapter XXXIII
Go Back The Way You Came

Big John rose from his knees and followed Pastor Truelove and two of his deacons out of the house and into the early morning sunshine. Head Lighter Man, Jed, and the three children crowded in close after them. They were on their way to preach in the Foggy Bottoms.

Big John thought back over the three prayer meetings they had had in the Pastor's home.

They had prayed yesterday when Pastor Truelove took them home with him. They had cried desperately for God to show them the way to go back home. They had also prayed earnestly for God to bless in that evening service—and in the preaching today in the Foggy Bottoms. When the Pastor's wife knew that the Pastor had asked them to go with him to the Foggy Bottoms, she had asked that the children be allowed to stay home with her, at least that little Alice be allowed to stay home with her. But Big John had declined her offer because the Holy Spirit had told him they would soon be going home, and had even told him the way they were to go home.

And then, after last night's service they had all prayed again—and the Spirit had again told him they were going home, and the way they were to go home.

And this morning in the prayer meeting, the Pastor's wife had renewed her kind offer, and had begged again that the children be allowed to stay with her while the men were preaching in the Foggy Bottoms.

But Big John had declined again, because, this morning the Spirit had again told him, very forcefully, that they were going home soon, and had told him the way again. The words of the Spirit were, "You know the way. Go back the way you came!"

Chapter XXXIV
The Devil's Lies

When they walked down into the Foggy Bottoms, they passed out of the light and down into a layer of fog that blotted out their vision of the sun. At times the sun tried to peek through, but as they went steadily downward the fog grew thicker until they could no longer see the sun.

And as they pressed downward into yet more fog, the houses appeared like phantoms, looming up toward them out of the fog.

Finally they went up a long rise through the fog until they came to a small park that was surrounded by houses built right up to the park. A huge sign in the middle of the park announced the settlement's long name: **SINCE I AM BORN WITH A SINFUL NATURE, AND CAN NEVER BE FREE FROM SIN, GOD ACCEPTS A FORM OF GODLINESS WITHOUT THE POWER THEREOF.** II Timothy 3:1-5

There were some children playing in the park; and when they saw the Preacher, they turned toward their houses and began calling out to their parents: "The Preacher is here! The Preacher is here! Come hear the Preacher!"

Immediately Pastor Truelove called out with a loud voice: "Come out and hear the Word of God! Call your friends, and bring them with you! I have a message from God's Word for you! All of you who want to hear God's Word, come out. We're going to start right now."

He gave his call twice, and immediately the people began filling the park.

One of the deacons opened the service in prayer. He had a clear, ringing voice that could be heard by everyone in the park. He lifted his voice to God with deep feeling, and this is the petition he made before God:

"Blessed God of grace and mercy, thou hast shown thy great love to us by giving thy Son to die for our sins. Oh God, show this people that true love is a willingness to sacrifice our own good for the good of others, as Jesus did when he died on the cross for our sins.

"Oh blessed Lord! Show us once again, that we know not what love is, and that we have no love for thee, if we live in disobedience to any of thy commandments. Thou hast said: 'This is the love of God that we keep his commandments.' (I John 5:2-3) O, righteous Lord! Convict us of sin, of righteousness, and judgment. Amen.'"

The second deacon now stepped forward with a hymnbook in his hand, and announced they would sing, The Old Rugged Cross:

On a hill far away stood an old rugged cross, The emblem of suffering and shame;
And I love that old cross where the dearest and best, For a world of lost sinners was slain.

So I'll cherish the old rugged cross, Till my trophies at last I lay down;
I will cling to the old rugged cross, And exchange it some day for a crown.

Oh, that old rugged cross so despised by the world, Has a wondrous attraction for me;
For the dear Lamb of God left his glory above, To bear it to dark Calvary.

So I'll cherish the old rugged cross, Till my trophies at last I lay down;
I will cling to the old rugged cross, and exchange it some day for a crown.

Big John was amazed at what he saw! Many of those who were seated or standing in the park had hymnals. And those without hymnals as well as those with hymnals were singing as if they knew the words by heart. Several of those singing were singing with heads turned up toward heaven and with their eyes closed. Others sang with tears streaming down their faces. Hadn't the Preacher said that the Foggy Bottoms were peopled with a mixed multitude of sinners—either with rank unbelievers or with backsliders from the Christian faith? John wanted to ask the Pastor about this, but the Pastor had just stepped forward and had opened his Bible to begin preaching.

But as the Pastor opened his Bible, a woman, and not just any woman, but one of the women from the Church of Ephesus (Revelation 2:1-7) stepped out in front of the Pastor as he was about to preach. And she began to testify. And as she testified she turned slowly about making eye contact with all those in the park. And this was her testimony:

"I love my Jesus. Oh, how I love him! To think he died for a sinner like me! The Apostle Paul said he was the chief of all sinners. (I Timothy 1:15) And the Psalmist David described himself as the most depraved sinner of all. (Psalm 51:5) But I know I'm a worse sinner than either David or Paul. But, praise God, the Bible says, 'Where sin abounded, grace did much more abound.' (Romans 5:20) So I know that God's grace reaches me, even though I am a sinner and sin every day!

"Oh, saints of God! Even though we are wicked sinners, and sin against God daily, Jesus still loves us! And now I want to sing the chorus that we all love so much: My Jesus I Love Thee.

And the woman from the church of Ephesus invited everyone to sing along with her. And tears began to stream down her face when she came to the last phrase: 'If ever I loved thee, my Jesus 'tis now.' And it was here that she broke down and wept, and had to blow her nose. But she composed herself, and finished with this fiery testimony:

"I hate all false religions, and false teachers, and false doctrines. I especially hate the doctrine of the Nicolaitans. And I hate the doctrine of law-works to be saved! Law-works is a lie! For the Bible says, 'we are saved by grace through faith, and that without the works of the law!' The law's been done away with! It doesn't exist for the Christian! And we don't have to keep it anymore! Oh, how I hate false apostles and false prophets! But, oh, how I love my sweet Jesus. I love him because he loves a sinner like me." Then she choked up again, after which she recovered long enough to quickly recite these closing words: "This testimony is for the honor and glory of God!"

The Preacher, standing, with open Bible, had patiently endured her testimony; but now he opened his mouth to read from the Bible. And again he was delayed.

For, some ten men and women, completely naked, stepped out into the vacant spot just in front of Pastor Truelove.

124

The twins gasped in surprise at the stark nakedness of the men and women. Big John and Jed also gasped in surprise, and were filled with anger and indignation at the shameless display of nakedness. And little Alice was so surprised and disturbed that she gave a small startled scream at the sight of the naked men and women.

Big John saw that some of the inhabitants of the Foggy Bottoms were also as indignant as he was. One yelled from the crowd, "Shameful! Shameful! Indecent! Indecent! Go home and put your clothes on!" Another man, near him, cried out, "I'm not a Christian! But if you're what Christians are, I'll never become a Christian!" A third person spoke out in disgust, "I don't know your God. But if you people are Christians, I don't want to know him." And he turned, and strode away.

Meanwhile the leader of the group announced: "We're going to sing, Onward Christian Soldiers. And he added with humility, "We didn't practice, so you'll have to forgive our singing. But we're singing for the honor and glory of God!"

As they began singing, they also began marching to the martial tempo of the Hymn. Back and forth they marched, without shame, in the limited space that they had.

And as they marched several more men and women turned away in disgust at the shameful display of nakedness.

Big John stepped to where Pastor Truelove stood with his open Bible. He touched his arm to gain his attention. Then asked, "why don't you tell them to leave? Why don't you tell them to go home and put some clothes on?"

"I have. But they swear that they are not naked! This group is from the Church of the Laodiceans. (Revelation 3:14-17) They don't even know they are naked! And, if you look closely you will see that they are blind! They can't see where they're going. See how they bump into each another—as well as into the people around them?"

And now John noticed that as they walked back through the crowd (for they had finished singing) that they did not walk straight. And he noticed that they were bumping into one another, as well as into other people who were in their way.

And then, as soon as the blind and naked singers had disappeared into the crowd, another group of fully clothed singers from the church of Sardis (Revelation 3:1-6) appeared and took their place. They stood there, very proud of their clothing. "See?" said their ashen faced spokesman, "We are not naked! We have on holy garments from God. They are whiter than any fuller on earth could white them!

"We will sing," he continued, "a liturgical canticle from the 17th century."

But John had learned to look closely at those who sang or testified. And he noticed that the song they sang was not a song at all. It was a chant, with beautiful harmony; but with the mournful sound of lifeless men chanting—repeating the same mournful words over and over again—from the depths of lifeless souls, begging God to pardon their never-ending sins.

And then John fastened his eyes on their garments. Their garments were not holy at all! They were indeed white! But they were so sullied by some awful defilement, that the contrast of the two made the defilement stand out in stark relief. And their eyes stared out from ashen faces, and were lifeless!

John sank to his knees, and cried out in horror: "Those men are not alive! They are chanting from the lifeless bodies of dead men!"

Chapter XXXV
God's Truth

Pastor Truelove was finally able to read from the Bible; and he read from one text after another without stopping:

'Unto the angel of the church of Ephesus write....I know thy works, and thy labor, and thy patience, and how thou canst not bear them which are evil: and thou hast tried them which say they are apostles, and are not, and hast found them liars....Nevertheless I have somewhat against thee, because *thou hast left thy first love*...Repent, and do the first works; or else I will come unto you quickly, and will remove thy candlestick out of his place, except thou repent.' Revelation 2:1-5

'And unto the angel of the church of the Laodiceans write....I know thy works, that thou art neither cold nor hot: I would thou wert cold or hot. So then *because thou art lukewarm, and neither cold nor hot, I will spue thee out of my mouth.* Because thou sayest, I am rich, and increased with goods, and have need of nothing; and knowest not that *thou art wretched and miserable, and poor, and blind, and naked...*' Revelation 3:14-17

'And unto the angel of the church in Sardis write; These things saith he that hath the seven Spirits of God, and the seven stars; I know thy works, that *thou hast a name that thou livest, and art dead*....Thou hast a few names even in Sardis which have not defiled their garments; and they shall walk with me in white: for they are worthy. He that overcometh, the same shall be clothed in white raiment; and I will not blot out his name out of the book of life, but I will confess his name before my Father, and before his angels.' Rev. 3:1-5

"You all know," Pastor Truelove said, "the messages to the seven churches. Two of the seven were faithfully serving God. But five were living in sin, and God warned them to repent and turn back to God!

"Some of you here are from the church in Sardis. And you know God's message to you—'**thou hast a name that thou livest, but art** dead.' And God has warned you that unless you repent, he will blot your name out of the book of life.

"But a few of you in Sardis have not defiled your garments, and God has words of encouragement for you:

> 'Thou hast a few names even in Sardis, which have not defiled their garments; and they shall walk with me in white: for they are worthy. He that overcometh, the same shall be clothed in white raiment; and I will not blot out his name out of the book of life, but I will confess his name before my Father, and before his angels.' Revelation 3:4-5

"Some of you are from the church of Laodicea. And, God has charged you with being lukewarm! Do you understand? *God has charged you with this sin*! It is not a man! *It is God*!

"*God* says you are lukewarm! Your obedience to God is partial. You do not obey God in everything. You're not on fire for God. You have no burning zeal to serve God and do his will. And God tells you he will spew you out of his mouth!

"Why? Because, *although you belong to God*, you are selfish and are living to please self!

> 'What? Know ye not that *your body* is the temple of the Holy Ghost...and *ye are not your own*? For *ye are bought with a price*: therefore glorify God *in your body, and in your spirit, which are God's*.' I Corinthians 6:19-20

"All our time, and all our possessions belong to God. Everything we own, everything we are, and everything we ever will be, belongs to God. And we owe everything we are and have to him, and should consecrate it to him. And if we don't consecrate everything we are and have to God, *we defraud God of what is rightfully his*!

"Have you never read in the Scriptures what the first of all the commandments is? Jesus tells us what the first of all the commandments is:

> 'The first of all the commandments is, Hear, O Israel; The Lord our God is one Lord: and thou shalt love the Lord thy

God with *all thy heart*, and with *all thy soul*, and with *all thy mind*, and with *all thy strength*: this is the first commandment.' Mark 12:29-30

"If you **do not serve God with all your heart**, you disobey the first commandment of God! With your selfish, half-hearted, halting, on-again-off-again service to God—with your *lukewarm* service to God—you insult God; and God will spew you out of his mouth!

"And some of you here today are from the church of Ephesus. Jesus has charged you with *leaving your first love*. What does Jesus mean when he says, 'Thou hast *left thy first love*?' He means you have left the great love you once had for God, when you first gave your heart to him!

"Those who have left their first love are like newlyweds, who, when wed, love each other with all their heart. But in the passage of time they find fault with one another; and separate, and go into the world, and give their love to strangers.

"The Apostle James describes the men or women who leave their first love for God, as adulterers and adulteresses:

'Ye *adulterers and adulteresses*, know ye not that the *friendship of the world is enmity with God*? Whosoever therefore will be a friend of the world *is the enemy of God.*' James 4:4

"Oh, my friends, did you know that the friendship of this world makes us *adulterers* and adultresses, and *enemies* of God?

"And, did you know that no one who loves this world will enter into heaven? I John 2:15-17

"We know we should love God with *all our heart, mind, soul, and strength*! Oh, dear friends, is there any reason *we should not love God with all that we have*? Is there any reason *we should not be holy, like God is holy*? Is there any reason *we should not be perfect, like our Father in heaven is perfect*?

'As he which hath called you is holy, so be ye holy. Because it is written, Be ye holy; for I am holy.' I Peter 1:15-16

'Be ye therefore perfect, even as your Father which is in heaven is perfect.' Matthew 5:48

'He that saith, I know him, and keepeth not his commandments, is a liar, and the truth is not in him.' I John 2:4

'Whosoever abideth in him **sinneth not**: whosoever sinneth hath not seen him, neither known him....He that committeth sin is of the devil....Whosoever is born of God doth not commit sin; for his seed remaineth in him: and he cannot sin, because he is born of God.'" I John 3:6, 8-9

Chapter XXXVI
The Devil's Lies

"My dear friends, a few of you have lived here in the Foggy Bottoms all your life. But most of you have come here from the Bright Regions, because you want to live in a place where your sins are licensed, approved, and excused!

"It is easy to see that your want your sins to be licensed, approved, and excused by looking at your signs. I have seen your sign here that says, WE ARE BORN SINNERS, SO IT IS IMPOSSIBLE FOR US TO OBEY GOD. Another sign says, WE ARE BORN WITH A NATURAL INABILITY TO OBEY GOD. Another sign says, THERE IS **NO BETTER EXCUSE FOR SIN** THAN TO BE BORN A SINNER.

"And the name of your settlement also shows that you want to have your sins licensed, approved and excused: **SINCE I AM BORN WITH A SINFUL NATURE, AND CANNOT LIVE WITHOUT SIN, GOD ACCEPTS A FORM OF GODLINESS WITHOUT THE POWER THEREOF.** II Timothy 3:1-5

"And I have seen the ugly signs put up by the homosexuals. And their signs show their great desire to have their sins *licensed, approved, and excused.* One sign says, GAY MARRIAGE IS NOW APPROVED AND LICENSED BY OUR STATE. Another sign says, IT'S NOT WRONG TO BE GAY—GOD CREATED ME THAT WAY. Another sign says, I'M PROUD OF THE NATURE GOD GAVE ME.

"And, just day before yesterday I saw the two huge signs where you use Scriptures to excuse your sins. But the Scriptures have words added to them that are not in the Bible. One sign says, THE HEART OF ALL CHRISTIANS IS DECEITFUL ABOVE ALL THINGS, AND DESPERATELY WICKED: WHO CAN KNOW IT? (Jeremiah 17:9) Another sign says, IF WE CHRISTIANS SAY THAT WE HAVE NO SIN, WE DECEIVE OURSELVES, AND THE TRUTH IS NOT IN US. I John 1:8

"Oh, friends, you add to the Scriptures, and take them out of context because you love your sins and want to excuse them! You speak glowingly of the grace of God, and salvation by faith alone. But your very statements about the grace of God, and salvation by faith alone, show that you have no clear idea of what the words, grace and faith, mean!

"I know, and I believe, as you do; that we are saved *by grace alone, through faith, and that without works.* But to add to this true doctrine, the false doctrine that the Christian cannot live without sin in this life, even with all the *grace and power* that God gives him, is a lie of the devil!

"God's grace saves us from all our sins! It is **by God's grace** that the Savior Jesus Christ saves his people from all their sins:

'And thou shalt call his name JESUS: for he shall save his people from their sins.' Matthew 1:21

'Whosoever committeth sin is the servant of sin....If the Son therefore shall make you free, *ye shall be free indeed.*' John 8:34, 36

'Much more they which receive *abundance of grace* and of *the **gift of righteousness*** shall *reign in life* by one, Jesus Christ.' Romans 5:17

'What shall we say then? Shall we continue in sin, that *grace may abound*? God forbid. *How shall we, that are dead to sin, live any longer therein*?' Romans 6:1-2

'Knowing this, that our old man is crucified with him, that the body of sin might be destroyed, that henceforth we should not serve sin. For he that is dead is *freed from sin.*' Rom. 6:6-7

'For **sin shall not have dominion over you**: for ye are not under the law, **but under grace**.' Romans 6:14

'Being then *made free from sin*, ye became the servants of righteousness.' Romans 6:18

'But now being *made free from sin*, and become servants to God, ye have your fruit unto holiness, and the end everlasting life.' Romans 6:22

"God's grace teaches us to deny ungodliness and worldly lusts. It teaches us to live soberly, righteously, and godly, in this present world:

'For the ***grace of God*** *that bringeth salvation* hath appeared unto all men, *teaching us that, denying ungodliness and worldly lusts, we should live soberly, righteously, and godly, in this present world.*' Titus 2:11-12

'For there are certain men crept in unawares...ungodly men, **turning the grace of our God into lasciviousness,** and **denying the only Lord God, and our Lord Jesus Christ.**' Jude 4

"You who talk so very glowingly about the grace of God, and yet go on living in sin, '**have denied** *the only Lord God, and our Lord Jesus Christ!*' You have '*counted the blood of Christ,* which cleanses us from sin and sanctifies us, *an unholy thing and have done despite unto the **SPIRIT OF GRACE**.*' Jude 4 and Hebrews 10:29

"You have also make God a liar! God promises to save all his people from their sins. (Matthew 1:21) But you refuse to believe God, making him a liar!

"But you do believe the devil! You believe the devil's lie that God will make his people holy only when he gets them to heaven.

"But God says that only those who are holy and righteous, now, will ever get to heaven! Hebrews 12:14, Revelation 21:27, Revelation 22:11-12, 14-15

"God saves his people from their sins, now, in this present life. And he does it by **grace alone**! *Everything we receive from God is by grace.* Everything!

'And *of his fullness* have all we received, and **GRACE FOR GRACE**.' John 1:16

'That *Christ may dwell in your hearts* **BY FAITH**...*that ye might be filled with all the fullness of God.*' Eph. 3:17, 19

'For *in him dwelleth all the fullness of the Godhead bodily.* And ye are **COMPLETE IN HIM**.' Colossians 2:9-10

'But unto every one of us *is **GIVEN GRACE** according to*

*the measure of the **gift of Christ**....*Till we all come...*unto a perfect man, unto the measure of the stature of the fullness of Christ.*' Ephesians 4:7, 13

"It is by grace that the *love of God is shed abroad in our hearts by the Holy Ghost which is **given to us**. Romans 5:5

"It is by grace that we drink into the one Holy Spirit and are made partakers of Christ's divine nature. I Corinthians 12:13, II Peter 1:3-4

"It is by grace that we are born again by the power of the Holy Ghost and become the sons of God and new creations in Christ Jesus. And it is by grace that we have been **glorified** and **translated**, and have been raised up together with Christ Jesus, and made to sit together in heavenly places in him.

'For *by one Spirit are we all baptized into one body...*and *have been all made to drink into one Spirit!*' I Corinthians 12:13

'His divine power *hath given unto us all things that pertain unto life and godliness,* through the knowledge of him that hath *called us to **glory** and **virtue**:* whereby are given unto us exceeding great and precious promises: that by these ye might be ***partakers of the divine nature,*** having escaped the corruption that is in the world through lust.' II Peter 1:3-4

'The *love of God is shed abroad in our hearts by the Holy Ghost which is **given unto us**.*' Romans 5:5

'Ye know that he was manifested to take away our sins; and in him is no sin. Whosoever abideth in him ***sinneth not***: whosoever sinneth hath not seen him, neither known him.' I John 3:5-6

'Little children, let no man deceive you: he that doeth righteousness is righteous, even as he is righteous. *He that committeth sin is of the devil*; for the devil sinneth from the beginning. For this purpose the Son of God was manifested, that he might destroy the works of the devil. *Whosoever is born of God doth not commit sin; for his seed remaineth in him: and he cannot sin, because he is born of God.* In this the *children of God* are manifest and the *children of the devil.*' I John 3:7-10

'*For whatsoever is born of God overcometh the world*: and this is the victory that overcometh the world, *even our faith.*' I John 5:4

'We know that *whosoever is born of God sinneth not*; but he that is begotten of God keepeth himself, and that wicked one toucheth him not.' I John 5:18

'…whom he justified, them he also *glorified.*' Romans 8:30

'And the *glory* which thou gavest me *I have given them.*' John 17:22

'Even when we were dead in sins, hath *quickened us together with Christ, (by grace ye are saved*;) and hath *raised us up together,* and *made us sit together in heavenly places in Christ Jesus.*'' Ephesians 2:5-6

"Oh, hallelujah!" Shouted the preacher. "God has given his Son, Jesus Christ, to free us from sin. He 'hath given unto us all things that pertain unto **life** and **godliness**' and 'hath called us to **glory** and **virtue**.' He 'hath given unto us exceeding great and precious promises; that by these we might be *partakers of the **divine nature**,*' and because we are partakers of his divine nature, we have 'escaped the corruption that is in the world through lust.'

'For the law of the **Spirit of life in Christ Jesus hath made me free** from the law of sin and death. For what the law could not do, in that it was weak through the flesh, God sending his own Son in the likeness of sinful flesh, and for sin, condemned sin in the flesh: *that the righteousness of the law might be fulfilled in us, who walk not after the flesh, but after the Spirit.* For they that are after the flesh do mind the things of the flesh; but they that are after the Spirit the things of the Spirit. For to be carnally minded is death; but to be spiritually minded is life and peace. Because the carnal mind is enmity against God; for it is not subject to the law of God, neither indeed can be. So then they that are in the flesh cannot please God. **But** *ye are not in the flesh, but in the Spirit, if so be that the* **Spirit** *of God dwell in you.* Now *if any man have not the Spirit of Christ, he is none of his.* And if Christ be in you, the body is dead because of sin; but the Spirit is life because of righteousness. But *if the Spirit of him that raised up Jesus from the dead dwell in you, he that raised up Christ from the dead shall also quicken your mortal bodies by his Spirit that dwelleth in you.* Therefore, brethren, we are debtors, not to the flesh, to live after the flesh. For if ye live after the flesh, ye shall die: but if ye through the Spirit do mortify the deeds of the body, ye shall live. For *as many as are led by the Spirit of God, they are the sons of God.*' Romans 8:2-14

'For whom he did foreknow, he also **DID PREDESTINATE TO BE CONFORMED TO THE IMAGE OF HIS SON**, *that he might be the firstborn among many brethren.* Moreover *whom he did predestinate, them he also called*: and *whom he called, them he also justified*: and *whom he justified,* **them he also glorified**....He that spared not his own Son, but delivered him up for us all, *how shall he not with him also freely give us all things?*' Romans 8:29-32

"Many of you here in this settlement, when you read, 'whom he justified, **them he also** *glorified*,' think it means, we will someday be glorified when we all get to heaven. But it means what it says, and what it says, is, that **God has already glorified his children now**! And God has glorified us by giving us his Spirit and dwelling in us!

'That they all may be one; as thou, Father, art in me, and I in thee, that they also may be one in us....And **the glory which thou gavest me I have given them**; that they may be one even as we are one: **I in them**, and **thou in me**....' John 17:22-23

'What? know ye not that **your body is the temple of the Holy Ghost which is in you**, which ye have of God, and ye are not your own?' I Corinthians 6:19

'For **ye are the temple of the living God**; as God hath said,

I will *dwell in them*, and *walk in them*; and I will be their God, and they shall be my people.' II Corinthians 6:16

'He that eateth my flesh, and drinketh by blood, *dwelleth in me,* and *I in him*....' John 6:56-57

"Oh, my friends! Do not reject the word I preach today! For it is God's word! It is God who tells you he will deliver you from all your sins. And he promises to **deliver you now, when you believe**:

'This only would I learn of you, *received ye the Spirit by the works of the law, or by the hearing of faith*?' Galatians 3:2

'*He therefore that ministereth to you the Spirit*, and *worketh miracles* among you, *doeth he it by the works of the law, or by the hearing of faith*?' Galatians 3:5

'Christ hath redeemed us from the curse of the law, being made a curse for us: for it is written, Cursed is every one that hangeth on a tree. That the blessing of Abraham might come on the Gentiles through Jesus Christ; *that we might receive the promise of the Spirit through faith*.' Galatians 3:13-14

THE LAW IS NOT AGAINST THE PROMISES OF GOD

'Is the law then against the promises of God? God forbid: for if there had been a law given which could have given life, verily *righteousness should have been by the law*. But the scripture hath concluded all under sin, that the *promise by faith of Jesus Christ* might be given to them that believe....For ye are all the children of God *by faith in Christ Jesus*.' Galatians 3:21-22, 26

'For we *through the Spirit* wait for the hope **of** *righteousness by faith*.' Galatians 5:5

'This I say then, *Walk in the Spirit*, and *ye shall not fulfil the lust of the flesh*....Now the *works of the flesh are manifest*, which are these; Adultery, fornication, uncleanness, lasciviousness, idolatry, witchcraft, hatred, variance, emulations, wrath, strife, seditions, heresies, envyings, murders, drunkenness, revelings, and such like: of the which I tell you before, as I have also told you in time past, that **THEY WHICH DO SUCH THINGS SHALL NOT INHERIT THE KINGDOM OF GOD.**' Galatians 5:16, 19-21

'But the *fruit of the Spirit* is love, joy, peace, long-suffering, gentleness, goodness, faith, meekness, temperance: against such there is no law. And they that are Christ's have crucified the flesh with the affections and lusts.' Galatians 5:22-24

'Be not deceived; God is not mocked: for whatsoever a man soweth, that shall he also reap. For he that *soweth to his flesh* shall of the flesh reap corruption (death); but he that *soweth to the Spirit* shall of the Spirit reap life everlasting.' Galatians 6:7-8

"God is not mocked! He that soweth to his flesh shall of his flesh reap death! And this death is the **second death**, everlasting punishment in the lake of fire and brimstone. Oh my friends do you realize that all of you, who are living in sin, are on a slippery slope that will take you down to everlasting punishment in the lake of fire and brimstone? Revelation 20:10 and Revelation 21:8

"Do you realize that you who are living in sin, *are of the devil* and not of God? '*He that committeth sin is of the devil*; for the devil sinneth from the beginning. For this purpose the *Son of God was manifested, that he might destroy the works of the devil.*' I John 3:8

"Do you realize that if you are living in sin, you are *not born of God*? 'Whosoever is born of God *doth not commit sin*; for his seed remaineth in him: and he cannot sin, because he is born of God. In this the *children of God are manifest,* and the *children of the devil*: whosoever *doeth not righteousness* is not of God, neither he that *loveth not his brother*.' I John 3:9-10

"Oh my friends, I want to warn you again! If you are living in the pleasures of sin, you are sliding down a slippery slope that will take you straight down to the lake of fire and brimstone!

"Friends, don't excuse your sins any longer. *There is no excuse for sin*! *If there were an excuse*, there would be no hell for the sinner! There would be no lake of fire and brimstone!

"Oh, friends! Flee from the wrath to come! Save yourself from the coming judgment! Repent, and give your heart to God. Believe on the Lord Jesus Christ, and he will save you from all your sins." Matthew 1:21

Chapter XXXVII
The Little Man Flees To The Foggy Bottoms

The Little Man opened his eyes. He pushed himself up to a sitting position.

It was growing light in the east. The sun would soon be up. Awful dread filled his heart. He looked over at the tunnel entrance from which he had emerged last night, and thought of its soothing darkness. Then he looked down to the low-lying expanse called the Foggy Bottoms. His father had warned him to stay away from it; that the darkness there was more deadly for the Christian than the darkness of the tunnels.

He stood quickly to his feet. "I will go down to the Foggy Bottoms for now. In the evening I will go up to the Bright Regions. There, I will find my enemies and kill them."

The Little Man happened upon the path that the Preacher usually took when he went to preach in the Foggy Bottoms. He also happened upon the same park where the Preacher usually stopped first to preach. And he came there less than an hour before the Preacher and the eight who were with him arrived. The park seemed to be empty, and the Little Man sat down on a bench to rest.

"Howdy neighbor!" Came a voice, not over 15 feet to his left. "You're a stranger here aren't you? And a mighty tiny stranger too, if you ask me. What's your name? What you doing in these here parts?"

Bitterness crept into the heart of the Little Man when he heard the voice speak of his tiny stature. And he turned, and was about to return insult for insult, when he saw, not an adversary, but an old man, tall and slim, with a smile and a very friendly face. He tried to hide his bitterness, and at the same time garner for himself the dignity and honor that his vanity and pride craved: "I'm Professor Judas. I'm the head Professor of the Psychology Department at the University of One Mile Circle. I'm here looking for some friends of mine. They are Christians."

"Oh, is that right? So, you're a Christian are you? And you say you're looking for some Christian friends here in the Foggy Bottoms? Friend, I'm afraid you're looking in the wrong place. There aren't any

Christians living here that I know of. Plenty of people claim to be
Christians, but I haven't seen one here yet that showed he was one.
Now I'm not a Christian. Never claimed to be one yet. But I know one
when I see one. When they don't stack up to what the Bible says, you
just know they aren't Christians. Now, there's a Preacher," he continued expansively, "comes through here most every day. Now, when
he converts somebody they become Christians, but they don't stay here
any time at all. They say the darkness here is killing them and they're
going to get shut of it and go where the light shines bright. So you
won't find any real Christians here.

"Say, little fellow, you hungry? I got coffee. And I think I could
scare up some eggs if you want." Without waiting for an answer, the
old man began walking toward his house, talking as he went. "You
know I've lived here all my life. And my daddy lived here before me.
So I know almost everyone for miles around. What's the name of those
friends you say are Christians? Maybe I know them."

The old man arrived at his house almost immediately. He opened
the door, went in, and then turned to the Little Man. "Come on in. Sit
here at the table and I'll fix some coffee. And, if you want, I'll fry you
up some eggs."

The Little Man sat down at the table and looked around. On the
wall he was facing, hung four rifles on supporting pegs. Beneath the
rifles stood a desk with its chair. And at the end of the room was a
large window looking out on the park. The Little Man was surprised to
see children now running and playing in the park. His eyes returned to
the rifles hanging above the desk. He looked upon them with a great
desire to possess just one of them. When the old man returned with
two cups of steaming coffee, the Little Man averted his eyes from the
guns and feigned interest in the table which was of hardwood,
fashioned with lovely carvings, and beautifully polished. "I've been
admiring your table." said the Little Man. "Did you make it yourself?"

"No, I didn't." said the old man. Then he added with great pride.
"My daddy made it. In fact, he built this house and made almost
everything in it. This is one of the first houses ever built here. And
you know, back then the Foggy Bottoms didn't exist. It was different
back then. Wasn't foggy like it is now. Why I remember, when I was
just a young man going hunting with my daddy, and this was one of the

best places for hunting in the country. But it isn't now. Game's all gone. Most of the trees and vegetation's dying. A clear stream used to run through here. But now it's turned into a swamp, and there's death now where there used to be life. I remember back when they started digging all those caves. About the same time they dug the long tunnel. That's when it all began—I don't know why, but that's when it began to change and became a swamp with all this fog."

"Are those the guns you used to hunt with?" asked the Little Man, pointing to the four guns hanging above the desk.

"Yes." replied the old man, turning to look upon the guns with great pride. "The shotgun and rifle on top was my daddy's. He gave me a rifle and shotgun when I was just sixteen. Taught me to shoot with his own guns until I was responsible enough to have my own."

"I'll give you $50.00 for just one of the rifles." the Little Man blurted out.

"Oh, no!" The old man answered quickly. "I would never part with my guns!"

"I'll double it. No, I'll triple it. I'll give you $150.00 for just one of the rifles."

"Oh, no! You don't understand." The old man responded slowly. "It's not just the money. I wouldn't sell my guns for any amount of money. They're gifts. They're from my daddy." The old man paused a moment, then added in a very quiet voice, "No, my daddy gave me those guns. And I would never part with'em." There was a far away look in the old man's eyes, and he dropped his head and fell silent.

After these words and the emotion shown by the old man, there was an embarrassing silence between the two men at the table. Then, suddenly, there was shouting from the children in the park. "The Preacher is here! The Preacher is here! Come hear the Preacher!"

After the shouting of the children, came the strong clear voice of Pastor Truelove: "Come out and hear the Word of God! Call your friends, and bring them with you! I have a message from God's Word.

All of you who want to hear God's Word, come out. We're going to start right now."

The old man lifted his head and said, "the Preacher's here. Let's go out and hear him."

He walked to the window and looked out. Then he turned to the Little Man and said, "He's got a big group with him today. Usually there are only one or two men with him. But today there must be around eight. Come on over, and look at them. Maybe your friends are with him. Come and take a look."

The Little Man stepped to the window and looked out. Instantly he saw his enemies. He backed quickly away from the window. So quickly did he back away, that the old man looked at him curiously and asked, "Are those your friends out there?"

"No!" lied the Little Man. "I've never seen any of those people before."

"Well, they're mostly new to me; so I thought maybe they might be your friends. But let's go hear the Preacher. He never wastes time in getting started." With these words the old man made his way outside. And the Little Man followed—very careful not to be seen by those who knew him so well.

Chapter XXXVIII
The Altar Call

Even though much time was taken up by the testimony of the woman from the Church of Ephesus, the singers from the Church of Laodicea, and the singers from the Church of Sardis, Pastor Truelove preached a lengthy message.

And at the end of his message, he urged the people not to excuse their sins any longer, but to turn from their sins and be saved from the wrath to come. And even as he called on sinners to repent, he fought back the urge to continue preaching. For he had an overwhelming desire to see the salvation of these people. And there in the park, moved by his great desire for their salvation, the Preacher fell to his knees in agonizing prayer.

One of the deacons stepped forward and called on the people to come forward to pray. "My friends," he said. You've heard God's Word. Come forward, kneel down here, and call on God for salvation. God has promised, 'Whosoever shall call on the name of the Lord shall be saved.'"

Three people stepped out of the crowd and knelt down to pray. The first to step out was the old man. Two young men followed him.

The old man knelt down next to the Preacher, and immediately began calling on God to forgive him and save him. Soon the Preacher began praying with him, and very soon the old man had prayed through and had the witness of the Spirit that he had been forgiven. But as he continued praying, his thoughts turned to his father, and he began struggling with the knowledge that his father had never been saved. Finally, troubled with this knowledge, he asked the Preacher, "My father was not saved when he died. Can he be saved now?"

"Oh, my dear friend," said the Preacher with compassion, "that is such a hard question to answer! Not because I don't know the answer! But, because none of us can bear to know our loved ones are lost! But my dear friend, if your father was unsaved when he died, there is nothing that we can do to save him now.

"Remember that God desires the salvation of every single soul upon this earth. The Apostle Peter said, "God is *not willing that any should perish*, but that *all should come to repentance*." (II Peter 3:9) And the Apostle Paul said, "(God) *will have all men to be saved*, and to come to the knowledge of the truth." I Timothy 2:4

The preacher paused for a few moments, and then said, "Have you prayed through? Do you have the witness of the Spirit that you are forgiven and that God has saved you?"

"Yes," replied the old man. "I know that God has saved me."

"Did you give your whole life to God? Are you ready to obey him in everything now?"

"Yes," said the old man, "I have held nothing back from God. I'm ready to obey him in everything."

"You know that Jesus commands you to be baptized in water?"

"Yes, I know that," said the old man. "I've heard you preach before, and I've seen you baptize others. And I'm ready now to obey God and be baptized." Having heard this, the Preacher rose to his feet. And the old man stood with him.

When the deacons saw the Preacher and the old man stand up, they brought the two young men to the Preacher and explained that they had both converted to Christ and desired to be baptized.

The Preacher lost no time, but took the three converts to a water tank close by and baptized them. Many from the crowd followed and looked on with interest.

After the three were baptized they begged leave to accompany the Preacher and his group, for they cared not to remain in the Foggy Bottoms but wanted to go immediately to the Bright Regions. And the old man asked that the Preacher wait just a few minutes while he gathered some personal belongings from his house.

And there, in his house, as he gathered his belongings into a sack, he discovered that one of the rifles was missing. And he discovered also, that the desk drawer had been left wide open, and a large box of ammunition was missing!

Chapter XXXIX
A Cry For Help

The twelve Christians made their way downward through ever increasing fog. The path leveled out, and through the fog they saw dead bushes and dead grass; and the skeletons of trees long since dead. Then in a clearing ahead three signs loomed up out of the fog.

The twelve stopped before the signs and looked up at them. The largest sign said, **WISDOM AND TEACHINGS OF THE CHURCH FATHERS**, and directly below those words, an arrow pointed to the left, with the distance, ½ mile.

Then in the middle was a smaller sign that said, **PLEASUREVILLE** 2½ miles, with an arrow pointing to the left also.

Then, a sign on the right side said, **SHORTCUT TO PLEASUREVILLE** ¼ mile, with an arrow pointing straight ahead.

The old man turned to the preacher, and asked, "Where do we go from here? **PLEASUREVILLE**, or **WISDOM AND TEACHINGS OF THE CHURCH FATHERS?**"

"We're going to **WISDOM AND TEACHINGS OF THE CHURCH FATHERS**," said the preacher. "Not because they have the wisdom and teachings of God. For they do not. Their teachings contradict the Word of God—And their settlement is filled with doctrines of devils. (I Timothy 4:1) Thank God there is a couple there now from the church of Smyrna (Revelation 2:8-11). They have been there a month, and are preaching the true gospel of Jesus Christ to those who are from the churches of Pergamos (Revelation 2:12-15) and Thyatira (Revelation 2:18-23). We go now to encourage them and help them."

Then the Preacher, indicating his two deacons, said, "We have preached in **PLEASUREVILLE** many times; but we have no time to go there today. And when we do go, we never take the shortcut. The shortcut is swampy land, and a death trap. Everybody knows it is filled with bogs and quicksand. But in spite of this, many men and women still take the shortcut and sink to their death in their hurry to reach **PLEASUREVILLE**. At these words, a solemn stillness settled over each of the Christians.

Then, suddenly, they all heard a voice cry out for help. "Help! Help! Help me! Help me!" Then there was silence!

One of the young converts said, "I'll go! I'll go help him!" The other young convert said, "I'll go too! Together we'll get him out." And they both made a move toward the sound of the voice.

"No!" Pastor Truelove yelled out. "You'll perish in the quicksand!"

At the same time, the old man yelled out too: "Stop! Stay here! Don't go down there!" Then he added, in a more moderated voice, "I've been all over areas like this in the Foggy Bottoms. It's dangerous. But I know what to do. I'll go!"

And having said this, the old man walked off the path to a stand of lodge-pole pines, long since dead, standing up out of the ground. He bent one down to the ground until it broke off just above the ground. Then he did the same with another until it also broke off just above the ground. He then had two poles just about 15 feet long. Taking one in each hand, he cautiously moved in the direction from which the cry for help had come.

The fog obstructed his view, and he paused and called out, "I'm coming to help you. But I can't see you. So yell, 'help!' so I'll know where you are."

Immediately the voice called out, and the old man moved in the direction of the voice.

The old man moved forward over ground that was so unstable it wobbled under his feet as if the ground were floating on liquid. The old man stopped momentarily, and peered ahead. Had he seen something move up ahead? Yes! And, now, as he drew nearer, carefully placing one foot before the other, fearful at any moment he might break through to quicksand below, the old man saw that it was the tiny man, that he had met this very morning in the park. And he saw also, that only the tiny man's big head and neck were still above the quicksand. But, he saw also that the tiny man was holding something just above his head. It was a rifle! It was the rifle that was missing from his home! The tiny man had stolen his rifle!

The old man saw that the tiny man could go under at any moment. But the ground between him and the tiny man was unstable, and had a frightening give to it. He put one of his poles down, and with the other reached out as far as he could. But still the pole came some five feet short of reaching the tiny man. He pulled the pole back and went down on hands and knees. Then with a hand on each pole he inched carefully forward on the shaky ground. When he had advanced another five feet, and had advanced as far as he dared to go, for the ground now trembled and shook beneath him with his slightest movement, he again reached out with one of the poles to the tiny man. "Take hold of the pole," he said, "and I'll pull you in to firmer ground."

"I can't," said the Little Man. "I've got a rifle in my hands."

"Throw down the rifle!" The old man commanded angrily. "It's the weight of the rifle that's taking you down further into the quicksand. Now throw it down and take hold of this pole!"

But the Little Man held stubbornly to the rifle!

Seeing that the Little Man was slowly sinking deeper and deeper, and would soon be swallowed up, the old man repeated his command, "Throw down the rifle, and take hold of this pole, before you go under!"

Still the Little Man would not let go, but held more desperately to the rifle, and even lifted it higher to keep it out of the quicksand.

But, when he lifted the rifle the inch or two needed to lift it out of the quicksand, his whole body sunk another inch or two deeper into the quicksand!

And the quicksand had now risen up to his chin and was about to reach his lips!

In fear of suffocating, he tilted his head back. And it was in this pitiable position, with his big head back, and his sorrowful eyes looking pleadingly up at the old man, that the Little Man finally released his grip on the rifle so that it was gobbled up by the quicksand. And the Little Man reached out to the pole, and was pulled in very cautiously by the old man to firmer ground.

Now the old man, still on hands and knees, with a pole under each hand, said, "Hey, little fellow you're safe now. But you're not out of the quicksand yet. Now, this is what you need to do. I'll hold on to the poles at this end, and back up. You hold on to the poles at that end and just ease yourself up on the ground, and forward out of the quicksand."

The Little Man obeyed, and, soon they were both on stable enough ground that they stood to their feet, and started back to the waiting group of Christians.

Chapter XL
"I Don't Have A Gun"

The Christians were all looking in the direction of the two men as they hurried back. They had all heard snatches of the words spoken by the two men. Especially the very clear and angry words of the old man when he had yelled, "Throw down the rifle. It's the weight of the rifle that's taking you further down into the quicksand."

And now, as they looked in the direction from which the conversation had come, they heard the squishing sound of walking in wet shoes; and then they saw the two men as they came into view through the fog.

The five Christians and Head Lighter Man were surprised when they saw the two men appear. It wasn't the contrast of a tiny midget walking beside a tall giant (and running at times in his squishy shoes to keep up) that surprised them or fastened their attention. And it wasn't the contrast in the demeanor of the two—for the tall giant radiated joy and happiness as he strode along, while the tiny midget exuded shame and embarrassment as he drew near and saw those who knew him. And it wasn't the filthiness of the Little Man that arrested their attention. Even though his filthiness did attract their attention. For his clothes were saturated with miry swamp mud, and every part of his body, from the top of his head to his feet and his shoes was covered with smelly, squishy mire. No part of his body was free from the sloppy, smelly mire except for his eyes and nose and mouth!

But none of those things commanded the attention of the six. What did command their attention was the fact that it was the Little Man himself that they were looking at—it was the Little Man who had tried to kill them, who was now walking toward them!

It was also the fact that the Little Man's presence here indicated he still wanted to kill them. And it was the fact that the Little Man had possessed the means to kill them. For they had heard the old man command the Little Man, not once, but twice, to "throw down the rifle." And it was the fact that the Little Man had a huge bulge in his left front pocket, which looked like it might be another pistol!

"Look!" said John. "It's the Little Man. And it looks like he's got a pistol in his front pocket.

"Pastor," said John as he turned to the Preacher. "That Little Man is dangerous. He's tried to kill us twice—with this pistol that I have here in my utility belt. And it looks like he's got another pistol now. We need to disarm him."

When the Little Man stood before the eleven Christians, all eyes were fastened upon him, and remained upon him. For, the Little Man—when he had seen his enemies—began to pull back behind the old man, and turned to one side to hide the huge bulge in his pocket.

"Little Man," asked the Pastor in a kind but serious voice, "Do you have a pistol in your pocket?"

"No!" answered the Little Man.

"Well, what's that big bulge there in your pocket?"

"It's nobody's business what I have in my pocket. I don't have a gun!"

"What were you doing with a rifle then? You did have a rifle, didn't you, that you were told to throw down? Where did you get it? What were you doing with it?"

The Little Man averted his eyes and hung his head and refused to answer further questions. But the old man broke the tense silence with the following words, "Pastor, I don't know why the little fellow stole my rifle. But I reckon he did. Because that was my rifle he was holding onto back there in the quicksand. And that's probably a box of bullets in his front pocket. Both were missing when I went to the house to get a few belongings for the trip to the Bright Regions."

The Little Man stood mute, shamed, and embarrassed; without any defense. And the six, who knew the Little Man well, did not doubt for one minute that the Little Man had a box of bullets in his pocket. But they felt such a keen sense of shame for the guilty man, that they did not insist (as they should have) that he suffer the shame of showing what was in his left front pocket!

Chapter IXL
The New Settlement

The thirteen walked slowly up the slight incline. They had been walking for some fifteen minutes, and were now beginning to pass the first signs of the new settlement. A few signs were copies of the signs in the first settlement, but most were new.

One of the new signs said, SHAPEN BY GOD IN INIQUITY, AND CONCEIVED BY MY MOTHER IN SIN. Another sign said, CREATED BY GOD WITH A NATURAL INABILITY TO OBEY HIM.

And then they saw many ugly signs put up by the homosexuals: GAY PRIDE, GOD MADE ME GAY, I'M GLAD GOD MADE ME GAY, IT'S NOT A SIN TO BE GAY—HOMOPHOBIA IS SIN.

Then they saw the two large signs with texts from the Bible, that had been changed and taken out of context to excuse sin: THE HEART OF CHRISTIANS IS DECEITFUL ABOVE ALL THINGS, AND DESPERATELY WICKED: WHO CAN KNOW IT? (Jeremiah 17:9) and, IF WE CHRISTIANS SAY THAT WE HAVE NO SIN, WE DECEIVE OURSELVES, AND THE TRUTH IS NOT IN US. I John 1:8

And then a huge sign that extolled the Church Fathers:

THE CHURCH FATHERS GAVE US THE DOCTRINE OF ORIGINAL SIN

Three signs were next to this huge sign, with doctrinal statements on original sin by three of the Church Fathers. The first was by Augustine, the most highly esteemed of all the Church Fathers:

'The whole human race existed as one moral person in Adam; so that in Adam's sin, we sinned, we corrupted ourselves, and we brought guilt and merited condemnation upon ourselves. Adam's will was the will of the species, so that in Adam's free act, the will of the race revolted against God and the nature of the race corrupted itself.' Doctrine of Augustine, fifth century A.D.

The second was by Cocceius:

'Adam was the Federal Head of the race, and God made a covenant with Adam, our Federal Head, agreeing to give eternal life to him and to all his descendants if he obeyed; but making the penalty for his disobedience the condemnation of all his descendants. Since our legal representative or Federal Head did sin, God imputes his sin, his guilt, and his condemnation to all his descendants.' Doctrine of Cocceius, 17th century A.D.

The third was by Placeus:

'Because Adam sinned, all men are born with a corrupt sinful nature and are guilty and condemned for that nature. They are not guilty for the sin of Adam, but are guilty only for the corrupt sinful nature they are born with. It is the corrupt nature, which they inherit from Adam, that is sufficient cause and legal ground for God to condemn them.' Doctrine of Placeus, 17th century A.D.

And then they went some twenty yards further, and the path widened. And, looking up, they saw another large sign suspended above them:

WISDOM AND TEACHINGS OF THE CHURCH FATHERS

And then both sides of the path were crowded with signs. Six signs quoted Augustine.

'Our nature sinned in Adam.' Augustine

'It was just, that after our nature had sinned…we should be born animal and carnal.' Augustine

'Our nature there transformed for the worse, not only became a sinner, but also begets sinners.' Augustine

'There is in us a *necessity* of sinning.' Augustine

'Unconscious infants, dying without baptism, are damned by virtue of their inherited guilt.' Augustine

'From this condemnation no one is exempt, not even newborn children.' Augustine

Two signs quoted Martin Luther:

'The nature and essence of man, is, from his birth, an evil tree and a child of wrath.' Martin Luther

'Even children, dying unbaptized, are lost.' Martin Luther

One sign quoted Calvin:

'Original sin is the hereditary depravity and corruption of our nature...which first makes us subject to the wrath of God, and then produces in us works which the Scripture calls works of the flesh.' Calvin

Then, there were many other signs with quotations from other highly esteemed sources:

'The sin of Adam is the immediate cause and ground of inborn depravity, guilt, and condemnation to the whole human race.' A. H. Strong, Systematic Theology, p. 611

'This evil tendency or inborn determination to evil, since it is the real cause of actual sins, must itself be sin, and as such must be guilty and condemnable.' A. H. Strong, Systematic Theology, p. 611

'Original sin is the corruption of man's nature, whereby he is utterly indisposed, disabled and made opposite to all that is spiritually good, and wholly inclined to evil, and that continually.' Larger Catechism

'From this original corruption whereby we are utterly indisposed, disabled and made opposite to all good, and wholly inclined to all evil, do proceed all actual transgressions.' Westminster Confession

'This corruption of nature, during this life, doth remain in those that are regenerated: and although it be through Christ pardoned and mortified, yet both itself, and all the motions thereof, are truly and properly sin.' Westminster Confession

Q. 16. Did all mankind fall in Adam's first transgression?

A. The covenant being made with Adam, not only for himself, but for his posterity; all mankind, descending from him by ordinary generation, sinned in him, and fell with him, in his first trangression. Shorter Catechism

Q. 19. What is the misery of that estate whereinto men fell?

A. All mankind by their fall lost communion with God, are under his wrath and curse, and so made liable to all miseries in this life, to death itself, and to the pains of hell forever. Shorter Catechism

'No man is able, either of himself, or by any grace received in this life, perfectly to keep the commandments of God, but doth daily break them in thought, word, and deed.' Larger Catechism

'They deplore their inability to love their Redeemer, to keep themselves from sin, to live a life in any degree adequate to their own convictions of their obligations...they recognize it as the fruit and evidence of the corruption of their nature derived as a sad inheritance from their first parents.' Charles Hodge, Systematic Theology, Vol. II, p. 273

The Preacher had read these signs aloud and without comment as he went from one sign to another. But now he turned to the twelve and cried out in anger, "These teachings are doctrines of the devil! **They are NOT IN THE BIBLE!**

"*Where in the Bible* does it say that 'the sin of Adam is the immediate cause and ground of inborn depravity, guilt, and condemnation to the whole human race?' *Where in the Bible* does it say that 'No Christian is able, by any grace of God received in this life, to keep the commandments of God?' *Where in the Bible* can it be found written that the Christian is, 'utterly indisposed, disabled and made opposite to all that is spiritually good, and wholly inclined to evil, and that continually?' These statements are not in the Bible and are repugnant to the Bible!

"The doctrine of original sin is a horrible doctrine that must **invent more false teachings** to cover up its fundamental disagreement with God's Word!

"The **Bible** says absolutely nothing of the 'Immaculate Conception.' (The 'Immaculate Conception' is the doctrine that Mary, the mother of our Lord Jesus Christ, 'was conceived free from any corruption of original sin' in order that she might be pure enough to be the mother of Christ.) The doctrine of the 'Immaculate Conception' is an **addition** to the Bible, made necessary by a belief in the doctrine of original sin.

"The **Bible** says absolutely nothing of the 'Baptism of Babies for the Remission of Original Sin.' This is another **invention,** and an **addition by men** to the doctrines of the Bible, made necessary by a belief in the doctrine of original sin.

"The **Bible** says absolutely nothing about 'Limbo.' 'Limbo' is **another invention** made necessary by a belief in the doctrine of original sin. ('Limbo' was invented for infants who have died without baptism. It is believed that 'Limbo' is a place where babies go, when they have died without baptism—and in place of going to either heaven or hell, they go to 'Limbo,' where 'neither the joys of heaven, nor the torments of hell prevail.')

"Again, the **Bible** never once mentions 'original sin.' It is a *term invented by men.* Surely the Bible would mention 'original sin' at least one time, if it were a Bible doctrine. But it does not! 'Original sin' is not a doctrine of the Bible! It is the doctrine of men, inspired by the devil!

"Again, the **Bible** does not mention or speak even one time about men being 'damned to hell' for the sin of Adam. On the contrary, it declares again and again that men are *condemned for their own sins*; and that *no man can be guilty for the sins of another man.* Ezekiel 18:2-4, 18:19-20; Deuteronomy 24:16; II Chronicles 25:4

"Over and over again, the **Bible** declares that God is our Creator. It declares that God created us 'good' and 'upright' and 'in his own image and likeness.' It never once speaks of 'God creating sinners!'

"There is not one verse in the entire Bible that says that we are 'born with a **sinful nature**.' Instead the Bible says that the '**good nature**,' given to us by God, urges us, even presses us, to obey the **law of God written in our hearts**. (Romans 2:14-15) Man is not created with a 'sinful nature.' Man is created 'in the image and likeness of God,' with a 'good nature,' which teaches him the difference between good and evil and right and wrong; and which approves of the good things he does, and disapproves of the evil things he does:

> 'For when the Gentiles...**DO BY NATURE** the things contained in the law, these, having not the law, are a law unto themselves: which show the work of **the law written in their hearts**, their **conscience** also bearing witness, **and their thoughts** the meanwhile **accusing** or else **excusing** one another.' Romans 2:14-15

"Does the **Bible** ever speak about men having the power to 'beget' either saints or sinners? Does the **Bible** ever use the term 'inborn sin nature' or 'Adamic sin nature'? Does the Bible mention 'original sin' or 'actual sin,' and make a distinction between the two? No! None of these doctrines and none of these terms can be found in the Bible. They are all inventions of men and additions by men to the doctrines of the Bible."

The preacher saw that several men from the new settlement had drawn near to hear him, and he saw that his preaching angered them. And looking upon them, he stopped his impassioned preaching momentarily; and then, continued in a more moderated voice, "No other doctrine has been so destructive to the clear teachings of the Holy Bible. And no other doctrine has been so destructive to good morals among Christians. The devil has used this false doctrine to deceive multitudes of people, both in the church and outside the church.

"But, look, we are about to enter the park! And, for now, we must give up further talk about this false doctrine that the devil has used to destroy the faith and walk of so many in the Christian church."

Chapter VIIIL
Strange And Startling Differences

They entered quickly into the park; a park much larger than the park they had preached in earlier.

And not only was the park much larger than the park they had preached in earlier, but there were large groupings of signs scattered all over the park. And men and women were gathered around the signs, arguing the different doctrinal points written on them. And the Christians were alarmed when they saw a violent argument irrupt in one of the gatherings that became so heated that several people began to curse and strike one another. They saw one man in his anger throw his neighbor to the ground; and then stand over him with a club, and threaten to beat him back to the ground if he got up without recanting his doctrinal beliefs. And this violent argument irrupted so near them that they feared for their safety, especially for the safety of the children. So they quickly moved away.

And as they went further into the park they observed other unusual things, things that were astonishing and inexplicable.

They observed a large house with a sign upon the door: 'House of Jezebel.' Revelation 2:20-23

Next to it, they came to a large building with a sign standing before it that said: 'Synagogue of Satan.' And there was writing upon the door that proclaimed: 'Enter to know the depths of Satan.' Revelation 2:9-11

And built right up next to the 'Synagogue of Satan' they saw another large building with a sign above its door: 'Non Denominational Fellowship Hall.' And underneath this sign, an explanatory subscript which said: 'Established July, 2012, by members of the Churches of Pergamos and Thyatira.' Revelation 2:12-29

And next to the Fellowship Hall, stood the greatest building of all. And from within this building could be heard the rumbling sound of presses printing out new translations of the English Bible—devious translations, corrupt translations—the first of which was the ERV, the English Revised Version (1881-1885); and its corresponding American translation, the ASV, the American Standard Version (1901).

158

There were numerous signs on either side of this building. And one of the signs said that the *King James Version of the Bible* had grave defects and inaccuracies in it. Another sign next to it said that the King James Bible was now out-of-date and needed to be replaced, because it had been translated before the discovery of *much earlier manuscripts* that were not available when it was translated.

The Preacher held a large King James Bible in one hand. And he turned and pointed to the two signs at the side of the great building, and cried out, "Those signs have not told the whole truth!

"They have not told the truth that when the King James Bible was translated (1611), that the 'earlier manuscripts' existed and were known to exist by the translators of the King James Bible. **And they were rejected by the King James translators** because they **knew they were corrupt!** And the translators of the King James Version did not use those **corrupt manuscripts**, but used others they **knew were not corrupt!**

"And none of these signs have told the truth about the man who had a hand in *corrupting those earlier Greek manuscripts*—Origen.

"**Origen** (185-254) edited a collection of Greek manuscripts of the Old Testament called the *hexapla*. Whether he had a direct hand in corrupting those manuscripts, or not, is not the most important point. What is most important is that his *hexapla* was a collection of six Greek manuscripts of the Old Testament that **were corrupt!** They had to be corrupt (at least five of them) because they were all different from one another!

WEBSTER'S NEW WORLD COLLEGE DICTIONARY, FOURTH EDITION, p. 670 gives a brief explanation of what the hexapla was:

> **hexapla** [Gr (*ta*) *hexapla*, title of Origen's edition, lit., sixfold, neut. Pl. of *hexaploos*...] 1 an edition having six versions arranged in parallel columns 2 [**H-**] Origen's edition of the Old Testament

WEBSTER'S NEW UNIVERSAL UNABRIDGED DICTIONARY, SECOND EDITION, p. 857 gives almost the same brief explanation:

Hexapla, n.pl. [construed as sing.] [Mod. L.;
Gr. Hexapla, neut. Pl. of hexaploos, hexaplous,
Sixfold; hexa, six, and –ploos, -fold.]
   1.   an edition having six versions arranged
        in parallel columns.
   2.   [H--] Origen's edition of the Old Test-
        ament.

"We know with certainty that the King James Version of the Bible is a true, inspired Version of the Word of God. Because God created all men with an **innate knowledge** of truth and error, right and wrong, good and evil, and justice and injustice. Gen. 1:26-27, Rom. 2:12-16

"For the same reason, we know with certainty that the corrupt Versions of the Bible are corrupt: for God created all men with an **INNATE KNOWLEDGE of truth and error, right and wrong, good and evil, and justice and injustice**. Gen. 1:26-27, Rom. 2:12-16

"And even more important to our **KNOWLEDGE OF TRUTH AND ERROR**: all true Christians **are BORN AGAIN OF GOD. *The Father, The Son, and the Holy Ghost LIVE, and DWELL, and WALK in us*!** We are **TAUGHT DIRECTLY BY GOD**. (John 6:45) We easily discern truth and error. We easily discern between the true Word of God and the corrupt Word of God!

'He that eateth my flesh, and drinketh my blood, **DWELLETH IN ME**, and **I IN HIM**.' John 6:56

'What? Know ye not that *your body is the TEMPLE OF THE HOLY GHOST*...and *ye are not your own*? For *ye are bought with a price*: therefore glorify God *in your body, and in your spirit, which are God's*.' I Corinthians 6:19-20

'What agreement hath the *temple of God* with idols? *For ye are the TEMPLE OF THE LIVING GOD; as God hath said, I will dwell in them, and walk in them; and I will be their God, and they shall be my people....And [I] will be a Father unto you, and ye shall be my sons and daughters, saith the Lord Almighty*. II Corinthians 6:16-18

''...When they deliver you up, take no thought how or what ye shall speak: for **it shall be given you** in that same hour what ye shall speak. *For it is not ye that speak, but the* *SPIRIT OF YOUR FATHER WHICH SPEAKETH IN* *YOU.*' Matthew 10:17-20

'I will pray the Father, and he shall give you **another Comforter**, that he may **ABIDE WITH YOU FOREVER**; even the **Spirit of truth**; whom the world cannot receive, because it seeth him not, neither knoweth him: but ye know him; for he **dwelleth with you**, and **shall be IN YOU**.' John 14:16-17

'But ye have an **UNCTION from the Holy One**, and **YE KNOW ALL THINGS**. I have not written unto you because **ye know not the truth, but because ye know it, and that no lie is of the truth**.' I John 2:20-21

"The Apostle Peter said that there were **false prophets** also among the people, even as there shall be **false teachers among you**, who privily **shall bring in damnable heresies**.

'But there were **FALSE PROPHETS ALSO** among the people, even as there shall be **FALSE TEACHERS among you**, who privily shall bring in **damnable heresies**, even denying the Lord that bought them, and bring upon themselves swift destruction. And many shall follow their pernicious ways; by reason of whom the **WAY OF TRUTH shall be evil spoken of**.' II Peter 2:1-2

"Wherever God's Word is preached or taught the devil is there to *corrupt* the Word of God, *resist* the Word of God, and *take away the Word of God* sown in men's hearts!

'But **when they have heard**, *Satan cometh immediately, and taketh away the word that was sown in their hearts.*' Mark 4:15

'Those by the wayside are they that hear; then *cometh the devil, and taketh away the word out of their hearts, lest they should believe and be saved.*' Luke 8:12

"But it is the **devil's children** who have corrupted **the written Word of God**. They have corrupted God's Word, by adding to, taking from, and changing God's Word.

They have changed God's Word, even though God has warned them not to change his Word!

> '*Ye shall not add unto the word* which I command you, *neither shall ye diminish ought from it,* that ye may keep the commandments of the Lord your God, which I command you.' Deuteronomy 4:2

> '*Every word of God is pure...Add thou not unto his words,* lest he reprove thee, and thou be found a liar.' Proverbs 30:6

> 'Also, read Revelation 22:18-19.'

"Codex Sinaiticus (Aleph) and Codex Vaticanus (B) are both corrupted Greek manuscripts of the Bible. There is proof beyond a reasonable doubt that they are descendants of Origen's hexapla. Codex Sinaiticus (Aleph) and Codex Vaticanus (B) were found by Tischendorf in 1844 A.D. The Vaticanus B Manuscript was found forgotten and in disuse in the Vatican Library, and the Sinaiticus Aleph Manuscript was found discarded in a wastebasket in a Catholic convent.

"In the late 1800's **Westcott/Hort** used these two corrupt Versions of the New Testament to create a new, New Testament Greek Text to supplant the Greek Text formerly used in translating the New Testament Scriptures.

"The Greek Text created by Westcott/Hort, and used to translate the English Revised Version—with its companion, the American Standard Version—altered the former Greek Text in over 5,000 places. And the English Revised Version was the predecessor to the New International Version, the New American Standard Version, the New World Translation, the Amplified Bible, and the Living Bible.

"There are some 200 places in some of the new English Versions of the New Testament where words, phrases, whole verses, and even a whole paragraph are omitted!

"And, as I said before, not only do they *omit God's word from the Bible,* they also **add words** *to the Bible,* **words that God has never said**!

"Just one example: the NIV and the Living Bible translate the word

162

σαρξ, which means *flesh*, as **sinful nature, evil nature**, or **old nature**. They add these words to the Bible, words that God has never said; and by doing so, teach that Christians have two natures at the same time—a **sinful nature** as well as a **holy nature**! Read the New International Version and the Living Bible in Romans 7:5, 18-25, Romans 8:1-13 and Galatians 5:16-24.

"Dear Christians, **It is impossible** for a Christian to have **two opposing natures at one and the same time**—a **holy nature** whose only fruit can be righteousness, and a **sinful nature** whose only fruit can be wickedness!

"Men are not created with a sinful nature. The devil himself was not created a devil! To say that we are created and born with a sinful nature is blasphemy against the God who has given us our nature! God created us in his own image and likeness with a nature like his—as free moral agents—with a free will, with a conscience, and with the law of God written in our hearts. The Bible says:

'For when the Gentiles...**DO BY NATURE** the things contained in the law, these, having not the law, are a law unto themselves: which shew the work of the *law written in their hearts*, their *conscience* also bearing witness, and their thoughts the mean while *accusing* or else *excusing* one another; in the day when God shall judge the secrets of men by Jesus Christ according to my gospel.' Romans 2:14-16.

"The Bible passage I have just read says that we **DO BY NATURE** the things contained in the law.

"Now, how could we **DO BY NATURE** the **THINGS CONTAINED IN THE LAW**, if we were **born with a sinful nature**? We couldn't if you were born with a sinful nature! Only if we were born with a good nature could we **do by nature** *the things contained in the law*. Also, the Bible teaches that *all sin goes against our nature*!

'God gave them up unto vile affections: for even their women did *change the natural use* into that which is **AGAINST NATURE**.' Romans 1:26

'Likewise also the men, *leaving the natural use* of the woman, *burned in their lust* one toward another.' Rom. 1:27

'What they know **naturally**, as brute beasts, in those things
THEY CORRUPT THEMSELVES.' Jude 10

'*All flesh* had **CORRUPTED HIS WAY** upon the earth.'
Genesis 6:12

"Dear Christians, avoid the *corrupt versions* of the Bible. For they
omit words, and **add words** to the Bible, teaching lies that contradict
the clear teachings of the Bible."

Once again a crowd had gathered to hear the impassioned words of
Pastor Truelove. And again, some in the crowd began to murmur
angrily at what he was saying. Two of them brandished clubs and
stepped up to Pastor Truelove with clubs raised: "Preacher," said the
meaner of the two, "you come to our settlement to preach, and you
think you own this place, and can say anything you want to!

"But you can't! You're not going to tell us what Bible we're going
to use. We like the one we're using. It's an up-to-date translation, and
not like the old one you're using.

"And you're not going to tell us the way we have to live. You
preach that we should be perfect and live without any sin at all. Your
beliefs are impossible to live by! We have our own beliefs, and we
have our own teachers, and we like what they teach us. I'm warning
you! Stop telling us that God created us with a good nature, and that
we can live without any sin. I can read! And, my Bible tells me that
God created us with a sinful nature. And that we will continue to sin as
long as we are in this life. Stop preaching holiness! Go someplace else
to preach, if you want to preach holiness!" Having said this, the man
turned, and strode away, followed by a large crowd of his supporters.

Pastor Truelove watched as the crowd went away. Then he saw his
friend, some distance away, hurrying toward him. He saw him meet
the angry crowd and exchange words with them; then hurry away from
them, coming on rapidly toward him and the Christians. Finally, he
arrived, quite out of breath, and stood before the group of Christians.

"Oh, Brother Truelove," said Faithful Witness, (for Faithful Witness
was his name) "I'm so glad to see you." And seeing there were
strangers with Pastor Truelove, he asked, "Are all these people with

you? I know Deacon Helps and Deacon Faith and Miracles, but who are all these people?"

Pastor Truelove introduced Faithful Witness to each person with him, and Faithful Witness shook hands with each one—but when he came to the Little Man, the Little Man refused to take his hand, saying he was covered with mud. And indeed he was covered with mud, and feeling very uncomfortable; and more uncomfortable every minute, for the mud was now dry and he was itching all over.

Now Faithful Witness turned to take the Christians to his house. And as they made their way, Faithful Witness began sharing his fears with Pastor Truelove. His words tumbled from his mouth, and in spite of the fact that they were meant specifically for Pastor Truelove, even so, everyone heard him: "Brother Truelove we have a serious problem, and we need to pray about it. You know that the people here claim to know God, even though they all live in open sin!

"And you know they have Bibles, and know their Bibles, and say they love every single word God has spoken; but from the first day we came here to this present, they have resisted the word of God we have preached to them.

"But now, things have gotten much worse! Now they have threatened to kill me for preaching what they don't like!

"They threatened to kill me for preaching that Jesus saves us from all our sins! Oh, how they hate the truth that God saves us from all our sins!

"They even threatened to kill me for preaching that our salvation is by grace alone, and wholly undeserved. And that if we got our just deserts we would all go to hell for our sins! Two men joined together to resist my sermon on salvation by grace alone. They stood in front of me, with their clubs raised, so that I could not continue preaching. And said, 'What you say cannot be true! God is our Creator. And *since God created us sinners*, God owes us salvation! And since *God owes us salvation*, salvation *cannot be by grace!*'

"They believe that salvation is *by justice*, and *not by grace*! They say it is *only just* for God to save those who are created and born sinners!

"They bring up the case of the heathen who have never heard the gospel of salvation. They say that *justice demands their salvation*! They say that it is *not just* that the heathen, who are created and born sinners, should go to hell without any hope of salvation! They say that *God owes them salvation*!

"Brother Truelove, their doctrine of created and born sinners makes God a monster! It makes God *unjust in all his ways*!

"But to go on—they threatened to kill me for preaching against Jezebel, who seduces the servants of God to commit fornication, and to eat things sacrificed to idols. Revelation 2:20

"And when I preached that the Synagogue of Satan, where many of them worship, is *not* a Synagogue of God—as they stoutly claim it is— they threatened to flog me.

"Then the men from the Nondenominational Fellowship Hall threatened to kill me if I ever preached again that their Fellowship Hall is a Fellowship Hall for sinners only, that excludes anyone who is committed to living a life without sin!

"Then, I preached against three of the corrupted Bible versions they use, and told them of the evil those corrupted versions cause in the work of God. And a delegation from the publishing house came to our house. And they threatened to flog me and my wife; and run us out of **WISDOM AND TEACHINGS OF THE CHURCH FATHERS** if we did not cease to speak out against the corrupted versions they sell!"

Faithful Witness stopped momentarily and pointed ahead: "We're home. And there's my wife. We'll have something to eat before the service today. But before we do, we need to pray. I fear someone will be seriously hurt, or possibly killed in the service today! We must pray! We must know what God wants us to do in the service today!"

Chapter VIIL
Sister Patience

Sister Patience met them with a happy smile and with handshakes and hugs; and was about to receive the Little Man with a Christian embrace, but he escaped by crying out, "I can't! I'm all muddy!"

"Why, you were muddy, but you're dry now!" observed Sister Patience. "Did you wander off the path the Lord has told us to walk in and fall into the slime pits?" She pointed to a shed out behind the house and said, "You can wash up back there in that shed, you and your clothes. And when you're through come on in the house. We'll have something to eat soon."

The house was small and there was little room for the dozen plus people in the prayer meeting. But they crowded into the small room and each one began calling upon God to protect them and show them what he would have them to do in the upcoming service. (Every one of them had seen enough physical violence in the park to know that the threats to kill and harm were serious.)

As they prayed the Spirit of God came upon them, and they began to praise and worship God. Then Jed Truly stood up and prophesied by the power of the Holy Spirit. I Corinthians 12:7-11

"Fear not, for not a hair of your head shall fall to the ground, and no man shall set on you to do you harm. Be not afraid, for I will make even your enemies to be at peace with you. Ye are my witnesses. Therefore hold not your peace, but preach my word. But be ye wise as serpents and harmless as doves. Preach my word today. But be ye wise as serpents and harmless as doves."

Then Brother Truelove received a word of wisdom (I Corinthians 12:8-11) and said, "I believe God is speaking to us as a body today. He wants us as the body of Christ to be witnesses for Jesus Christ. The Holy Spirit told us twice to be 'wise as serpents, and harmless as doves.' I believe that the Holy Spirit is telling Faithful Witness and me not to preach today. The people have already expressed anger with Faithful Witness and me for our preaching. We must be wise as serpents and harmless as doves. There are others here who are called to preach. Let them preach. But I believe God has warned Faithful

Witness and me not to preach today. The only thing I ask of you who do preach, is that you preach with the Holy Ghost sent down from heaven. (I Peter 1:12 and I Peter 4:11) And that whatever any of you do, whether you testify or preach or read a Scripture or do anything; that you do it only in the power of the Spirit, and that you minister only according to the measure of your faith and the gift of God given to you. Romans 12:6-7, I Peter 4:11, I Corinthians 12:8-11

Chapter VIL
The Little Man Buys A Gun

The Little Man hurried on to the Bright Regions. The sun was high in the sky. The light hurt his eyes. It was driving him crazy! He stopped a moment, unbuttoned his shirt, took it off, and tried to arrange it over his head so that it would keep the light from his eyes. Then he swore when it wouldn't stay in place.

He should have stayed at the preacher's place. The sun shone through the fog there only for short times, and then not strong enough to hurt his eyes.

But it had become necessary to leave the place quickly, without anyone knowing. Time was short. He must buy a gun and ammunition. He had learned from Head Lighter Man that he was taking the five Christians back into the tunnels! Well, he would be waiting for them when they came back into the tunnels!

He must buy the gun first! Then he must get to the tunnels before they did! He must hurry. But, oh, how the sun hurt his eyes!

*** *** ***

"I want that rifle!" The Little Man screamed.

"But you haven't got enough money," replied the merchant. "That rifle costs almost $400.00. And it's as big as you are. You could hardly carry it, you're so small. And the money you do have doesn't look very good. It looks like it's gone through the wash. Now here's a small pistol, 38 caliber. I can let you have it for just $180.00. And I'll throw in this box of shells at no extra cost."

After the sale was made, and the Little Man had gone out through the door of Plary's Guns and Hunting Equipment, his son, X. M. Plary, stepped up to the counter where his father stood looking out at the Little Man. "Dad," he said. "I know that man. I know him very well. He was one of my teachers in Psychology. I think he's crazy. He was screaming and cursing and talking to himself when I came into the classroom where he was tied up. He told me he was going to the Bright Regions to kill some enemies. He commanded me to stay in the tunnels until he got back. He said that when he got back from killing his enemies, he was going back to teaching Psychology.

"Dad he's crazy. He's unbalanced. He's completely detached from reality. And he needs something more than the help of a Psychiatrist. I know now that he needs God. I think he's out to destroy others who will not conform themselves to his own perverted views of truth and reality.

"Dad, I'm going to follow him. I'm going after him. He bought that gun from you because he wants to kill some enemies. I don't know when I'll be back. But I'll be back as soon as I can."

*** *** ***

The Little Man did not turn around and look back as he stepped from the bright sunshine into the mouth of the dark tunnel. Had he done so, he would have seen X. M. Plary following him at a far enough distance so as not to be easily recognized. But the Little Man did not turn around to look back. Nor did he hesitate. But he stepped quickly out of the bright sunlight into the soothing darkness of the tunnel's mouth.

Two minutes later X. M. Plary stepped up to the tunnel's mouth. There he stopped and considered. The Little Man had said he was going to the Bright Regions to kill some enemies. Yet now he had gone back into the tunnels. Had he already killed the enemies he was after? Or were his enemies now back in the tunnels?

X. M. Plary considered a while longer, and came to a logical conclusion: The Little Man had bought the gun in order to kill his enemies; enemies who must still be alive. For he had bought the gun only some 15 minutes earlier. Reluctantly, X. M. Plary stepped into the hated darkness of the tunnels.

Chapter VL
Little Alice Sings

Faithful Witness placed a table in the park for a pulpit, and placed his big black Bible on top of it. Pastor Truelove and the other Christians sat in chairs behind the table. Faithful Witness's wife sat at one side with her accordion.

A few people had drawn close out of curiosity just to get a better look at the large group of visitors. But the great mass of people hung back in sullen disapproval.

Faithful Witness prayed. After he had prayed he turned the service over to Pastor Truelove to introduce the visitors.

"We have nine visitors with us today." began Pastor Truelove. "All are Christians. Three of them were saved in the service we just came from in the settlement of: **SINCE I AM BORN WITH A SINFUL NATURE, AND CANNOT LIVE WITHOUT SIN, GOD ACCEPTS A FORM OF GODLINESS WITHOUT THE POWER THEREOF** (II Timothy 3:I-5)

"Another of our visitors was saved yesterday, in the dark tunnels where the University of One Mile Circle is. He has since come out, and has brought five Christians out with him. The five Christians say they fell into the dark tunnels from their School, Lynwood Christian Elementary School, which is built right over the tunnel they fell into. And they all come from strange cities I have never heard of before. All of them were forced to stand trial by a depraved Psychology Professor, under penalty of death if they did not deny their faith in God. None of them denied God! God has delivered them, and brought them out, to be with us, here, today!"

Still, the mass of people hung back in sullen disapproval. Until Pastor Truelove introduced little Alice as the youngest of those who had been tried for believing in God. Little Alice walked up and stood behind the table, looking out at the people who stood very far away. She stood straight and tall, but her head and shoulders barely showed above the table. But when she held the Bible in her two hands and lifted it high over her head and began to sing with a clear, strong voice, the B-I-B-L-E, the resistance in the crowd was broken, and the crowd began drifting closer to see and hear her. Sister Patience joined in immediately with the accordion as little Alice sang the B-I-B-L-E.

> The B-I-B-L-E,
> Yes that's the Book for me.
>
> I stand alone on the Word of God,
> The B-I-B-L-E.

Then, little Alice lowered the Bible to the table, opened it to John 3:16, and read:

> 'For God so loved the world, that he gave his only begotten Son, that whosoever believeth in him should not perish, but have everlasting life.' John 3:16

Little Alice closed the Bible, lifted it lovingly to her right shoulder, and sang:

> Jesus loves me, this I know,
> For the Bible tells me so.
>
> Little ones to him belong,
> They are weak, but he is strong.
>
> Yes, Jesus loves me. Yes, Jesus loves me. Yes, Jesus loves me. The Bible tells me so.

Alice set the big black Bible back on the table, and turned to go back to her seat. Immediately the crowd, enthralled with her happy yet solemn performance, began to applaud and continued excitedly until well after she was seated.

Chapter IVL
Bill Becker Testifies

Bill Becker stepped up to the table with a desire to testify of the great joy of his salvation, but fearful he would not be able to well express it.

"My name is Bill Becker." he said.   "I go to the Christian Elementary School the Pastor talked about. But more important than the fact I go to a Christian School is the fact that I'm saved, and that God has given me real joy.

"Before I was saved I thought that the Christian life was a sad, unhappy life of trying to serve and obey God; a life of sacrifice and suffering, without any joy at all.

"Christians didn't smoke or drink. They didn't dance or go to the movies. They didn't watch TV. They didn't cheat, or lie, or steal, or disobey their parents.   And they didn't tell dirty jokes or use bad language. About the only thing they did do was go to church and pray and read the Bible. And I didn't like doing any of those things. I thought religion was just for old men and old women.

"But then I got saved.   And I found out that there's real joy in serving God!

"There's real joy in knowing your sins are forgiven, and knowing you're going to heaven, and not going to hell.

"Also, before I was saved, I thought that the Christian life was impossible to live. I remember saying to a friend of mine, before I was saved, It's too hard. I don't think I can live it!

"But, praise God, everything changed when God saved me, for I was *born again and made a new person by the Spirit of God.* Titus 3:5

"And I found that the bad things I loved before, I didn't love anymore! And the good things I hated before, I didn't hate anymore! I didn't want to do the bad things I loved to do before. I didn't want to steal anymore. I didn't want to tell lies anymore. I didn't want to tell dirty jokes anymore.

"Now, *I wanted to pray*, and *read my Bible*, and go *to church*. Now, *I wanted to obey God and do his will*. Now, I had the Holy Spirit dwelling in me, and I had the *joy unspeakable and full of glory* that Peter talks about in I Peter 1:8.

"Praise God for his *wonderful salvation*, and the *joy unspeakable and full of glory* that God gives us! Praise the Lord!"

Chapter IIIL
Bob Preaches

Bill Becker walked back to his seat and sat down. Many young people had drawn closer. They had never heard a young person testify before. And they could not remember anybody testifying about the joy they had in being a Christian.

Now Bill's twin brother, Bob, stood to his feet and walked to the table. He opened the big black Bible to I Timothy 1:5-11. He looked out over his audience momentarily. Then he read his text:

> 'Now the end of the commandment is *charity out of a pure heart*, and of a *good conscience*, and of *faith unfeigned*: from which some having swerved have turned aside unto vain jangling; desiring to be teachers of the law; understanding neither what they say, nor whereof they affirm. But we know that the law is good, if a man use it lawfully; knowing this, that *the law is not made for a righteous man, but for the lawless and disobedient, for the ungodly and for sinners, for unholy and profane, for muderers of fathers and murderers of mothers, for manslayers, for whoremongers, for them that defile themselves with mankind, for menstealers, for liars, for perjured persons, and if there be any other thing that is contrary to sound doctrine;* according to the glorious gospel of the blessed God, which was committed to my trust.' I Timothy 1:5-11

"What is the simple straight-forward message of the text I have just read? It is that *the law is not made for any man who is righteous*, but that it is *made only for a sinner*!

"And what does the law tell every sinner?

"It tells him, you are cursed and you are condemned, and you are on your way to hell; for you have not continued in all the things that are written in the law to do them. It says to him:

> 'Cursed is everyone that continueth not in all things which are written in the book of the law to do them.' Galatians 3:10

"The law has one message and only one message for the sinner. Its message is, 'The wages of sin is death.' (Romans 6:23) Its message is,

'Cursed is everyone that continueth not in all things which are written in the book of the law to do them.'

"Its message never changes. Its message is always the same. Its message is one of condemnation and woe to the sinner. Its promise to the sinner is *death and judgment and everlasting punishment!*

"The law cannot save the sinner. It cannot give life to the sinner. The sinner can faithfully do all that the law commands for the rest of his life, and he is still under its curse, unless he has come to Jesus Christ for pardon and deliverance from his sins.

"The law was never given to give life to the sinner. It was given to show the sinner his need of the Savior, and to shut him up to faith in the Savior Jesus Christ!

'For if there had been a law given which could have given life, verily righteousness should have been by the law....Wherefore *the law was our schoolmaster to bring us unto Christ*, that we might be justified by faith.' Galatians 3:21, 24

"The sinner can never be justified by the law! The law can only justify a man who has never sinned!

"If the sinner were to live a perfect life, for the rest of his life, with no more sin—the law would still continue to condemn him forever for the sins he has already committed.

"What? Can the convicted murderer stand before the judge and say, 'Look, your honor, I'm not going to commit murder again for the rest of my life, so you must drop all charges against me, and let me go free'?

"Sinner, once you have sinned the law must condemn you forever! The law has no power to extend grace and mercy to the sinner!

"Paul taught that the sinner can never earn grace, or mercy, or justification, or righteousness, or life, or any gift of God by doing good works! On the contrary, he taught that the sinner receives grace, and life, and mercy, and all the gifts of God *by faith in the Savior Jesus Christ*:

176

'This only would I learn of you, received ye the Spirit by the works of the law, or by the *hearing of faith*?' Galatians 3:2

'For by grace are ye saved *through faith*; and that not of yourselves: it is the gift of God: not of works, lest any man should boast. For we are his workmanship, *created in Christ Jesus* unto good works.' Ephesians 2:8-10

"The law can never pardon or give life to the sinner; only Jesus Christ can pardon the sinner and give him life.

'Much more they which receive *abundance of grace* and of the **GIFT OF RIGHTEOUSNESS** shall reign in life by one, Jesus Christ.' Romans 5:17

'For *whatsoever is born of God overcometh the world*: and *this is the victory that overcometh the world, even our faith. Who is he that overcometh the world, but he that believeth that Jesus is the Son of God*?' I John 5:4-5

'And the very *God of peace sanctify you wholly*, and I pray God your whole spirit and soul and body *be preserved blameless* unto the coming of our Lord Jesus Christ. *Faithful is he that calleth you, who also will do it*.' I Thessalonians 5:23-24

'Now unto *him that is able to keep you from falling, and to present you faultless* before the presence of his glory with exceeding joy, to the only wise *God our Savior* be glory and majesty, dominion and power.' Jude 24-25

'He that is dead is *freed from sin*...Being then made *free from sin*, ye became the servants of righteousness...But now being *made free from sin*, and become servants to God, ye have your fruit unto holiness, and the end everlasting life.' Romans 6:7, 18, 22

"Does God deceive us when he tells us *he has freed us from sin*? I want to read more from the Bible about the *sanctifying power of God* that makes the believer holy:

'His divine power hath given unto us all things that pertain unto life and godliness, through the knowledge of him that hath *called us to glory and virtue*. Whereby are given unto us exceeding great and precious promises: that by these ye might be *partakers of the divine nature*, having escaped the corruption that is in the world through lust.' II Peter 1:3-4

'For in him dwelleth all the fullness of the Godhead bodily. And ye are *complete in him*.' Colossians 2:9-10

'That ye might be *filled with* **all the fullness of God**.' Ephesians 3:19

'And *of his fullness have all we received*, and *grace for grace*.' John 1:16

'Verily, verily, I say unto you, He that believeth on me hath everlasting life. I am the living bread which came down from heaven: if any man eat of this bread, he shall live forever: and the bread that I will give is my flesh....Then Jesus said unto them...Except ye eat the flesh of the Son of man, and drink his blood, ye have no life in you....He that eateth my flesh, and drinketh my blood, *dwelleth in me, and I in him. As the living Father hath sent me, and I live by the Father: so he that eateth me, even he shall live by me*.' John 6:47, 51, 53, 56-57

"Now, I want to say just a few more words about the full gospel of God; and compare it with the deficient and altogether negative gospel that is preached here.

"**You do preach Christ**. But you preach a powerless Christ, a dead Christ—a Christ yet in the tomb—with no power to save his people from their sins.

"You **do not preach** a resurrected, living Christ with unlimited power to save you from your sins!

"The signs you have displayed all around you show you **do not believe** that God is able to save you from your sins, at least not in this life. For one of your signs says, 'CREATED BY GOD WITH A NATURAL INABILITY TO OBEY HIM.'

"You believe that God created you with a 'sinful nature,' and that you have a 'natural inability' to obey God. You believe that you are, 'by nature,' unable to obey God. You believe that you will be a slave to sin all your life, until you die and go to heaven!

"Yes! You believe that *God must wait until you die and go to heaven,* before he can deliver you from your sins!

"And, because you believe *the false teachings of the Church Fathers,* **you cannot believe the true teachings of God,** that you have **complete victory over all sin** *through faith in the Savior Jesus Christ.*

"And, so, believing as you do, that you can never live without sin in this life, you give only the **husks, peels,** and **shells of the gospel** to your people. While you hide from them **the heart and soul of the gospel**, which is a life of complete victory over sin through faith in the Savior Jesus Christ.

"Sirs, what would you think of a man who carefully peeled a banana, threw the heart away, and then ate the peelings?

"Or, a man who cracked a few walnuts, then threw the meats away, and then ate the shells?

"Or, a man who brought in his wheat, separated the wheat from the chaff, then threw the wheat away and used the chaff to make his bread?

"But aren't you foolish, as well as guilty, when you preach a gospel that is only the husks, and shells, and peelings, and not the whole gospel? Aren't you foolish and guilty when you preach, 'We Christians are all sinners; and will be as long as we are here on earth'? Or worse yet, when you declare: 'We are all just sinners saved by grace, but *God will change us when we all get to heaven'*?

"What? Is God so impotent that he cannot change us now? Must he wait until he gets us to heaven to change us? Must we all live in rebellion against our Savior until we die and go to heaven? Is that the gospel of Jesus Christ?

"How horrible is this philosophy that teaches that we must live our whole life in disobedience to God until we die and go to heaven!

"This philosophy makes *death* our sanctification! Think of it! We must *die* and go to heaven before we can be sanctified wholly!

"But the Bible teaches that it is God who sanctifies us; and that he sanctifies us now, in this life, and before we die and go to heaven.

'And the very God of peace **sanctify you wholly**; and I pray God your **whole spirit and soul and body** be preserved blameless *unto the coming of our Lord and Savior Jesus Christ*. Faithful is he that calleth you, who also will do it.' I Thessalonians 5:23-24

"Sirs, *you do know* that you are withholding the very heart of the gospel from your people, don't you?

"Sirs, *you do know* that you are giving only the husks of the gospel to your people, don't you? *You do know* that when you preach a gospel that *only pardons* the sinner, but leaves him still bound by sin, you have given him only the hard shells of the gospel? *You do know* that when you preach a gospel of the God of 'yesterday' and 'tomorrow,' but not a gospel of the God of 'today,' you have given only the husks and peelings of the gospel?

"Christ is the same **yesterday**, and **today**, and **forever**! (Hebrews 13:8) But you have 'limited the HOLY ONE of Israel!' (Psalm 78:41) You have made God the God of the 'past' and the 'future,' but not the God of 'today.'

"You preach a mighty, miracle-working God of 'yesterday' and 'tomorrow.' You preach a miracle-working God of the 'past' and the 'future.' but not a miracle-working God of 'today.'

"Men were saints in days of yore. And, we shall be saints in the sweet by and by. But, not now! Christ has no power, now, to sanctify us! His grace is not sufficient, now, to make us holy!

"All this negative preaching comes from **unbelief**. The greatest sin in the church today is **unbelief**. Jesus promised 'all power' to the believer. Jesus promised 'life' and 'more abundant life' and a 'well of water springing up into everlasting life' and 'rivers of living water' to the **believer**.

"He promised to give us *another Comforter to abide with us forever*. He promised to baptize *all who believe in Jesus Christ* with the Holy Ghost

> 'He that **believeth** on me as the scripture hath said, out of his belly shall flow **rivers of living water**. (But this spake he of the Spirit, which they that **believe on him** should receive: for the Holy Ghost was not yet given; because that Jesus was not yet glorified.)' John 7:38-39

"Oh, my friends! The only thing that keeps you from entering into all the fullness of Christ is **unbelief**! God has promised to free you from all your sins if you come to Jesus Christ in faith. He has promised to give you life and make you more than a conqueror if you believe in his Son Jesus Christ. But you respond to God's promises by saying, 'God, I can't believe you! What you say can't be true! For I believe the teachings of the Church Fathers that we are born with a sinful nature and cannot live without sin.'

"Oh, how you defame and dishonor God with your unbelief! You make God a liar with your unbelief!

> 'He that believeth on the Son of God hath the witness in himself: he that believeth not God **hath made him a liar**; because he believeth not the record that God gave of his Son. And this is the record, that God hath given to us eternal life, and this life is in his Son. He that hath the Son hath life; and he that hath not the Son of God hath not life.' I John 5:10-12

> 'Of how much sorer punishment...shall he be thought worthy, who hath trodden under foot the Son of God, and hath counted the blood of the covenant, wherewith *he was sanctified*, an unholy thing, and hath done despite unto the Spirit of grace....Now the just shall **LIVE BY FAITH**: but if any man draw back, my soul shall have no pleasure in him.' Hebrews 10:29, 38

"Your unbelief is sin! There is no greater sin than unbelief! Because of your unbelief you will neither enter into the fullness of Christ yourselves, nor permit others who are entering, to enter in. You have taken away the key of knowledge with your unbelief. You will not enter into the fullness of Christ yourselves; nor permit others, who are entering to enter in. And Jesus pronounces a woe upon you for your **stubborn unbelief**:

> 'Woe unto you, lawyers! for ye have taken away the key of knowledge: ye entered not in yourselves, and them that were entering in ye hindered.' Luke 11:52

> 'But woe unto you, scribes and Pharisees, hypocrites! For ye shut up the kingdom of heaven against men: for ye neither go in yourselves, neither suffer ye them that are entering to go in.'" Matthew 23:13

Chapter IIL
God Speaks To His People

Not a person moved. Not a person spoke.

Pastor Truelove was in a quandary. He could see that the sermon just preached had taken a mighty hold on the listeners. Conviction showed on the faces of the listeners, especially the faces of the young people. He did not want to grieve the Holy Spirit by continuing with more testimonies, or even more preaching. But he had practically told the Christians earlier that they would all minister in one way or another.

He leaned over to Faithful Witness and asked in a low voice, "What do we do now? Do we continue as before, or should we call on the people to come forward and pray for salvation?"

As Pastor Truelove was consulting with Faithful Witness, Deacon Faith and Miracles stepped to the pulpit and cried out with a loud voice, "Ye have heard the words of my three servants. And yet there are two more who must testify of me. Hear ye them! For I have brought them from a secret place that ye know not of, that they might be a sign, a wonder, and a marvel unto you. And that they might testify and preach my word to a rebellious and hard-hearted people"

Chapter IL
John Frank Preaches

John Frank stepped to the makeshift pulpit and opened the big black Bible to John's gospel. He looked out at the great crowd of people, and said, "I will read two portions of the Bible today. They are closely related, because both have to do with the Christian's **salvation from sin**. The first is John 3:3, 5, 7; and the second is Hebrews 2:3.

> 'Verily, verily, I say unto thee, **Except a man be born again, he cannot see the kingdom of God**...Verily, verily, I say unto thee, Except a man be born of water and of the Spirit, **he cannot enter into the kingdom of God**...Marvel not that I said unto thee, *Ye must be born again.*' John 3:3, 5, 7

> '**How shall we escape**, if we neglect SO GREAT SALVATION?' Hebrews 2:3

"The most amazing thing about this '**so great salvation**' of God is the instantaneous, miraculous change that God makes in our lives. It is a change so immediate, so complete, and so miraculous that only God could do it. God is the God of miracles! And if you don't believe that the **new birth** is a miracle you just don't believe what the Bible says. There is no miracle of God more miraculous than the miracle of being changed overnight from a vile, low-down sinner, to a saint, by the power of the Holy Ghost.

"I know! Because I know what I was before God saved me!

"I was a vile, low-down sinner until God got a hold of me. I was bound and shackled by sin and selfishness.

"But, thank God, I came to know what it was to have the shackles of my sin broken off of me. I heard the gospel of Jesus, and I heard the words, '**Ye must be born again.**' And I believed God's Word, and experienced the miracle of the new birth. God made me a new creature in Christ Jesus. Old things passed away; all things became new.

"Did you know that as long as you are bound by selfishness and sin, you can never go to heaven? That's why Jesus said, '*Ye must be born again.*' For the **sinner must be changed—transformed and made righteous, pure, and holy**—before he can **enter into the kingdom of**

184

God. To be **born again** means to be radically changed by God's power. It means to be changed from a sinner into a saint. It means to be made holy like our Savor Jesus Christ.

"Did you know that Jesus died to *save us from our sins*?

"Yes, it's true that Jesus died to save us from hell! But he died to save us from something even more horrible than hell! He died to save us from ourselves! He died to save us from our own wickedness and hatred and envy and pride and selfishness. Jesus died to save deceitful and desperately wicked men from their own sinful and desperately wicked hearts. Jesus died on the cross to *save us from our sins*!

'Thou shalt call his name JESUS: **for he shall save his people from their sins.**' Matthew 1:21

'He was manifested *to take away our sins.*' I John 3:5

'He that committeth sin is of the devil; for the devil sinneth from the beginning. *For this purpose* the Son of God was manifested, *that* he might destroy the works of the devil.' I John 3:8

'Who gave himself for our sins, *that he might deliver us from this present evil world.*' Galatians 1:4

'Christ also loved the church, and gave himself for it; *that he might sanctify and cleanse it* with the washing of water by the word, *that he might present it to himself a glorious church*, not having spot or wrinkle, or any such thing; but *that it should be holy and without blemish.*' Eph. 5:25-27

'Who gave himself for us, *that he might redeem us from all iniquity, and purify unto himself a peculiar people, zealous of good works.*' Titus 2:14

'He died for all, *that they which live should not henceforth live unto themselves, but unto him which died for them, and rose again.*' II Corinthians 5:15

'God, having raised up his Son Jesus, *sent him to bless you, in turning away everyone of you from his iniquities.'* Acts 3:26

"Jesus promised to give us his life, his fullness, his divine nature!

'He that eateth my flesh, and drinketh my blood *DWELLETH IN ME, AND I IN HIM. As the living Father hath sent me, and I live by the Father: SO HE THAT EATETH ME, EVEN HE SHALL LIVE BY ME.'* John 6:56-57

'And **of his fullness** *have all we received.'* John 1:16

'In him dwelleth all the *fullness of the Godhead bodily.* And ye are *complete in him.'* Colossians 2:9-10

'*...filled with all the fullness of God.'* Ephesians 3:19

"Jesus promised to baptize us with the Holy Ghost and empower us to preach his gospel in all the world with miracles and signs and wonders and gifts of the Holy Ghost.

'Verily, verily, I say unto you, He that *believeth on me*, the works that I do shall he do also; and greater works than these shall he do; because I go unto my Father.' John 14:12

'God also bearing them witness, both with signs and wonders, and with divers miracles, and gifts of the Holy Ghost.' Hebrews 2:4

'And these signs shall follow them that believe; In my name shall they cast out devils; they shall speak with new tongues; they shall take up serpents; and if they drink any deadly thing, it shall not hurt them; they shall lay hands on the sick, and they shall recover.' Mark 16:17-18

"Now let's look at the text in Hebrews 2:1-3, which warns Christians of the wrath and judgment of God upon them **if they neglect this SO GREAT SALVATION we have been reading about**!

'Therefore **WE** ought to give the more earnest heed to the things which **WE** have heard, lest at any time **WE** should let them slip. For if the word spoken by angels was steadfast, and every transgression and disobedience received a just recompense of reward; how shall **WE ESCAPE**, if **WE NEGLECT SO GREAT SALVATION.**' Hebrews 2:1-3

'Take heed, **BRETHREN**, lest there be in any of you an evil heart of unbelief, in **DEPARTING FROM THE LIVING GOD**. But exhort one another daily, while it is called Today; lest any of you be hardened through the deceitfulness of sin. For we are made partakers of Christ, if we hold the beginning of our confidence steadfast unto the end.' Hebrews 3:12-14

'For it is impossible for those who were once enlightened, and have tasted of the heavenly gift, and were made partakers of the Holy Ghost, and have tasted of the good word of God, and the powers of the world to come, if they shall fall away, to renew them again unto repentance....For the earth which drinketh in the rain that cometh oft upon it, and bringeth forth herbs meet for them by whom it is dressed, receiveth blessing from God: *but that which beareth thorns and briers is rejected, and is nigh unto cursing; whose end is to be burned.*' Hebrews 6:4-8

'For if we sin willfully after that we have received the knowledge of the truth, there remaineth no more sacrifice for sins, *but a certain fearful looking for of judgment and fiery indignation, which shall devour the adversaries.*' Hebrews 10:26-27

'He that despised Moses's law died without mercy under two or three witnesses: of how much sorer punishment, suppose ye, shall he be thought worthy, who hath trodden under foot the Son of God, and hath counted the blood of the covenant, wherewith he was sanctified, an unholy thing, and hath done despite unto the Spirit of grace? For we know him that hath said, Vengeance belongeth unto me, I will recompense, saith the Lord. And again, *The Lord shall judge his people.* It is a fearful thing to fall into the hands of the living God.' Hebrews 10:28-31

'Now the just shall live by faith: but if any man draw back, my soul shall have no pleasure in him; but we are not of them that draw back unto perdition; but of them that believe to the saving of the soul.' Hebrews 10:38-39

'Follow peace with all men, and holiness, without which no man shall see the Lord: looking diligently lest any man fail of the grace of God; lest any root of bitterness springing up trouble you, and thereby many be defiled; lest there be any fornicator, or profane person, as Esau, who for one morsel of meat sold his birthright. For ye know how that afterward, when he would have inherited the blessing, he was rejected: for he found no place of repentance, though he sought it carefully with tears.' Hebrews 12:14

'See that ye *refuse not him that speaketh*. For if they escaped not who refused him that spake on earth, much more shall not we escape, if we turn away from him that speaketh from heaven....let us have grace, whereby we may serve God acceptably with reverence and Godly fear: for our God is a consuming fire.' Hebrews 12:25-29

"Oh, my friends, please do not consider me an enemy because of what I preach. For I preach what I preach because I love you and am concerned for your eternal wellbeing. So I must tell you that if you go on living in sin, you will spend eternity in hell!

"You know that Jesus loved you so much that he laid down his life to save you. But he also loved you so much that he forewarned you that if you do not turn from all your sins, and do not do all the will of your Father which is in heaven; he will say to you on that day of judgment: 'Depart from me, ye that work iniquity.' Jesus said it in the sermon on the mount:

'...I never knew you: *depart from me, ye that work iniquity.*' Matthew 7:21-23

"And he said:

'Depart from me, ye cursed, into everlasting fire, prepared for the devil and his angels.....And these shall go away into ever-lasting punishment: but the righteous into life eternal.' Matthew 25:41, 46

"But God loves you, even though you are sinning against him, and his '*so great salvation*.' And he wants to save you, dear friend. God loves you; and his Son Jesus Christ loves you; and will save you from all your sins if you will only come to him. Oh, listen to the words of Jesus as he tells of God's great love for you:

> 'For God so loved the world, that he gave his only begotten Son, that whosoever believeth in him should not perish, but have everlasting life. For God sent not his Son into the world to condemn the world; but that the world through him might be saved. He that believeth on him is not condemned: but he that believeth not is condemned already, because he hath not believed in the name of the only begotten Son of God.' John 3:16-18

"Oh, how Jesus loves you! He loves you so much, that he calls you, now, in your present condition of sin: 'Come unto me, all ye that labor and are heavy laden, and I will give you rest. Take my yoke upon you, and learn of me; for I am meek and lowly in heart: and ye shall find rest unto your souls. For my yoke is easy, and my burden is light.' Matthew 11:28-30

"Come to him, dear friend. He is your Savior. He wants to save you from an eternity in hell. He will take you in his arms as a child, and carry you to the Father."

189

Chapter L
The New Covenant In The Blood Of Jesus

Again, the crowd made no movement. Deep conviction had fallen upon them. They stood solemnly as if at a funeral. John Frank's last few words on the love of Christ had moved some to tears. Almost all stood with heads bowed, afraid to make eye contact with John.

Jed saw all this as he stepped to the makeshift pulpit. "I'm grateful to the Pastors," he began, "for allowing me to preach. And I'm so glad that all of you have turned out to hear God's word today." He paused a moment, then bowed his head and prayed, "Lord, empower me to preach your word. Keep me from the errors of men. And let me speak only thy truth. In Jesus name I pray. Amen."

Then he said, "I'm preaching today on the *new testament* in the blood of Jesus. So I'm reading the words of Jesus from Matthew, Mark, and Luke; and also the words of Paul in first Corinthians on the *new testament.* Then I will read Hebrews 8:8-12 on the *new covenant* in the blood of Jesus.

'For this is my blood of the *new testament*, which is shed for many for the remission of sins.' Matthew 26:28

"And he said unto them, This is the blood of the *new testament*, which is shed for many.' Mark 14:24

'This cup is the *new testament* in my blood, which is shed for you.' Luke 22:20

'After the same manner also he took the cup, when he had supped, saying, This cup is the *new testament* in my blood.' I Corinthians 11:25

"Now I will read the passage in Hebrews 8:8-12 that speaks of the *new covenant* in the blood of Jesus:

'For *finding fault with them*, he saith, Behold, the days come, saith the Lord, when I will make a *new covenant* with the house of Israel and with the house of Judah: Not according to the covenant that I made with their fathers in the day when I took them by the hand to lead them out of the land of Egypt;

because they continued not in my covenant, and I regarded them not, saith the Lord. For this is the covenant that I will make with the house of Israel after those days, saith the Lord; *I will put my laws into their mind, and write them in their hearts*: and *I will be to them a God, and they shall be to me a people*: and they shall not teach every man his neighbor, and every man his brother, saying, Know the Lord: *for all shall know me, from the least to the greatest.* For I will be merciful to their unrighteousness, and *their sins and their iniquities will I remember no more.*' Hebrews 8:8-12

"The word **testament** and the word **covenant** are both translated from the same Greek word *diatheke*, and mean a contract, a will, a testament, or a covenant. Our translators translated the word *diatheke* as **a testament in the context of Christ's shed blood and death**, because the word **testament** is associated with **a will** in which the **death** of the testator is necessary before the **will** can be in force.

'For where a **testament** is, there must also of necessity be the **death of the testator**. For a testament is of force after men are dead; otherwise it is of no strength at all while the testator liveth.' Hebrews 9:16-17

WHAT IS A COVENANT?

"A covenant is a *contract or an agreement* made between two or more persons to buy, sell, or do something for one another. Generally, a person must give value for value in these agreements.

"You agree to paint your neighbor's house for $900 dollars. He agrees to pay you $900 dollars for painting his house. This is a simple covenant, contract, or agreement.

"You are a carpenter, and you are employed to help build a house for a certain man. Your employer agrees to pay you a certain amount of money for a 40-hour week. You agree to work the 40-hour week for that amount of money. This is another simple covenant.

"Or you go to the market to buy some groceries. The groceries you buy total $57.62. You pay over the $57.62 and take your groceries. You have just fulfilled your part of a contract by giving the value in money equal to the value of the groceries you took from the market.

"But *the new covenant in the blood of Jesus Christ* is not at all like these three examples! The new covenant in the blood of Jesus is a covenant of pure promise, without works. We pay God nothing in this new covenant! It is all a gift of God! It is pure mercy and pure grace. It is promised to us without money and without price, and it is received by faith alone, and not by works.

"So, before we look at the promises of the new covenant in the blood of Jesus, we need to have firmly in mind that the new covenant in the blood of Jesus is a covenant of pure promise. That it is the gift of God. And that it is received by faith alone, and not by works.

'Not by works of righteousness which we have done, but according to his mercy he saved us, by the washing of regeneration, and renewing of the Holy Ghost; which he shed on us abundantly through Jesus Christ our Saviour.' Titus 3:5-6

'For by grace are ye saved through faith; and that not of yourselves: it is the gift of God: not of works, lest any man should boast. For we are his workmanship, created in Christ Jesus unto good works, which God hath before ordained that we should walk in them.' Ephesians 2:8-10

WHAT DOES GOD PROMISE IN THE NEW COVENANT?

"He promises to save his people from all their sins. He promises to write his law in the heart and in the mind of all his people. He promises to put his Holy Spirit within his people so that they will be holy. He promises to pour out his Spirit upon all his servants and upon all his handmaidens. He promises that he will be our God and we will be his people. He promises to give us the life of the Father, the life of Son, and the life of the Holy Ghost. He promises that he will be our Father and we will be his sons and his daughters. He promises life, and power, and complete victory over sin. He promises the complete eradication of sin in the heart and life of his people. The promise of complete salvation from all sin, and stability in holiness, is the heart and soul of the new covenant in the blood of Jesus.

"We will look at this sweeping promise, of complete deliverance from sin, and stability in holiness, in Jeremiah 31:31-34:

'Behold, the days come, saith the Lord, that I will make a new covenant with the house of Israel, and with the house of Judah: not according to the covenant that I made with their fathers in the day that I took them by the hand to bring them out of the land of Egypt; which **my covenant they brake**, although I was an husband unto them, saith the Lord: but this shall be the covenant that I will make with the house of Israel; After those days, saith the Lord, I will put my law in their inward parts, and write it in their hearts; and will be their God, and they shall be my people. And they shall teach no more every man his neighbor, and every man his brother, saying, Know the Lord: for they shall all know me, from the least of them unto the greatest of them, sayeth the Lord: for I will forgive their iniquity, and I will remember their sin no more.' Jeremiah 31:31-34

"This is a promise of God to put within his people a holy mind and a holy heart. God's people were not faithful and did not obeyed him under the covenant of the law, so God made a new covenant with them, one in which they would obey him, and keep his law.

"God made this new covenant with Israel for one reason only. The old covenant did not save them from their sins—they were unfaithful to God, and did not obey his law—so God made a new covenant with them, one in which they would be faithful, and keep his law.

'For if the first covenant had been faultless, then should no place have been sought for the second. For *finding fault with them*, he saith, Behold, the days come, saith the Lord, when I will make a new covenant with the house of Israel and with the house of Judah....*Because they continued not in my covenant*....' Hebrews 8:7-9

"Now, let us look at another new covenant promise from Jeremiah:

'And they shall be my people, and I will be their God: and I will give them **one heart**, and **one way**, that they may *fear me forever*, for the good of them, and of their children after them: and I will make an *EVERLASTING COVENANT* with them, that I will not turn away from them, to do them good; but *I will put my fear in their hearts, THAT THEY SHALL NOT DEPART FROM ME.*' Jeremiah 32:38-40

"This is the new covenant promise of God to every member of the Church of Jesus Christ. He says, 'I will give them **one heart**, and **one way**, that they may **FEAR ME FOREVER**.' God promises to give us one heart. Not two hearts! Not a heart that is for God today and a heart that is against God tomorrow. But one heart that we may **fear God forever**. And God promises to give us one way. Not two ways. Not God's way today and the devil's way tomorrow. But one way and one heart that we may **fear God forever**!

"God gives us **one heart**, which is a pure heart. He gives us **one way**, which is a holy way. And he gives us only this one heart and only this one way, so that we might **fear him forever**. And then he adds, 'I will put my fear in their hearts, **that they shall not depart from me**.'

"Do you believe this? Do you believe that God will give you a single heart and a single way so that you will fear him forever? Do you believe that God will put his fear in your heart so that you will never depart from him? That is what he has promised in this new covenant that he says is an **everlasting covenant**. And this covenant is the **everlasting covenant** in the blood of Jesus. For it is mentioned in Hebrews 13:20-21 as the **everlasting covenant** in the blood of Jesus: 'Now the God of peace, that brought again from the dead our Lord Jesus, that great shepherd of the sheep, through the blood of the **everlasting covenant**, make you perfect in every good work to do his will, working in you that which is well-pleasing in his sight, through Jesus Christ; to whom be glory for ever and ever. Amen.' Hebrews 13:20-21

"Ezekiel also prophesied of the new covenant in the blood of Jesus, a new covenant in which God will cleanse his people from all their filthiness and from all their idols:

'Then will I sprinkle clean water upon you, and ye shall be clean: from *all your filthiness*, and from *all your idols*, will I cleanse you. A new heart also will I give you, and a new spirit will I put within you: and I will take away the stony heart out of your flesh, and I will give you an heart of flesh. And I will put my Spirit within you, and cause you to walk in my statutes, and ye shall keep my judgments, and do them.' Ezekiel 36:25-27

"God promises to completely cleanse his people from all their sins! He says, 'Then will I sprinkle clean water upon you, and ye shall be clean: from *all your filthiness*, and from *all your idols*, will I cleanse you.' God promises to give his people a new heart, and put a new spirit within them. He also promises to take away the stony heart out of their flesh, and give them a heart of flesh. And finally he says, 'And I will *put my Spirit within you*, and cause you to walk in my statutes, and ye shall keep my judgments and do them.'

"God says *he will do all this*! He does not say, 'If you will do such and such for me, I will do this.' He simply promises to all those who will believe, 'I WILL cleanse you from all your filthiness and from all your idols. I WILL give you a new heart. I WILL put my Spirit within you. I WILL give you life. I WILL make you holy. I WILL put my fear within you so that you will not depart from me.' These are the *new covenant promises* in the blood of Jesus!

"The prophet Joel also proclaimed the *new covenant promise* of God, that he would **pour out his Spirit upon all flesh** in the last days:

'And it shall come to pass afterward, that I will **pour out my Spirit upon all flesh**; and your sons and your daughters shall prophesy, your old men shall dream dreams, your young men shall see visions: and also upon the servants and upon the handmaids in those days will I **pour out my Spirit**. And I will shew wonders in the heavens and in the earth, blood, and fire, and pillars of smoke. The sun shall be turned into darkness, and the moon into blood, before the great and terrible day of the Lord come. And it shall come to pass, that whosoever shall call on the name of the Lord shall be delivered: for in mount Zion and in Jerusalem shall be deliverance, as the Lord hath said, and in the remnant whom the Lord shall call.' Joel 2:28-32

"Deliverance! That is what God has promised his people in the new covenant. Supernatural deliverance through the power of the Holy Ghost! 'Whosoever shall call on the name of the Lord shall be delivered: for in mount Zion and in Jerusalem shall be deliverance, as the Lord hath said, and in the remnant whom the Lord shall call.'

"Remember, dear friends, God made a *new covenant* with Israel for one reason only. And that was because the old covenant, the covenant of the law, *did not save Israel from their sins*!

'For **if the first covenant had been faultless, then should no place have been sought for the second**. But finding fault with them, he saith, Behold, the days come, saith the Lord, when I will make a new covenant with the house of Israel and with the house of Judah: not according to the covenant that I made with their fathers in the day when I took them by the hand to lead then out of the land of Egypt; **Because they continued not in my covenant**...For this is the covenant that I will make with the house of Israel after those days, saith the Lord; I will put my laws into their mind, and write them in their hearts.... " Hebrews 8:7-12

"Israel continually broke the covenant of the law. And the law itself could do nothing to make Israel obedient and holy. The law has no motives in it to make the sinner holy. The law can give no life to the guilty sinner. It can only condemn the guilty sinner and pronounce judgment upon him. It can only say, 'The soul that sinneth it shall die' and 'Cursed is everyone that continueth not in all things which are written in the book of the law to do them.'

"So God promised a new covenant in the blood of Jesus. A new and a better covenant that not only pardons the sinner, but also cleanses the sinner from all his filthiness and all his idols. A covenant that gives the sinner life, and a covenant that gives the sinner stability in holiness and righteousness. This new and better covenant is established on better promises. God promises us a new birth. He promises us life and holiness in his Son. He promises us singleness of heart and stability and faithfulness. He promises to write his law in our heart and mind. He promises to give us a new heart and a new spirit. He promises to make us drink of the Holy Spirit, and also promises to baptize us with the Holy Ghost. He promises that he will be our God, and that we will be his people. He promises to give us one way and one heart, and he promises to put his fear in our hearts so that we will not depart from him. He promises to **dwell in us** and **walk in us FOREVER!**

'What? know ye not that *your body is he temple of the Holy Ghost which is in you, which ye have of God*, and ye are not your own?' I Corinthians 6:19

'What agreement hath the *temple of God* with idols? *For ye are the temple of the living God; as God hath said, I will dwell in them, and walk in them; and I will be their God* ....

And *I will be a Father unto you, and ye shall be my sons and daughters, saith the Lord Almighty*. Having therefore these promises, dearly beloved, let us cleanse ourselves from all filthiness of the flesh and spirit, perfecting holiness in the fear of God.' II Corinthians 6:16-7:1

"My dear friends here in **WISDOM AND TEACHINGS OF THE CHURCH FATHERS**, you hold as a basic tenet that God created you with a sinful nature, and that your sinful nature makes it impossible for you to live in holiness and righteousness before God.

"But my dear friends, the idea that you were born with a sinful nature, and cannot live without sin is a lie of the devil. **Your belief that you were born with a sinful nature**, makes it *impossible for you to believe any of the clear promises of the new covenant in the blood of Jesus Christ*! For the sum total of all the promises of the new covenant are that God completely delivers you from every sin in this life, and preserves you in holiness and righteousness, without fault or blame, until the coming of our Lord and Savior Jesus Christ!

'And the very God of peace *sanctify you wholly*; and I pray God your whole spirit and soul and body be *preserved blameless* unto the coming of our Lord Jesus Christ. Faithful is he that calleth you *who also will do it*.' I Thessalonians 5:23-24

'Now unto him that is *able to keep you from falling*, and *to present you faultless* before the presence of his glory with exceeding joy...' Jude 24-25

"My dear friends, you are very religious! But your religion is only an empty shell without any life! You know that your religion has not saved you from your sins! Your own testimony is that you are still a slave to sin, that you sin daily, and that you can never be free from sin.

"And dear friends, with sin in your lives you are not saved! As long as you are living in sin, you are lost and on your way to hell.

"Oh, my dear friends, come to Jesus! Only through faith in him, and his new covenant promises, can you be saved and delivered from all your sins."

Chapter LI
Delivered From Demon Possession

Jed Truly went back to his seat and sat down after his sermon on the new covenant. He saw that there was general conviction among the people. But he saw also that some of the men in the crowd had become very agitated by his final words when he told them that their religion was only an empty shell without any life. And that they must believe in Jesus and the new covenant in his blood; and that only if they believed in Jesus would God set them free from their sins.

With these final words, some of the men in the crowd had made menacing motions toward the pulpit. And Jed saw that these men carried clubs. Although he wanted to kneel and pray, he remained seated, for fear he would not see, if any of the men with clubs came down upon the Christians to do them harm.

Pastor Truelove now stepped up to the table. He saw that there was great conviction among the people.

But he saw, also, that there was a group of angry men, railing against the preaching. And he recognized in this group the same two men who had threatened him earlier for preaching against the corrupted versions of the Bible. The two men carried clubs, and the meaner of the two swung his club angrily toward the pulpit, saying something to his companion.

But now Pastor truelove spoke: "You have heard the preacher's words. And you know that Jesus loves you and will forgive your sins if you will come to him with faith and repentance. Will you come now? Come forward now. Come, and kneel before God. Ask God to forgive you. and he will forgive you and cleanse you from all your sins."

After this simple invitation, seven young men came down to pray. Pastor Truelove stepped around the table to kneel and pray with them, but stood frozen when he saw the same two men who had resisted him earlier, approaching with clubs lifted high above their heads.

At that moment an anguished scream rent the heavens. And Pastor truelove saw a youth running full tilt toward the two men with clubs. They turned around and faced the oncoming youth. The youth let loose

198

another earth rending scream; then threw himself to the ground; and wallowed there, gnashing his teeth, and foaming at the mouth.

Immediately, Deacon Faith and Miracles ran to where the youth had thrown himself to the ground. When he got there, he saw that the two men with clubs were standing over the youth, and were watching him with evident concern. "Do you know this young man?" asked Deacon Faith and Miracles.

"Yes." Conceded the meaner of the two with sorrow; and with not a little shame. "This is my only son. This came upon him just a short time after we moved here from the Bright Regions. My wife also suffers like attacks as my son, but her attacks are even worse. The spirits tear her continually, and throw her sometimes into the fire and sometimes into the water to destroy her; and in the last attack she fled from here screaming in great torment, and I know not where she is now."

"Oh my friend, if you can believe, all things are possible to him who believeth. Will you now believe all that Jesus has said here today?"

Immediately the mean man replied, "In the past I have picked only what I wanted to believe. But now I will believe everything that Jesus has said." And the mean man dropped his club, fell to his knees next to his son, and began to pray.

At this, Deacon Faith and Miracles looked down at the youth, and cried out with a loud voice, "I command you, tormenting spirit, in the name of Jesus Christ, come out of him and torment him no more."

Immediately the tormenting spirit left the young man. And he stood slowly to his feet and began thanking God for his deliverance.

Now that the seven young men had prayed through, Pastor Truelove rose from prayer and returned to the pulpit. There he made a call for the new converts to be baptized in water. He said, "Jesus commanded all who believe in him to be baptized in water. I want all of you who have given your hearts to God, and are ready to obey the command of Jesus, to come and stand in front of this pulpit."

Pastor Truelove watched with gladness, as, without hesitation, the seven young men rose to their feet to stand before the pulpit.

But Pastor Truelove watched with even more gladness as he saw the once mean man, along with his son, come and stand with the seven others who were ready to obey Christ's command to be baptized.

Then, suddenly, angry shouts erupted from the crowd. And an angry group of men pushed through the crowd and drew near. When the leader spoke, his words were measured and conciliatory. He said, "We teach only what the Church Fathers have taught. They taught that we are born sinners and cannot help but sin. They taught that we have a sinful nature, and will have it as long as we are in this world. We know that what they have taught is true. But you come with a new doctrine, and teach that we are not born with a sinful nature.

"Why don't you stay in your own church and preach your doctrine there?" He paused, and indicated the nine people who stood ready to be baptized. "You see that you are confusing and dividing the church of Jesus Christ with your divisive doctrine! Why don't you preach something else besides your doctrine of living free from sin? We wouldn't mind you preaching here, if you would preach something else besides living without sin."

Here, the father of the young man, out of whom the devil had gone, broke in, and said, "Oh, no! Noble Teacher of Tradition and Dogma, we have been wrong. I know I have been wrong! And now I repent of my disobedience to God.

"Look at my son! He has been delivered from demon possession. God has done a great miracle today, and we cannot gainsay it. Neither can we gainsay any of the preaching today. It's all in the Bible. We cannot live in sin and be right with God. We must give up all our sins, once and for all, and forever!"

Upon hearing Enforcer of Tradition and Dogma speak thus (for, Enforcer of Tradition and Dogma was his name), Teacher of Tradition and Dogma exploded into a hate filled diatribe against him. He spat out his words: "Have care that you do not die for your treachery," he warned. "Everyone knows that the Church has held the traditions and dogmas we teach, from its very inception. We cannot turn from the traditions and dogmas of the Church, and remain guiltless.

"Besides, we all know it's impossible to live without sin! Have you ever seen anyone who has lived for even one day without sin? I haven't! And the very idea of living a sinless life is foolish. The doctrine of sinless perfection is heresy! Even the Apostles did not live **free from sin**? Jesus was the only man who ever lived **free from sin**! No one else can live **free from sin**, for we are all born with a sinful nature!"

Enforcer of Tradition and Dogma felt a quickening of the Holy Spirit as he heard his former teacher repeat three times the three words, "*free from sin*." Then he said the three words, "*free from sin*!" Then he repeated the words again, even more forcefully, "***free from sin***! That shall be my new name!" he cried. "For I am done with the name, Enforcer of Tradition and Dogma. Henceforth my name shall be *Freed From Sin*, or, *Made Free From Sin*; names that accord with those who have been delivered from their sins by the Savior Jesus Christ. For do you remember, Noble Teacher, the sermon just preached by the young man? He quoted Romans 6:7, which declares:

'For he that is dead is **freed from sin**.' Romans 6:7

"And, he quoted Romans 6:18, which says:

'Being then made **free from sin**, ye became the servants of righteousness.' Romans 6:18

"And, he quoted Romans 6:22, which says:

'But now being made **free from sin**, and become servants to God, ye have your fruit unto holiness, and the end everlasting life.' Romans 6:22

"Oh, Noble Teacher!" begged the man who was no longer mean, and whose heart was now filled with the love of God, and who had chosen the Christian name, **Freed From Sin**: "Please turn with us to God. For God is a God of love and mercy, and will forgive our sins. Repent of your sins, and turn with us, and call on the name of the Lord for salvation, and be baptized according to his command."

His former teacher was furious. He felt insulted and demeaned by the words of Freed From Sin. "What? You ask me to repent and be baptized like some common ordinary sinner? Not I! And neither will you be baptized! Nor any of these standing here with you! Not here, in Wisdom And Teachings Of The Church Fathers. No one with your heretical beliefs will ever be baptized here! And if you do not recant your heretical beliefs you will be expelled from our communion, or stoned to death! Go! Get out while you are still alive. I will kill you myself if you attempt to be baptized here. Go! Get out!"

Teacher of Tradition and Dogma now turned to the eight young men and began to rebuke them, trying to turn them from their new faith in Jesus Christ. At the same time Freed From Sin exhorted the young men not to listen to Teacher of Tradition and Dogma, but to continue believing in the miracle working Jesus, who saves sinners from their sins.

But the voice of Teacher of Tradition and Dogma was more powerful than the voice of Freed From Sin; And his voice drowned out the voice of Freed From Sin. And seeing this, Deacon Faith and Miracles drew near to Teacher of Tradition and Dogma; and, filled with the Holy Ghost, cried out with a loud voice: "Thou child of the devil. Thou enemy of all righteousness. Why wilt thou pervert the right ways of the Lord? Behold, the hand of the Lord is against thee. And thou shalt be dumb for a season, that thou mightest know that it is God, and not man, against whom thou fightest."

And, immediately, Teacher of Tradition and Dogma was struck dumb. He grunted and groaned, and contorted his face, making unintelligible noises; but could not speak another word. He ran around in small circles, grunting and groaning and clasping his hands and swinging his arms through the air in an effort to speak, but to no avail. Finally he fled in shame because of the spectacle he was making. And his supporters followed after him, to find out what was wrong with him.

Chapter LII
On To The Next Settlement

Faithful Witness and his wife, Patience, stayed on in **WISDOM AND TEACHINGS OF THE CHURCH FATHERS**, in spite of much concern for their safety.

And Pastor Truelove and the large group of Christians with him went on to the next settlement.

And so quickly did they move, that in a very short time, they began seeing signs, indicating that they were nearing the next settlement. And the signs were prolific, as prolific as they had been in the last settlement.

Bob Becker commented on the many signs they were seeing: "We must be getting fairly close to the next settlement—from the looks of the many signs! And he pointed to a very large sign that he had never seen before, and began reading:

CHRIST'S IMPUTED RIGHTEOUSNESS, POSITIONAL HOLINESS, AND PROGRESSIVE SANCTIFICATION

"Is that the name of the new settlement?" asked Bob.

"Yes," replied Pastor Truelove. "That's its name. And the foundation of that name is the blasphemous lie that God created us with a corrupt, sinful nature that makes sin a necessity in our lives.

"So, although you will see many of the old signs as before; you will also see many new signs that agree with the name they have given this new settlement."

Then Bob saw three very lengthy signs, that blamed God and excused the sinner, with wording he had never seen before: NOT BY OUR OWN CHOICE WERE WE CREATED AND BORN SINNERS; BUT BY THE CHOICE OF GOD AND OUR PARENTS. For Psalm 51:5 declares, BEHOLD, I WAS SHAPEN IN INIQUITY BY GOD; AND IN SIN DID MY MOTHER CONCEIVE ME.

The second sign said: GOD CREATED US WITH A SINFUL NATURE, EVEN THOUGH HE KNEW WE COULD NOT LIVE WITHOUT SIN—SO JUSTICE REQUIRES HIM TO SAVE US.

And the third sign said: THE SINFUL NATURE GOD CREATED US WITH, MAKES ALL OUR SINS EXCUSABLE. FOR NO ONE CAN BE BLAMED FOR A NATURE HE WAS BORN WITH.

When Bob read these last three signs he cried out with indignation: "What? Justice saves sinners? The Bible says it is not justice that saves sinners; but God's mercy and grace! There is not one place in the entire Bible where God excuses sin or says we are saved by justice!"

And then, both sides of the path were crowded with signs from the Church Fathers. Again, six signs quoted Augustine:

'Our nature sinned in Adam.' Augustine

'It was just, that after our nature had sinned…we should be born animal and carnal.' Augustine

'There is in us a <u>necessity of sinning</u>.' Augustine

'Our nature there transformed for the worse, not only became a sinner, but also begets sinners.' Augustine

'Unconscious infants, dying without baptism, are damned by virtue of their inherited guilt.' Augustine

'From this condemnation no one is exempt, not even newborn children.' Augustine

Two signs quoted Martin Luther:

'The nature and essence of man is, from his birth, an evil tree and a child of wrath.' Martin Luther

'Even children, dying unbaptized, are lost.' Martin Luther

One sign quoted Calvin:

'Original sin is the hereditary depravity and corruption of our nature…which first makes us subject to the wrath of God, and then produces in us works which the Scripture calls works of the flesh.' Calvin

And then there followed a large sign on the origin of the original sin doctrine just like the one in the settlement they had just come from:

THE CHURCH FATHERS GAVE US THE DOCTRINE OF ORIGINAL SIN

Next to this large sign, were the doctrinal statements on original sin by three church fathers. The first was by the most highly esteemed of all the church fathers. The second and third were by men hardly recognized in church history.

The first said:

'The whole human race existed as one moral person in Adam; so that in Adam's sin we sinned, we corrupted ourselves, and we brought guilt and merited condemnation upon ourselves. Adam's will was the will of the species, so that in Adam's free act, the will of the race revolted against God and the nature of the race corrupted itself.' Doctrine of Augustine, fifth century AD

The second said:

'Adam was the federal head of the race and God made a covenant with Adam, our federal head, agreeing to give eternal life to him and to all his descendants if he obeyed; but making the penalty for his disobedience the condemnation of all his descendants. Since our legal representative or federal head did sin, God imputes his sin, his guilt, and his condemnation to all his descendants.' Doctrine of Cocceius, 17th century A.D.

The third said:

'Because Adam sinned, all men are born with a corrupt sinful nature and are guilty and condemned for that nature. They are not guilty for the sin of Adam, but are guilty only for the corrupt, sinful nature that they are born with. It is the corrupt nature, only, which they inherit from Adam, that is sufficient cause and legal ground for God to condemn them.' Doctrine of Placeus, 17th century AD

Then, after these statements, followed the testimony of the Shorter Catechism on original sin:

Q. 16. Did all mankind fall in Adam's first transgression?

A.   The covenant being made with Adam, not only for him-self, but also for his posterity; all mankind, descending from him by ordinary generation, sinned in him and fell with him, in his first trangression. Shorter Catechism

Q. 19 What is the misery of that estate whereinto men fell?

A.   All mankind by their fall lost communion with God, are under his wrath and curse, and so made liable to all miseries in this life, to death itself, and to the pains of hell forever. Shorter Catechism

Then, there were many other signs with quotations from other highly esteemed sources:

'The sin of Adam is the immediate cause and ground of inborn depravity, guilt, and condemnation to the whole human race.' A. H. Strong, Systematic Theology, p. 611

'This evil tendency or inborn determination to evil, since it is the real cause of actual sins, must itself be sin, and as such must be guilty and condemnable.' A. H. Strong, Systematic Theology, p. 611

There was a tendency now to **underline certain words** that was not done in the first two settlements. Bob had noticed that the underlining of these words emphasized the **complete inability of Christians to live free from sin**. Two glaring examples that he had observed: 'inborn determination to evil', and an earlier statement by Augustine, 'There is in us a necessity of sinning.'

And Bob also noticed that although some of the signs they had seen

before in WISDON AND TEACHINGS OF THE CHURCH
FATHERS seemed now to be missing, that the signs that spoke of the
utter inability of Christians to obey God seemed to super-abound. In
fact, as Bob read the next five signs, he was filled with alarm at the
rational dementia, and moral madness of men who could believe that
the nature given to them by God, made it impossible for them to obey
him:

> 'Original sin is the corruption of man's nature, whereby he is
> utterly indisposed, disabled and made opposite to all that is
> spiritually good, and wholly inclined to evil, and that
> continually.' Larger Catechism

> 'From this original corruption whereby we are utterly
> indisposed, disabled and made opposite to all good, and
> wholly inclined to all evil, do proceed all actual transgres-
> sions.' Westminster Confession

> 'This corruption of nature, during this life, doth remain in
> those that are regenerated: and although it be through Christ
> pardoned and mortified, yet both itself, and all the motions
> thereof, are truly and properly sin.' Westminster Confession

> 'No man is able, either of himself, or by any grace received in
> this life, perfectly to keep the commandments of God, but
> doth daily break them in thought, word, and deed.' Larger
> Catechism

> 'They deplore their inability to love their Redeemer, to keep
> themselves from sin, to live a life in any degree adequate to
> their own convictions of their obligations…they recognize it
> as the fruit and evidence of the corruption of their nature
> derived as a sad inheritance from their first parents.' Charles
> Hodge, Systematic Theology, Vol. II, p. 273

Now Pastor Truelove advanced a few more steps, and pointed
angrily at several more signs. "See the verses of Scripture on those
signs? Those are some of the verses they change and take out of context
to support their doctrine of a **natural inability to obey God:**

> 'The heart **of all God's people** is deceitful above all things,
> and desperately wicked: who can know it?' Jeremiah 17:9

'If we **Christians** say that we have no sin, we deceive ourselves, and the truth is not in us.' I John 1:8

'If they sin against thee, for there is *no man that sinneth not.*' I Kings 8:46

'For there is *not a just man upon the earth, that doeth good, and sinneth not.*' Ecclesiastes 7:20

'There is no **Christian** righteous, *no, not one.*' Romans 3:10

"Then, as they advanced yet further, they came up to a number of other signs, signs they had never seen before. And, again, the Christians were appalled as they read the signs:

ONCE I AM SAVED, I AM ALWAYS SAVED AND ETERNALLY SECURE, EVEN THOUGH I SIN DAILY AGAINST GOD.

I AM BORN AGAIN, AND I CAN NEVER BE UNBORN! I MAY BE A DISOBEDIENT CHILD OF GOD, BUT I AM FOREVER HIS CHILD!

GOD IMPUTES THE RIGHTEOUSNESS OF CHRIST TO ME; SO EVEN THOUGH I SIN DAILY, I AM STILL AS RIGHTEOUS AS CHRIST.

I BELIEVE IN POSITIONAL HOLINESS. I AM HOLY BECAUSE OF MY POSITION IN CHRIST. I AM HOLY EVEN THOUGH I HAVE A SINFUL NATURE AND SIN DAILY.

I BELIEVE IN PROGRESSIVE SANCTIFICATION: GOD KNOWS I AM BORN WITH A SINFUL NATURE AND CANNOT LIVE WITHOUT SIN; SO GOD IS SATISFIED IF I MAKE PROGRESS IN SANCTIFICATION AND BECOME A LITTLE BIT HOLIER EACH DAY.

Chapter LIII
Reverend Nicolaitan And Water Baptism

The Christians went up a final hill, and then quickly descended into the park against cold gusts of wind and swirling fog.

This was a strange phenomenon, for before entering into the park, there had been no cold wind or swirling fog; and the sun had even managed to peek through the fog from time to time.

But aside from the strange phenomenon of the swirling fog and the cold gusts of wind, this park was much like the park in **WISDOM AND TEACHINGS OF THE CHURCH FATHERS**. For it had the same groupings of signs in the park, with people standing about them, debating and arguing the doctrinal points taught by the different signs.

When Bob saw the people arguing, he asked, "Do we need to fear violence from these people? I see they are arguing quite heatedly."

"Oh, no!" said Pastor Truelove. "And you're not likely to see them brandishing clubs here. But the people here are sticklers for doctrinal perfection, and spend much of their time arguing their doctrinal positions. It's sad they are not as scrupulous for Christian perfection. Nay, they seem to hate the very thought of Christian perfection." And after a slight pause, he added with finality, "And Christian perfection is the one thing that God cares for in his people!"

And with these words he headed toward a group of men standing around a group of signs, who were arguing the doctrinal points of water baptism. And among them was a man looking toward Pastor Truelove with recognition and some amazement.

"Reverend Truelove!" the man exclaimed. "That's an awful big group of people you have with you today. And you're later than usual. I was hoping we could have a public debate today and debate the doctrine of water baptism. But you can choose the doctrine. Whether it be the doctrine of original sin, the doctrine of a natural inability to obey God, the righteousness of Christ imputed to believers, the 30, 60, and 100 fold Christian, the impossibility of Christian perfection, or the doctrines of positional and progressive sanctification. You can choose. But I would like to debate the doctrine of water baptism; because I believe water baptism communicates all the graces of Christ to believers."

"No!" cried out Pastor truelove. "I will not debate doctrines with you! God has not called me to debate doctrines, but to preach his Word. But I will say a few words on water baptism in just a minute, for we have nine converts here, whom Christ commands us to baptize in water. And," he added, "if God wills, and there is time later, I will also preach on the *three baptisms* that belong to every believer."

And with these words he led off toward the baptismal tank, which was only a few hundred feet from the park. As they went he leaned over to Nicolaitan, (for Nicolaitan was the man's name) and in a low voice he said, "Elder Nicolaitan, you are true to your name. You desire to be over the laity, and be elevated above the laity; and be revered and worshipped when only God should be revered and worshipped. You want the laity to call you by the name, Reverend. But that name belongs to God, and God alone. Psalm 89:7 and Psalm 111:9

"And I told you when I first came here that I could not, and would not, address you as Reverend, and I told you I did not want anyone to address me as Reverend. So, please, do not address me as Reverend again! And do not use other terms that men use to worship men. Jesus warned us against this:

> 'And (they) love the uppermost rooms at feasts, and the chief seats in the synagogues, and greetings in the markets, and to be called of men, Rabbi, Rabbi. But be ye not called Rabbi: for one is your Master, even Christ; and all ye are brethren. And call no man your father upon the earth: for one is your Father, which is in heaven. Neither be ye called masters: for one is your Master, even Christ.' Matthew 23:6-10

"So do not call me Father, or Holy Father, or Master, or Reverend, or The Right Reverend, or The Most Reverend, or The Most Holy and Reverend; for such appellations belong only to God, who alone is to be worshipped! If you must call me by some name use the biblical names of Elder, Pastor, or even Preacher. But Jesus suggested the common name, Brother, for we believers are all brothers in Christ."

But now they were at the baptismal tank, and a big crowd had followed them to witness the baptism of the new converts.

Pastor Truelove opened his Bible and read a text:

> 'I marvel that ye are so soon removed from him that called you into the grace of Christ unto another gospel: which is not another; but there be some that trouble you, and would pervert the gospel of Christ. But though we, or an angel from heaven, preach any other gospel unto you than that which we have preached unto you, **LET HIM BE ACCURSED**. As we said before, so say I now again, If any man preach any other gospel unto you than that ye have received, **LET HIM BE ACCURSED**.' Galatians 1:6-9

"Paul was angry with the men who were preaching another gospel which was not the *gospel of the grace of Christ*. He said, '**LET THEM BE ACCURSED**.' They were preaching that in addition to believing in Jesus Christ to by justified and saved, it was necessary to be circumcised and keep the law!

"Paul emphatically denounced this false teaching, and said that it was a perversion of the *gospel of the grace of Christ*. And, his words concerning any man who would preach such a perverted gospel were, '**LET HIM BE ACCURSED**.' He said:

> 'Though we, or an angel from heaven, preach any other gospel unto you than that which we have preached unto you, **LET HIM BE ACCURSED**. As we said before, so say I now again, If any man preach any other gospel unto you than that ye have received, **LET HIM BE ACCURSED**.' Galatians 1:8-9

"The true gospel of Christ is the good news that salvation is the free gift of God, and not of works lest any man should boast. And it is received only by simple faith in Christ without any works. Paul said, 'For by grace are ye saved through faith; and that not of yourselves: it is the *gift of God*: not of works, lest any man should boast. For we are his workmanship, created in Christ Jesus unto good works, which God hath before ordained that we should walk in them.' Ephesians 2:8-10

"There is only one way to be saved and receive any life, or grace, or gift from God. It is only through simple faith in Jesus Christ the Savior. Anyone, who preaches another way of salvation, such as by keeping the law, or by being circumcised, *or by being baptized in water,* is cut off from the grace of Christ, and **IS ACCURSED!** He is accursed because *ALL HAVE SINNED; are under the curse of the law; and can only be saved by faith in the Savior Jesus Christ!*

"The nine men who are here to be baptized in water, are not here to be saved by water baptism! They are saved already by faith in Jesus Christ. They were saved today when they put their faith in the Savior Jesus Christ. And they are going to be baptized now because Christ commands all those who believe in him to be baptized.

"Jesus, himself, was baptized by John the Baptist—not to be saved, but to 'fulfill all righteousness.' And these men will be baptized—not to be saved, but in obedience to Christ's command, and to thus 'fulfill all righteousness.'" Matthew 3:13-15

212

Chapter LIV
Three Christian Baptisms For Today

After Pastor Truelove had baptized the nine converts, they all went back to the park for the preaching.

The fog was still swirling about in a strange way. Elder Nicolaitan brought a pulpit and set it up for Pastor Truelove to preach from. A great crowd had gathered for the preaching. The crowd was filled with a heightened curiosity, both because of the water baptism and because of the large number of visitors. (All the inhabitants of CHRIST'S IMPUTED RIGHTEOUSNESS, POSITIONAL HOLINESS, AND PROGRESSIVE SANCTIFICATION had an excessive and unnatural desire to hear new preachers in the hope that they might hear some new or unusual doctrinal teaching. They had an unnatural desire to hear some 'new revelation.')

The fog continued to swirl about in its strange and unnatural way. Pastor Truelove shivered from the cold gusts of wind. He looked at the thick fog as it swirled about. Then he noticed that four men were approaching through the swirling fog. They wore T-shirts with printing front and back. And as they approached between the pulpit, and the crowd, they turned slowly about, shuffling sideways to show off the messages printed on their T-shirts.

One T-shirt said, 'BE PATIENT WITH ME, GOD IS NOT FINISHED WITH ME YET.' Turning, it said, 'I NOW SIN EVERY DAY; BUT WHEN GOD TAKES ME UP TO HEAVEN, I WON'T SIN ANYMORE.'

A second T-shirt said, 'EVEN THE GREAT APOSTLE PAUL CONFESSED HE WAS A SLAVE TO SIN.' (Romans 7:14-25) Turning, it said, 'AND THAT MAKES ME FEEL A WHOLE LOT BETTER ABOUT MY SINS.'

A third T-shirt said, 'WE SIN BECAUSE WE HAVE A SINFUL NATURE.' Turning, it said, 'BUT, BE OF GOOD CHEER, OUR POSITION IN CHRIST MAKES US AS HOLY AS CHRIST IS HOLY.'

The fourth T-shirt said, 'GOD KNOWS WE CANNOT OBEY HIM PERFECTLY.' Tuning, it said, 'SO GOD ACCEPTS A PARTIAL

OBEDIENCE—A PROGRESSIVE SANCTIFICATION—GOD JUST
ASKS US TO OBEY HIM A LITTLE BIT BETTER EACH DAY.'

After seeing the T-shirts, Pastor Truelove called on everybody to
pray. He said, "Let us pray now. Let us ask God to lead us and direct
us. Let us ask God to tell us exactly what he wants us to preach, and
who he wants to preach. Let's call on God to show us his will for
today!"

And having spoken these words he fell on his face and began to
implore God for help and direction. And there was a low murmur as
the crowd also began to pray.

Pastor Truelove's prayer was very short. After praying he asked
Deacon Faith and Miracles to preach. He also asked Jed Truly to
preach. And finally he asked Bob to preach.

Then he stepped to the pulpit and announced the order of the
service:

"Today we have five visitors with us. All five testified and
preached in the service in **WISDOM AND TEACHINGS
OF THE CHURCH FATHERS**. God told us there that he
had sent them to the Foggy Bottoms to be a sign and a wonder, and to
preach his word to a rebellious and hard-hearted people.

"And I believe God has sent them to preach his word here also. So I
have asked two of them to preach here, along with Deacon Faith and
Miracles.

"So, God willing, there will be three and possibly four sermons
preached here today. Brother Jed Truly will preach first. He is the
Science and Bible teacher at the Lynwood Christian Elementary School
in Lynwood, California. Bob Becker is an eighth grade student in the
same School, and will preach next. Then Deacon Faith and Miracles
will preach. And, if there is time, I will preach also on the Three
Christian Baptisms."

Brother Truelove turned to Jed Truly, and said, "Brother Truly,
please come now, and preach to us the word that God has laid on your
heart."

Before Jed could take a step toward the pulpit, Elder Nicolaitan, being at the forefront of the crowd, and close by, raised his voice and said: "Brother Truelove, we are glad you have brought these visitors with you today. We are also glad that two of them will be preaching today.

"But we want you to preach first so we can be sure you preach your sermon on the three baptisms. We know that Ephesians 4:5 says that there is only 'one baptism.' So we know that, that 'one baptism' has to be water baptism.

"The Bible also talks about a baptism with the Holy Ghost. But that baptism was only given for the early church, and is now done away with. So there is really only one baptism for today's church. I certainly do not know of three baptisms for today! So, please, tell us now about the three baptisms you believe in."

Pastor Truelove paused for just a moment, to consider. And then answered, "All right, Elder Nicolaitan, I will preach now. I will preach on the three Christian baptisms for today. But I am not preaching this to be contentious, or to prove you or anybody else wrong. I am preaching it only because it is the word of God and the truth; and because God wants all his people to know the truth."

Pastor Truelove now turned to Jed Truly and said, "Excuse me Brother Truly for preaching before you." He then opened his big black Bible and read two texts:

'There is...**one baptism**.' Ephesians 4:5

'...the doctrine of **baptisms**.' Hebrews 6:2

"Ephesians 4:5 says, 'There is...one baptism.' But Hebrews 6:2 also speaks of baptisms in the plural, meaning that there are at least two baptisms. And we will soon find that the Bible clearly teaches that there are three baptisms that belong to every Christian believer today!

"But, Ephesians 4:5 does say, 'There is...one baptism.' Is, then, the one baptism of Ephesians 4:5 water baptism? No. The one baptism of Ephesians 4:5 is not water baptism. Well then, if the one baptism of Ephesians 4:5 is not water baptism, is it the baptism with the Holy Ghost? No! It is not the baptism with the Holy Ghost either.

"If the one baptism of Ephesians 4:5 is neither water baptism, nor the baptism with the Holy Ghost, then what baptism is it?

"I will tell you in one moment. But first, I must say that nobody who has been a Christian for very long at all should even have to ask, what baptism Ephesians 4:5 speaks of when it speaks of only 'one baptism.' Every Christian should know within a very short time after his conversion, through the teaching of the church, and through careful study of his Bible, what baptism Ephesians 4:5 is speaking of when it says, 'There is…one baptism.'

"But sadly, the one baptism of Ephesians 4:5 is almost unknown among Christians. Yet, it should be the most well known of the three; for it is the most important of the three Christian baptisms!

"It is the most important of the three baptisms, because it always takes place first in the life of the believer. It is the baptism in which the believer is baptized into Christ, in which he receives new life in Christ, and in which he is born again.

"It is the most important of the three baptisms because it is the beginning of life for the believer. Without the one baptism of Ephesians 4:5 no one is saved or can be saved. In the one baptism of Ephesians 4:5 the believer in Christ Jesus shares in the very life of Christ, is pardoned and saved, is born again, and becomes a saint and a child of God—all at the same instant he believes in Jesus Christ!

"What is the one baptism of Ephesians 4:5? It is the baptism into Jesus Christ! It is the baptism into the body of Jesus Christ! It is the baptism into the quickening, life-giving body of our Lord and Savior Jesus Christ!"

> 'For **BY ONE SPIRIT** are we **ALL BAPTIZED into one body**, whether we be Jews or Gentiles, whether we be bond or free; and have been all made to drink into one Spirit.' I Corinthians 12:13

"Now let's look in our Bibles. And we will see that it plainly teaches that there are **THREE DIFFERENT BAPTISMS**. And we will see also that it plainly teaches that there are **THREE DIFFERENT BAPTIZERS; a DIFFERENT BAPTIZER doing the baptizing** in each of the three different baptisms."

216

THE BAPTISM WITH WATER

"First, the Bible tells us there is a baptism with water, and it tells us that it is **man who baptizes** with water.

'Then went out to him Jerusalem, and all Judaea, and all the region round about Jordan, and were **baptized of him** in Jordan, confessing their sins.' Matthew 3:5-6

'And the eunuch said, See, here is water, what doth hinder me to be baptized?...and they went down both into the water, **both Philip** and the eunuch; and **he baptized him**.' Acts 8:36,38

'Go ye therefore, and teach all nations, **baptizing them** in the name of the Father, and of the Son, and of the Holy Ghost.' Matthew 28:19

THE BAPTISM WITH THE HOLY GHOST

"The Bible tells us there is a **baptism with the Holy Ghost**, and that it is **Jesus, the Son of God, who baptizes** with the Holy Ghost:

'**I indeed baptize you with water** unto repentance: but he that cometh after me is mightier than I, whose shoes I am not worthy to bear: **He** shall **baptize you with the Holy Ghost**, and with fire.' Matthew 3:11

'And I knew him not: but he that sent me to baptize with water, the same said unto me, Upon whom thou shalt see the Spirit descending, and remaining on him, the same is **he that baptizeth with the Holy Ghost. And I saw and bare record that this is the Son of God.**' John 1:33-34

'**This Jesus** hath God raised up, whereof we are all witnesses. Wherefore being by the right hand of God exalted, and having received of the Father the promise of the Holy Ghost, **he hath shed forth this, which ye now see and hear.**' Acts 2:32-33

'It is expedient for you that I go away: for if I go not away, the comforter will not come unto you; but if I depart, **I WILL SEND HIM UNTO YOU.**' John 16:7

THE BAPTISM INTO THE BODY OF JESUS CHRIST

The Bible tells us that it is the **Holy Spirit** who **baptizes believers into the body of Jesus Christ**.

'For **BY ONE SPIRIT** are we **all baptized into one body**, whether we be Jews or Gentiles, whether we be bond or free; and have been all made to drink into one Spirit.' I Corinthians 12:13

Before we examine the four other passages from the Bible that speak of our baptism into the body of Christ, I want to comment on some important truths we have seen in the Scriptures we have looked at thus far:

We have certainly seen three altogether different baptisms for the Christian believer:

We have seen a baptism of believers in water, **done by man**.

We have seen a baptism of believers with the Holy Ghost, **done by the Lord Jesus Christ.**

And we have seen a baptism of believers into the body of Christ, **done by the Holy Spirit.**

"**Man** does not baptize believers with the Holy Ghost. Only Jesus baptizes believers with the Holy Ghost.

"**Man** does not baptize believers into the body of Christ (or into the church which is the body of Christ). Only the Holy Spirit baptizes believers into the body of Christ.

"**Jesus** does not baptize believers into his own body. It is the Holy Spirit who baptizes believers into the body of Christ.

"**The Holy Ghost** does not baptize believers with himself. It is Jesus who baptizes believers with the Holy Ghost.

"Men may be so conceited as to think that they give the Holy Ghost by the laying on of hands. But they don't. (The laying on of hands

218

is scriptural, and God answers the prayer of faith with the laying on of hands. But only Jesus the Son of God baptizes with the Holy Ghost.)

"And men may be so conceited as to think that they are adding new members to the church when they baptize believers in water. But they are not. It is only the Holy Spirit who adds new members to the church, which is the body of Christ; and he adds them when they first believe in Christ, and not later when they are baptized in water."

THE BAPTISM INTO THE BODY OF JESUS CHRIST (CONTINUED)

"We have already seen I Corinthians 12:13. Which tells us that the **Holy Spirit baptizes believers into the body of Jesus Christ**. Now we will look at four more passages that speak of our baptism into Christ:

'For ye are all the children of God by faith in Christ Jesus. For as many of you as have been **baptized into Christ** have **put on Christ**.' Galatians 3:26-27

"Here Paul speaks of believers who are *children of God by faith*, and believers who have been *baptized into Christ* and have *put on Christ*. He is not talking about water baptism, a work that men do; he is talking about **the baptism into Jesus Christ**, a work that the Holy Spirit does. This is not water baptism, which is the work of men. It is **baptism into Christ**, the work of the Holy Spirit."

"The next passage that speaks of our *baptism into Jesus Christ* is found in Romans 6:3-6:

'Know ye not that so many of us as were **baptized into Jesus Christ** were baptized into his death? Therefore *we are buried with him by baptism into death: that like as Christ was raised up from the dead by the glory of the Father, even so we also should walk in newness of life. For if we have been planted together in the likeness of his death, we shall be also in the likeness of his resurrection: knowing this, that our old man is crucified with him that the body of sin might be destroyed, that henceforth we should not serve sin.'* Romans 6:3-6

"Many Christians think of 'water' every time they see the word 'baptism.' But this passage is not talking about water. It is talking about Jesus Christ, and Jesus Christ is not water. Neither is a baptism into Jesus Christ a baptism into water.

"And, of course, we know that water baptism does not accomplish the great work of God that Paul talks about in Romans 6:3-6. That work, and every work of God's grace in the believer, is accomplished only by faith in the Lord Jesus Christ: 'For ye are all children of God **by faith in Christ Jesus**. For as many of you as have been **baptized into Christ** have put on Christ.' Galatians 3:26-27

"It is by **faith alone** and not by water baptism that we become children of God. Before the believer has obeyed the command to be baptized in water he has **already trusted** the Savior and has become a child of God. So it is not when the believer is baptized in water that he becomes a child of God, but when he first trusts in the Savior Jesus Christ.

"And Paul is telling us in Romans 6:3-6 of the mighty work that God works in us when we first believe in Jesus Christ, and **are baptized into him**: we are crucified with him, we die with him, we are buried with him, and we are raised up with him to newness of life. Paul tells us in Romans 6:3-6 that in our baptism into Christ, and in our union and oneness with Christ in that baptism, we share with Christ in his life and receive all the provision and work of Christ done for us. So that in our union with Christ we are 'crucified with Christ that the body of sin might be destroyed, that henceforth we should not serve sin.' And that we die and are 'buried together with him,' and that we are 'raised up together with him to walk in newness of life.'—A new victorious sin-free life!

"I know that many preachers use Romans 6:3-6 to preach on water baptism. But they shouldn't. This passage has nothing to do with water baptism. It does not speak of water baptism. It does not allude to water baptism. Nor is it a picture of water baptism.

"It speaks only of our baptism into Christ and of our complete salvation and total deliverance from sin in him!

"Romans 6:3-6 does not describe a visible work that men can see. It describes an invisible work, yet a very real work of God done in the life of the believer when he has been baptized by the Holy Spirit into the body of Jesus Christ. In our union with Christ we are transformed from wicked sinners ('crucified with him, that the body of sin might be destroyed, that henceforth we should not serve sin') to saints. In our union with Christ we receive new life and are born again. But this is all a spiritual work that cannot be seen by the physical eye.

"Everything that Paul describes in Romans 6:3-6 is unseen. But men are not comfortable with the unseen. For the only way that the unseen can be seen is by faith. Men are comfortable with water baptism because it is something physical, something they can see, feel, and touch. But in Romans 6:3-6 Paul speaks of a baptism that men cannot see, feel, or touch; because it isn't a physical work, but a spiritual work. We know that we were not physically crucified with Christ some 2000 years ago. We know that we were not physically buried with Christ some 2000 years ago. We know that we did not rise from the dead with Christ in our physical bodies some 2000 years ago.

"But because the work done in us is spiritual and moral, and not physical, does not make it any less real. Paul insists that in our baptism into Christ there has been a real spiritual and moral work accomplished in the believer. Romans 6:3-6 talks about an unseen, but real, sin-destroying, life-giving work of God accomplished in the believer when he is baptized into Jesus Christ!

"Let us look at the next passage of Scripture which speaks of our baptism into Christ:

'For in him (in Christ) dwelleth all the fullness of the Godhead bodily. And ye are complete in him which is the head of all principality and power. In whom also ye are circumcised with the circumcision **made without hands**, in putting off the body of the sins of the flesh by the circumcision of Christ: **buried with him in baptism**, wherein also ye are risen with him through the faith of the operation of God, who hath raised him from the dead. And you, being dead in your sins and the uncircumcision of your flesh, hath he quickened together with him, having forgiven you all trespasses.' Colossians 2:9-13

"This is another passage of Scripture that is usually misinterpreted to be water baptism. Christians see the word 'baptism' in verse twelve, 'buried with him in baptism,' and immediately think 'water.' But the context and subject of which Paul was speaking was not water, but **Jesus Christ** and the **body of Jesus Christ** and the **fullness of the Godhead in the body of Jesus Christ**, and our union with him and our completeness in him and our circumcision in him. Hence the many phrases, 'in him,' 'in whom,' 'with him,' and 'together with him,' which refer to our union with Christ through our **baptism into him**. Let's look again at the full context of this passage, and see if this passage could possibly be anything else but **baptism into Christ**:

'...after the **tradition of men**, after the **rudiments of the world**, and **NOT AFTER CHRIST**. *For in him dwelleth all the fullness of the Godhead bodily. And ye are complete in him which is the head of all principality and power: in whom also ye are circumcised with the circumcision made without hands in putting off the body of the sins of the flesh by the circumcision of Christ: buried with him in baptism; wherein also ye are risen with him through the faith of the operation of God, who hath raised him from the dead. And you, being dead in your sins and the uncircumcision of your flesh, hath he quickened together with him, having forgiven you all trespasses.'* Colossians 2:8-13

"It is impossible that Colossians 2:8-13 can be talking of water baptism! Oh, Christian, think! If the baptism spoken of in Colossians 2:8-13 is not baptism into Christ's body, but is instead water baptism, then it is not in Christ but in water that we are made complete in 'the fullness of Christ's body.' (verse 9) And it is not in Christ but in water that 'we are made complete in Christ.' (verse 10) And it is not in Christ but in water that we are 'circumcised with a circumcision made without hands in putting off the body of the sins of the flesh.' (verse 11) And finally, if the baptism spoken of here is not into Christ's body, but is instead baptism into water, then it is through **water baptism** that we have been 'quickened together with him' and have been 'forgiven all trespasses.' (verse 13) If water baptism does all these things, we don't need Christ! All we need is water baptism! Water baptism becomes our **Savior**, and we become **Idolaters** who worship water baptism!

"Oh, dear Christian, think of what you are saying if you say that the baptism spoken of here is water baptism. You are saying that it is not Christ who is your Savior, but water baptism! You are saying that water baptism does what Christ came into the world and died on the cross to do! You are saying that faith in the crucified and resurrected Son of God is unnecessary—that the sinner is quickened to new life and forgiven all his trespasses in water baptism!

"But, it is impossible that this passage could be talking of water baptism. For it is clear that the Apostle Paul ascribed to the baptism spoken of in this passage all the works of God he had enumerated in Colossians 2:9-13.

"If water baptism brings forgiveness of sins, and the new birth, and holiness of life (all of which the believer is said to have through the baptism spoken of in this passage), then we do not need Christ, and he has died in vain.

"Oh, Christian! Water baptism does not save us. It does not wash our sins away. It does not make us God's children. We do not receive new life and we are not born again in water baptism. Our name is not written in the Lamb's book of life when we are baptized in water. Water baptism does not sanctify us. It does not deliver us from the world, the flesh, or the devil. It does not destroy the body of sin, the old fleshly nature, or the old carnal man. Water baptism does not crucify the old sinful man. Our old sinful man is not buried in water baptism and we are not then raised again to walk in newness of life through water baptism. Water baptism does not work a circumcision in us and cut away the body of the sins of the flesh. It does not impart to us any life, or any grace, or any power, or any gift from God. Water baptism does not, and cannot, do any of those things.

"All of those things were done in us before we were baptized in water, when we first believed in Jesus Christ and the Holy Spirit baptized us into the body of Christ, and we received of his life and fullness. At the very moment we placed our faith in Jesus Christ the Holy Spirit baptized us into Christ, and in him we now partake of all his grace, and life, and fullness.

"There is one more passage from the Bible that speaks of our baptism into the body of Jesus Christ. It is the verse of Scripture in Ephesians 4:5, which says: 'There is…*one baptism.*'

"We know that this verse is talking about baptism into the one body of Christ, and not water baptism, because of its context. The context of this text says nothing about water; but it speaks of the **one body of Christ** and the **one Spirit who baptizes all believers** with **one and the same baptism into the one body of Christ**:

> 'Endeavoring to keep the **unity of the Spirit** in the bond of peace. There is **one body**, and **one Spirit**, even as ye are called in **one hope** of your calling; **one Lord, one faith, one baptism, one God and Father** of all, who is above all, and through all, and **IN YOU ALL.**' Ephesians 4:3-6

"Also, we know that Ephesians 4:5 is talking about the **one baptism** into the **one body of Christ** because of what I Corinthians 12:13 says. It says, 'by **one Spirit** are we **all baptized into one body**.' Oh, Christians, if we are **all baptized into one body** there has to be only **one baptism**! And that **one baptism** is the baptism of **all believers** by **one Spirit** into the **ONE BODY OF CHRIST**.

"The Holy Spirit is *not divided*, and Christ is *not divided*; so there is only one baptism by one Spirit into the one body of Christ.

"Yet there are countless Christians who still think that the 'one baptism' spoken of in Ephesians 4:5 is water baptism. But water baptism is not the subject of discourse in this passage. Water is not mentioned nor alluded to in all the context of this passage. And water baptism is absolutely foreign to and repugnant to the context of this passage. The subject matter of this passage is the **unity and oneness** of believers **in the one body of Christ**. Paul is arguing for unity among all the believers in Christ, because we are **all one in Christ**. There is **one** baptism by **one** Spirit into the **one body** of Christ!

"The Holy Spirit does not have one hundred different baptisms—he has only one! He does not baptize Presbyterian believers into a Presbyterian body of Christ. He does not baptize Baptist believers into a Baptist body of Christ. He does not baptize Pentecostal believers into a Pentecostal body of Christ. He does not have a different baptism for the Presbyterian body of Christ, a different baptism for the Baptist body of Christ, a different baptism for the Congregational body of Christ, and so on through the Methodists, the Lutherans, and all the other different denominations in the body of Christ. But the Holy Spirit has only ONE baptism. The body of Christ is ONE, and there is only **one baptism** by **one Spirit** into the **one body of Christ**."

CLOSING REMARKS

"The Bible teaches that there are three baptisms that belong to every Christian.

"Two of these baptisms minister life and grace to the believer. They are the **baptism into the body of Jesus Christ,** and the **baptism with the Holy Ghost.**

"**Water baptism** does not minister any life or grace to the believer. Water baptism, like circumcision, was not commanded by God to give life, but rather to be the believer's **act of commitment** and **obedience to God.** (That is why believers were always commanded to be baptized in water the very same day they were saved.)

"**Baptism into Christ** is always the first baptism that takes place in the life of the believer. It always takes place at the very moment the sinner repents and believes the gospel. It is the most important of the three baptisms for the simple reason that it is through this baptism that the believer receives fullness of life, and all the provisions and gifts of God that are given to him in his baptism into the body of Jesus Christ.

"Our baptism into Christ, with all the life and grace and provision that we receive in him, is the **heart and soul** of the gospel of Jesus Christ.

"If we have not been baptized into Christ and have not received of his life—if we have not had the radical change of the new birth—we do not know the gospel of Jesus Christ! (John 1:12-13, 16-17)

"If we have not been baptized into Christ, and have not been crucified with him, that the body of sin might be destroyed, that henceforth we should not serve sin, we do not know the gospel of Jesus Christ! (Romans 6:3-22)

"If we have not been baptized into Christ, and buried with Christ, and then, raised up together with Christ, to walk in newness of life, we do not know the gospel of Jesus Christ! (Romans 6:3-22)

"If we have not been baptized into Christ, and have not experienced a circumcision made without hands, in putting off the body of the sins of the flesh by the circumcision of Christ, we do not know the gospel of Jesus Christ! (Col. 2:9-13)

"And if we have not been baptized by the one Spirit of God into the one body of Christ, and know by experience what it is to drink into the one Spirit of God, we do not know the gospel of Christ. (I Corinthians 12:13)

"And finally, if we have not been baptized by the one Spirit of God into the one body of Christ, and know by experience what it is to walk in love and fellowship and unity with all the saints of God, we do not know the gospel of Jesus Christ. Ephesians 4:1-7

"When we are baptized into the body of Jesus Christ, our whole life is transformed!"

Chapter LV
Jed Truly Preaches

Pastor Truelove wasted no time; but as soon as he had finished preaching, he turned to Jed Truly and said, "Brother Truly, come now, and preach to us the word God has laid on your heart."

Jed truly stepped to the pulpit, and said, "Thank you Pastor Truelove for giving me the opportunity to preach God's word today. He then looked out at the great crowd and said, "Open your Bibles to the first epistle of John. And I will read the first four verses of his first epistle.

> '*That which was from the beginning*, which we have heard, which we have seen with our eyes, which we have looked upon, and our hands have handled, of the *word of life*. (*For* the *life* was manifested, and we have seen it, and bear witness, and *shew unto you that eternal life*, which was with the Father, and was manifested unto us;) That which we have seen and heard declare we unto you, that ye also may have fellowship with us: and truly *our fellowship is with the Father, and with his Son Jesus Christ*. And these things write we unto you, that your joy may be full.' I John 1:1-4

"What was John speaking of when he said, 'That which was from the beginning.'?

"You who know your Bibles, know immediately that he was speaking of God. For you know that only God is *from the beginning*. And you know the first words in the Bible, '*In the beginning God...*' (Genesis 1:1) And you also know John 1:1, which says, '*In the beginning was the Word*, and the *Word* was with God, and *the Word was God*.'

"So we know that when John spoke in his first epistle, and said, 'That which was from the beginning,' that he was speaking of God. He was speaking of **Jesus Christ, who is God manifested in the flesh.**

"Next John speaks about the *Word of life*, and *the life*, and *the eternal life* that **Jesus Christ is**:

> 'That...which we have looked upon, and our hands have handled, of the *Word of life*; (for the *life* was manifested, and we have seen it, and bear witness, and shew unto you *that*

eternal life, which was with the Father, and was manifested unto us.)' I John 1:1-2

"John speaks of the *eternal life* that Jesus Christ **is**—not just so his readers will know that Jesus Christ **is eternal life**, but to make his readers know the glad tidings that Jesus Christ *shares his eternal life* with all those who believe in him!

"John's gospel confirms this:

'*Of his fullness have all we received*, and grace for grace. For the law was given by Moses, but *grace and truth came by Jesus Christ*.' John 1:16-17

"And John declares in first John 5:11-12:

'And this is the record, that God hath given to us *eternal life*, and this **life** is in his Son. *He that hath the Son hath life*; and he that hath not the Son of God *hath not life*.' I John 5:11-12.

"Additional testimony of Jesus and the Apostle Paul:

'Except ye eat the flesh of the Son of man, and drink his blood, **ye have no life in you**. Whoso eateth my flesh, and drinketh my blood, **hath eternal life**....He that eateth my flesh, and drinketh my blood, dwelleth in me, and I in him. As the living Father hath sent me, and I live by the Father: so he that eateth me, even he shall live by me.' John 6:53-57

'That ye might be **filled with all the fullness of God**.' Ephesians 3:19

'For ye are the **temple of the living God**; as God hath said, **I will dwell in them, and walk in them; and I will be their God, and they shall be my people**.' II Corinthians 6:16

'Whereby are given unto us exceeding great and precious promises: that by these ye might be **partakers of the divine nature**.' II Peter 1:4

"Eternal life describes duration of life—the **everlasting life** we will live in heaven.

"But eternal life also describes the nature and character of God's life that he shares with his people right now. It describes the divine nature of the life Jesus shares with his people!

'Whosoever hateth his brother is a murderer: and ye know that *no murderer hath eternal life abiding in him.*' I John 3:15

"Jesus spoke very emphatically of the sinner's need to have God's life within him, when he spoke of the necessity that the sinner **be born again of God.**

'**Verily, verily**, I say unto thee, **Except a man be born again**, he cannot see the kingdom of God....**Verily, verily**, I say unto thee, **Except a man be born of water and of the Spirit**, he cannot enter into the kingdom of God. That which is born of the flesh is flesh; and **that which is born of the Spirit is spirit**. Marvel not that I said unto thee. **Ye must be born again.**' John 3:3-7

"Finally, John *declares to his readers the reason he has written to them of Jesus Christ and the eternal life that he is.* It is that they all might know the glad truth that God gives his eternal life to all who believe in the Son of God. And that they all might have fellowship with the Father, and with his Son Jesus Christ—and that, thus, their joy might be full. He says:

'That which we have seen and heard declare we unto you, that *ye also may have fellowship with us*: and truly *our fellowship is with the Father, and with his Son Jesus Christ.* And these things write we unto you **that your joy may be full.**' I John 1:3-4

The Evidence That God's Life Is in Us:

"John tells us that we cannot have God's life abiding in us, without having real evidence of the life of God that abides in us. And he tells us that the *evidence that God's life is in us,* is that we *no longer walk in sin*, but that we *walk in holiness and righteousness like God who dwells in us*!

"So John puts the lie to your doctrine that you were born with a sinful nature, and cannot obey God. For John teaches that those who have God's life in them *do not sin, and cannot sin*! I John 3:6, 9

"Dear friends here in Christ's Imputed Righteousness, Positional Holiness, and Progressive sanctification—*it is impossible to live in sin* while God's life is in you! For the evidence that God's life is in you, *is that you do not walk in sin, but that you live and walk like God*!

"So, the Apostle John tells us in this Epistle *what the evidences are* of those who are *God's children*, and *those who are not God's children*.

"He tells us *what the evidences are* of those who *know God*, and he tells *what the evidences are* of those who *do not know God*.

"He tells us *what the evidences are* of those who *are born of God*, and *what the evidences are* of those who *are not born of God*.

"And he tells us *what the evidences are* of those *who have fellowship with God*, and those who *do not have fellowship with God*.

"Now let's read I John 1:5-6.

'This then is the message which we have heard of him, and declare unto you, that *God is light, and in him is no darkness at all*. **IF WE SAY** that we **HAVE FELLOWSHIP WITH HIM**, and **WALK IN DARKNESS**, we lie, and do not the truth.' I John 1:5-6

"It is **easy to say** that we have fellowship with God. But what is *the evidence* that we have fellowship with God? It is *walking in light*, and *not walking in darkness*. For 'God is light, and in him is no darkness at all. **IF WE SAY** that we have **FELLOWSHIP WITH HIM**, and walk in darkness, we lie, and do not the truth.'

"*Walking in the light* is walking in holiness, righteousness, and truth. *Walking in darkness* is walking in sin and ungodliness. '**If we say** that we **have fellowship with him** and walk in **sin and ungodliness, WE LIE**, and do not the truth!'

"Now let's look at I John 1:8 where John continues with the truth that '**God is light, and in him is no darkness at all**.'

'**IF WE SAY** that we have no sin, we deceive ourselves, and the truth is not in us.' I John 1:8

"This verse is written in the context of the three previous verses, which speak of those who walk in darkness instead of walking in light. So it is saying, 'If we walk in darkness instead of walking in the light, and **say that we have no sin,** we **deceive ourselves,** and **the truth is not in us.**' Sometimes professing Christians, who are walking in the darkness of sin, will deny they are sinning. But God's word says, '**If we say** that we have no sin (when we are walking in darkness), we **deceive ourselves,** and **the truth is not in us.**'

"Now let's look at I John 1:10:

'**IF WE SAY** that we have not sinned, **we make him a liar,** and his word is not in us.' I John 1:10

"John is still talking in the context of those who are walking in darkness, and still **say that they have not sinned.** In verse eight he says that those who walk in darkness, and say that they have not sinned '**deceive themselves,** and the truth is not in them.' But in verse ten he says that those who walk in darkness, and say they have not sinned, '**make God a liar,** and his word is not in them.'

"Sinner, you should know that you are **calling God a liar,** when you walk in darkness, and say you have not sinned! For God says that when you walk in darkness, you have sinned—and if you deny what God has said, **you call God a liar!**

"Now, let's read I John 2:4:

'**He that saith,** I know him, and keepeth not his command-ments, is a liar, and the truth is not in him.' I John 2:4

"Sinner, you are a liar, if you say you know God, and do not keep his commandments. For **the evidence** that you know God, is that you keep his commandments. This is made even plainer by the verse that precedes verse four:

'Hereby we do know that we know him, **if we keep his commandments.** He that sayeth, I know him, **and keepeth not his commandments,** is a liar, and the truth is not in him.' I John 2:3-4

"Now, look at verse six:

'**He that saith he abideth in him** ought himself also so to walk, even as he walked.' I John 2:6

"Dear friends, here in Christ's Imputed Righteousness, Positional Holiness, and Progressive Sanctification, are you abiding in Christ? You are, if you are walking as Christ walked! And how did Christ walk? He always did the Father's will and walked in the light of all his commandments. So **the evidence that we abide in Christ** is that we do the Father's will, and walk in all God's commandments.

"Now look at verse nine:

'**He that saith** he is in the light, and hateth his brother, is in darkness even until now.' I John 2:9

"Oh, how plain and easy to understand, is God's word! God comes directly to the point, and tells us the plain truth about ourselves. He tells us that if we hate anyone, but especially someone close like a brother, (or a sister, or a mother, or a father, or a husband, or a wife), we are not in the light, but in total darkness even until now! For the evidence that we are in the light is that we love our brother even as we love ourselves!

"And dear friends, John continues to talk about both love and hate in verses 10 and 11:

'He that loveth his brother abideth in the light, and there is none occasion of stumbling in him. But he that hateth his brother is in darkness, and walketh in darkness, and knowth not whither he goeth, because that darkness hath blinded his eyes.' I John 2:10-11

"Oh, my dear friends, if you hate anyone you are walking in darkness and do not know God, for God is love:

'We know that we have passed from death unto life, because we love the brethren. He that loveth not his brother abideth in death. Whosoever hateth his brother is a murderer: and ye know that **NO MURDERER HATH ETERNAL LIFE ABIDING IN HIM.**' I John 3:14-15

232

'Beloved, let us love one another: for love is of God; and every one that loveth is born of God, and knoweth God. **He that loveth not knoweth not God**; for God is love.' I John 4:7-8

"Now let's read I John 2:15-17:

'Love not the world, neither the things that are in the world. **If any man love the world, the love of the Father is not in him**. For all that is in the world, *the lust of the flesh, and the lust of the eyes*, and *the pride of life*, is not of the Father, but is of the world. And the world passeth away, and the lusts thereof: but he that doeth the will of God abideth forever.' I John 2:15-17

"John places all the sins of the world under three headings: 'the lust of the flesh,' and 'the lust of the eyes,' and 'the pride of life.' And he tells us that the evidence of whether we do or do not love God is whether we do or do not love the world and the things that are in the world. John tells every worldly Christian, 'If any man love the world, **the love of the Father is not in him**!' Dear professing Christian, if you love the world, you do not love the Father!

"Now let's read I John 2:29:

'If ye know that he is righteous, ye know that everyone that doeth righteousness is born of him.' I John 2:29

"John tells us here that we can know when someone is born of God and when they are not born of God. He says, 'If ye know that he (God) is righteous' then 'ye know that every one that doeth righteousness **is born of him**.'

"And John tells us later in I John 3:10, that 'whosoever doeth not righteousness **is not of God**.'

'Whosoever doeth not righteousness is not of God, neither he that loveth not his brother.' I John 3:10

"Now let's go to I John chapter three, and read verses five and six:

'And ye know that he was manifested to take away our sins; and in him is no sin. Whosoever abideth in him **sinneth not**:

whosoever sinneth *hath not seen him, neither known him.*'
I John 3:5-6

"The evidence that we abide in him, and see him and know him, is
that we **sin not**. Those who know him **do not sin**. Those who see him
do not sin. Those who abide in him **do not sin**. 'Whosoever abideth
in him **sinneth not**.' 'Whosoever sinneth **hath not seen him, neither
known him**.' I John 3:6

"Now let's go to verses seven and eight:

'Little children, let no man deceive you: he that doeth righteousness
is righteous, even as he is righteous. He that committeth sin **is of
the devil**; for the devil sinneth from the beginning. For this purpose
the Son of God was manifested, that he might destroy the works of
the devil.' I John 3:7-8

"John warns the Christians not to be deceived by anyone about sin
and righteousness. He says, 'Little children, **let no man deceive you**.'
I John 3:7

"The reason he warns them not to be deceived, was because some
teachers were teaching (the Gnostics taught) that man cannot be
righteous. They taught that man's flesh was sinful by nature; so they
taught that Christ did not 'come in the flesh,' for, if he had come in the
flesh, he would have been sinful like other men. They taught that
Christ was not a real man, like other men; but that he only 'appeared' to
have a flesh and blood body like other men. (See I John 4:1-3 and II
John 7-11) So John warns the Christians against this antichrist
doctrine, inspired by the devil, and tells them that through Christ *they
are able to be righteous even as Christ Jesus is righteous*:

'Little children, **let no man deceive you**: he that doeth righteousness **is righteous**, even as **he is righteous**.' I John 3:7

"**Jesus delivers us from our sins!** '**He was manifested to take
away our sins**.' (I John 3:5) 'For this purpose the Son of God was
manifested, that he might destroy the works of the devil.' (I John 3:8)
'Thou shalt call his name JESUS: for he shall save his people from
their sins.' Matthew 1:21

"Now let's read I John 3:9-10:

'Whosoever is born of God **doth not commit sin**; for his seed remaineth in him: and **he cannot sin**, because he is born of God. In this the children of God are manifest, and the children of the devil: whosoever doeth not righteousness is not of God, neither he that loveth not his brother.' I John 3:9-10

"Dear friends, do you believe what God says in I John 3:9-10? 'Whosoever is born of God **doth not commit sin**; for his seed remaineth in him: and **he cannot sin,** because he is born of God.'

"Dear friends, do you realize that what God says in I John 3:9-10 **CANNOT BE TRUE**, if what you teach here in the settlement of Christ's Imputed Righteousness, Positional Holiness, and Progressive Sanctification is true?

"For you teach that 'There is in us a '**NECESSITY OF SINNING.**' But God's word teaches something completely different! God's word says, 'There is in us a '**NECESSITY OF NOT SINNING.**' God's word says, the born again Christian '**CANNOT SIN**, because he is born of God.' I John 3:9

"Oh my dear friends! This message is for you! It is for you who are standing here in this park today! Do you realize that you are either a child of God, or a child of the devil? You cannot be both at the same time!

'**He that committeth sin IS OF THE DEVIL**; for the devil sinneth from the beginning. For this purpose the Son of God was manifested, that he might **destroy the works of the devil**. Whosoever is born of God **DOTH NOT COMMIT SIN**; for his seed remaineth in him: and **HE CANNOT SIN**, because he is born of God. *In this the children of God are manifest*, and *the children of the devil*: whosoever doeth not righteousness is not of God, neither he that loveth not his brother.' I John 3:8-10

"The children of God do righteousness like their Father. The children of God **DO NOT LIVE IN SIN!** The children of the devil live in sin like their father the devil. The children of the devil **DO NOT DO RIGHTEOUSNESS**. We know who is a **child of God**, and we know who is a **child of the devil** by the works they do!

"The verses of Scripture we have looked at in I John 3:6-10 clearly teach that we **ARE NOT BORN OF GOD**, and we **DO NOT KNOW GOD** if we **ARE LIVING IN SIN**.

"Two of the verses in chapter three have been very difficult for Christians to understand. They are I John 3:6 and I John 3:9. I John 3:6 seems to teach that any Christian who commits a sin never really knew God in the first place; and I John 3:9 seems to teach that it is absolutely impossible for the Christian ever to commit a sin. These teachings are counter intuitive, so we know that what they seem to teach cannot be true. An understanding of the **perfect tense** of the **Greek verb** does away with all the difficulty in understanding these two verses:

"In I John 3:6 the verb form μένων is a present participle which emphasizes continuous action in the present. It means *is abiding* or *is remaining*. The verb form αμαρτάνει is the present active. It can denote either continuous or simple action in the present. It means *sins* or *is sinning*. Next, the verb form αμαρτάνων is used. It is a present participle which denotes continuous action in the present. It means *is sinning*. The last two verb forms in I John 3:6 are εώρακεν and έγνωκεν. They are both **perfect active**. The **perfect** denotes a completed action in the past that continues into the present. So that εώρακεν means *has seen and continues to see,* and έγνωκεν means *has known and continues to know*. First John 3:6, then, has the following meaning:

> "Whosoever *is abiding* in him *sins* not: whosoever *is sinning has not seen him and continued to see him*, neither *known him and continued to know him*." I John 3:6

"So the fact that a Christian may commit sin does not mean that he never really saw and knew God in the first place. What it does mean is that by living in present sin he *no longer continues* to see and know Christ, whom *he once saw and knew*. You cannot be sinning against God and continue to see and know him at the same time!

"In I John 3:9 the verb form γεγεννημένος is a **perfect passive participle** which speaks of completed action in the past that continues into the present. It means *has been born and continues to be born*. The verb forms ποιεί, μένει, and δύναται are all present active which can

236

denote either simple or continuous action in the present. The meaning of each one, in succession, is: *do* or *is doing*, *remain* or *is remaining*, and *can* or *is able*. The verb form αμαρτάνειν is a present infinitive which emphasizes continuous action. It means *to continue to sin or to go on sinning*. The verb form γεγέννηται is the **perfect passive**. It denotes completed action in the past that continues into the present. It means *has been born and continues to be born*. First John 3:9, then, has the following meaning:

"Whosoever *has been born of God and continues to be born of God* does not continue *doing sin*: for his seed *remains* in him: and *he cannot continue to do sin*, because he *has been born of God and continues to be born of God*." I John 3:9

"This verse does not teach that it is impossible for the Christian ever to sin. What it does teach is that it is impossible for the Christian to stand begotten of God while he is living in sin. To stand begotten of God and to live in sin are two self-excluding opposites. One cannot exist where the other exists. If you have the seed of God (which is the life of God) in you, you cannot continue in sin. If you do continue in sin, you do not have God's eternal life in you. God's eternal life within you, and the willful committing of sin are as incompatible as light and darkness. One cannot exist where the other exists.

"Now let's read I John 4:7-8, I John 4:12, I John 4:16, and I John 4:20-21 which tell us that we must love both God and man to have **any evidence at all that we know God** and **that God dwells in us**:

'Beloved, let us love one another: for love is of God; and everyone that loveth is born of God and knoweth God. He that loveth not knoweth not God; for God is love.' I John 4:7-8

'No man hath seen God at any time. **If we love** one another, **GOD DWELLETH IN US**, and **his love is perfected in us**.' I John 4:12

'God is love; and **he that dwelleth in love dwelleth in God, and GOD IN HIM**.' I John 4:16

'**If a man say**, I love God, and hateth his brother, he is a liar:

for he that loveth not his brother whom he that seen, how can he love God whom he hath not seen? And this commandment have we from him, That he who loveth God love his brother also.' I John 4:20-21

"Now let's read I John 3:24:

'*He that keepeth his commandments DWELLETH IN HIM*, and *HE IN HIM*. And hereby we *know that he abideth in us*, *by the Spirit* which he hath given us.' I John 3:24

"My dear friends, we know that *we dwell in God*, and that *God dwells in us* when we *keep his commandments*. And, my friends, we know (have evidence) that *God abides in us by the Holy Spirit he hath given us*.

"You will never **keep God's commandments** *until you dwell in God, and God dwells in you*! Only those with **GOD DWELLING IN THEM** overcome sin and keep his commandments!

'Know ye not that **YOUR BODY is the TEMPLE OF THE HOLY GHOST**?' I Corinthians 6:19

'For ye are the **temple of the living God**; as God hath said, *I will dwell in them, and walk in them*; and I will be their God, and they shall be my people. Wherefore come out from among them, and be ye separate, saith the Lord, and touch not the unclean thing: and I will receive you, and will be a *Father unto you*, and *ye shall be my sons and daughters*, saith the Lord Almighty.' II Cor. 6:16-18

'Ye are not in the flesh, but in the Spirit, if so be that the **SPIRIT OF GOD DWELL IN YOU**. Now if any man have not the Spirit of Christ, he is none of his. And if **CHRIST BE IN YOU**, the body is dead because of sin; but the Spirit is life because of righteousness. But if the *SPIRIT OF HIM THAT RAISED UP JESUS FROM THE DEAD DWELL IN YOU*, he that raised up Christ from the dead shall also quicken your mortal bodies **BY HIS SPIRIT THAT DWELLETH IN YOU**....For as many as are **led by the Spirit of God**, they are the **sons of God**.' Romans 8:9-14

"Now let's go to I John 5:3-5.

'For this is the love of God, **that we keep his command-ments**: and his commandments are not grievous. For ***WHOSOEVER IS BORN OF GOD OVERCOMETH THE WORLD***: and this is the victory that overcometh the world, even our faith. *Who is he that overcometh the world, but he that believeth that Jesus is the Son of God?*' I John 5:3-5

"Now let's read I John 5:10-13:

'He that **believeth on the Son of God** hath the witness in himself: he that believeth not God hath made him a liar; because he believeth not the record that God gave of his Son. And this is the record, that God hath given to us *eternal life*, and *this life* is *in his Son*. He that hath the Son *hath life*; and he that hath not the Son of God *hath not life*. These things have I written unto you that believe on the name of the Son of God; that ye may know that ye **have eternal life, and that ye may believe on the name of the Son of God.**' I John 5:10-13

"This passage is key—it sums up the whole message of I John. 'God gave his Son so that we could have eternal life. He that believeth the record that God gave of his Son hath eternal life. He that believeth not the record hath made God a liar. And this is the record, that God hath given to us eternal life, and *this life is in his Son.*' I John 5:10-13

"My friends, read these words over and over again! Memorize them! Hide them in your heart! '*For this is the record, that God hath given to us eternal life, and this life is in his Son. He that hath the Son hath life; and he that hath not the Son of God hath not life.*'

"Now let's read the final passage of John's First Epistle, I John 5:18-21

'**WE KNOW** that *whosoever is born of God sinneth not*; but he that is begotten of God *keepeth himself, and that wicked one toucheth him not*. And **WE KNOW** that *we are of God,* and the whole world *lieth in wickedness*. And **WE KNOW** that *the Son of God is come,* and *hath given us an understanding, that we may know him that is true*, and we are *in him that is true, even in his Son Jesus Christ*. This is

THE TRUE GOD, and ETERNAL LIFE. Little children, keep yourselves from idols. Amen.' I John 5:18-21

"Praise God! We who KNOW GOD know some things! And we *know them with certainty*!

"WE KNOW that WHOSOEVER IS BORN OF GOD SINNETH NOT!

"WE KNOW that he that is begotten of God KEEPETH HIMSELF, AND THAT WICKED ONE TOUCHETH HIM NOT.

"And WE KNOW THAT WE ARE OF GOD, and THE WHOLE WORLD LIETH IN WICKEDNESS.

"And, praise God, WE KNOW that the SON OF GOD IS COME, and HATH GIVEN US AN UNDERSTANDING, THAT WE MAY KNOW HIM THAT IS TRUE, AND WE ARE IN HIM THAT IS TRUE, EVEN IN HIS SON JESUS CHRIST.

"And WE KNOW, praise God, that JESUS CHRIST IS THE TRUE GOD, and ETERNAL LIFE!

"Dear friends, this epistle ends with an exhortation that may seem strange and out of place to you. John ends this epistle with the words, 'Little children *keep yourselves from idols*. Amen.'

"What a contrast! Jesus Christ, *THE TRUE GOD*, *and ETERNAL LIFE—contrasted with idols*!

"Lifeless idols, that cannot see, hear, walk or talk; that must be born on the shoulders of their worshippers if they are to be moved! Idols that cannot save or deliver! Idols that can give no life, because *they have no life*! "Contrasted with the *resurrected Savior, who lives forever*, who *IS THE TRUE GOD and ETERNAL LIFE,* and who *GIVES ETERNAL LIFE to all those who believe in him*!"

240

Chapter LVI
Not Finished Preaching

Jed was finished preaching from the First Epistle of John. But he was not finished preaching!

He felt constrained by the Holy Ghost to show the people their awful guilt, and the terrible punishment that would fall upon them on the judgment day if they continued in their sins. He picked up the big black Bible and moved from one side of the pulpit to the other as he continued to preach.

"Most of you moved here from five other churches, because you could not abide the plain preaching in those churches, that named your individual sins. And you are here—because, here, your sins are tolerated and excused.

"Here, you are taught that you sin by nature. You are taught that you cannot help but sin. And you are taught that once you believe in Jesus you are eternally secure even though you go on living in sin.

"But the doctrine of the eternal security of the believer *while you live in sin*, is an evil doctrine, inspired by the devil. It is a doctrine founded on a lust for sin. It is a doctrine that dishonors God and his whole moral government of law, mercy, and grace. It is a doctrine that encourages supreme selfishness in the hearts of sinners, who don't really love God, but still want to be assured that they are secure with God while they live in sin!

"I believe in the eternal security of the believer! For the eternal security of the believer is clearly taught in the Bible! But there is no eternal security for the sinner! Ever! The sinner is not a believer. He is an unbeliever! And eternal security is only for those who believe.

"Jesus taught the eternal security of the believer in the tenth chapter of John's gospel. But I want to call your attention to who is a believer and who is not a believer according to the words of Jesus in John 10:26-30. For only the believer, and not the unbeliever, is eternally secure according to Jesus.

"Jesus said in verse 26 to those who *did not believe*, 'Ye *believe not*, because ye are *not of my sheep*, as I said unto you. **My sheep *hear my* *voice*, and **I know them**, and *they follow me*: and *I give unto them eternal life*; and *they shall never perish*, neither shall any man pluck them out of my hand. My Father, which gave them me, is greater than all; and no man is able to pluck them out of my Father's hand. *I and my Father are one*.' John 10:26-30

"Eternal security is only for sheep that belong to Jesus. And the sheep that belong to Jesus are the sheep that **believe him, follow him,** and **obey him. But the sinner does not believe God**, for he **does not obey him**!

"Oh, it's true that sinners have faith after a fashion, but it is the same faith that the devils have. And it is the same faith that makes the devils tremble. And James says that that kind of faith, a faith that does not obey God, is a dead faith. He says, 'faith without works, is dead, being alone.'

> 'Faith, if it hath not works, is dead, being alone…Thou believest that there is one God; thou doest well: the devils also believe, and tremble. But wilt thou know, O vain man, that faith without works is dead?…For as the body without the spirit is dead, so faith without works is dead also.' James 2:17, 19-20, 26

"Do you dare call yourself a believer and a man of faith, when you **do not believe** what God says about deliverance from sin in the epistle of I John? Do you dare say, here in the presence of Almighty God, that you are a believer, and a man of faith, when to this present day **you have not believed** the gospel message of total salvation from sin through Jesus Christ?

"If you really did believe God you would believe all of God's Word! You would not pick and choose what you want to believe. But you would believe everything God says. You would believe his Word that teaches that all sin is inexcusable. You would believe his Word that teaches that there is absolutely no security for anyone living in sin. And you would believe his Word that tells of everlasting punishment in hell for every sinner who dies in his sins!

"But, you sirs, are so bent on eternal security, *while you live in sin*, that you have embodied it in the very name of your settlement: CHRIST'S IMPUTED RIGHTEOUSNESS, POSITIONAL HOLI-

NESS, AND PROGRESSIVE SANCTIFICATION—a three-legged stool that supports unrestrained wickedness!

"Your doctrine of eternal security, while you live in sin, is a lie of the devil! And your doctrines of Christ's Imputed Righteousness, Positional Holiness, and Progressive Sanctification are three more lies that prop up the first lie!

"You teach that the righteousness of Christ is imputed to you while you continue to live in sin. But the Bible, in no place, says that Christ's righteousness is imputed to us! What it does say, is, that '**OUR FAITH is imputed to us for righteousness.**' Romans 4:1-25

"You teach a positional holiness in Christ, that hides the sins you refuse to give up! But, again, the Bible in no place teaches that our sins are hidden from God by our position in Christ! What the Bible does teach, is that when we are **baptized into Christ** we *receive all the fullness of God in Christ Jesus,* and are **made holy and righteous in him**! John 1:16; Colossians 2:9-13; Romans 6:3-18

"You also teach a progressive sanctification—but not the sanctification that the Bible teaches! The sanctification taught in the Bible is a growth from one plateau of holiness to another plateau of holiness. (See II Peter 3:17-18) But the sanctification you teach allows you to go on living in your sins—as long as you **progressively** prune away some of your sins!

"you also teach the lie that you need not worry about your present sinful life, because God will change your character and make you holy when you get to heaven. But God says he will not change the character of anyone when he gets to heaven! Listen to what Revelation 22:11-15 says:

'He that is unjust, let him be unjust still: and he which is filthy, let him be filthy still: and he that is righteous, let him be righteous still: and he that is holy, let him be holy still. And, behold, I come quickly; and my reward is with me, to give to every man according as his work shall be. I am Alpha and Omega, the beginning and the end, the first and the last. *Blessed are they that do his commandments, that they may have right to the tree of life, and may enter in through the gates into the city.* For without are dogs, and sorcerers, and whoremongers, and murderers, and idolaters, and whosoever loveth and maketh a lie.' Revelation 22:11-15

"It is true that God will change the believer at the rapture. But this change is not a change in character. It is a change from a **corruptible** body to an **incorruptible**, and from **mortality** to **immortality**!

'For the trumpet shall sound, and the dead shall be raised incorruptible, and we shall be changed. For this **corruptible** must put on **incorruption**, and this **mortal** must put on **immortality**.' I Corinthians 15:52-53

"Oh, my friends! You must be holy as God is holy! You must be perfect as your Father in heaven is perfect; or you will be shut out of heaven forever! And if you are shut out of heaven, you will be cast into the lake of fire and brimstone, where you will be tormented day and night, forever and ever. Jesus said:

'And the **devil that deceived them** was cast into the lake of fire and brimstone, where the beast and the false prophet are, and shall be tormented day and night forever and ever.' Revelation 20:10

'But the fearful, and unbelieving, and the abominable, and murderers and whoremongers, and sorcerers, and idolaters, and all liars, shall have their part in the lake which burneth with fire and brimstone: which is the second death.' Revelation 21:8

"One day a scribe came to Jesus and asked him, 'Which is the **first** of all the **commandments**?' Jesus said, 'Thou shalt love the Lord thy God **with all** thy heart, and **with all** thy soul, and **with all** thy mind, and **with all** thy strength.' Mark 12:30

"In this **first and great commandment**, God comes to each and every one of us, right where we are, and just as we are. And he says to each one of us, 'love me **with all** that you have: **all** your heart, **all** your soul, **all** your mind, and **all** your strength.' He does not require **more** than we have. He just asks for **all** that we have. Something that *everybody is able to do.*

"He comes to a little baby, whose moral faculties are not yet developed and who has not yet reached the age of accountability. He comes to him in this stage of physical, mental, and moral predevelopment, and says, 'Love me with all your heart, mind, soul, and strength.' And since the little baby has no capacity either of heart, mind, soul, or strength—that is all that God requires! He does not require that the baby give him more than he has. He merely says, 'Whatever is **thy strength**, of body, soul, and mind—love me with all of it.

"He comes to a grown man, right where he is, and says, 'love me with all you have.' He does not say, 'You must love me with the strength of an angel.' Neither does he say, 'You can love me with the strength of a baby. A grown man is bound to love God with **ALL HIS HEART, MIND, SOUL, AND STRENGTH.**

"God comes to each one of us, wherever we are, whatever our capacities, and commands us to dedicate everything we are and have to him. He **does not require more** than we have, and he **will not accept less** than we have.

"But you sirs, here in CHRIST'S IMPUTED RIGHTEOUSNESS, POSITIONAL HOLINESS, AND PROGRESSIVE SANCTIFICA-TION, believe that your selfish, half-hearted, partial service to God is acceptable to him! You believe that you can serve two masters, both self and God, and that God will to be satisfied with that!

"And you continue to reject the biblical teaching that all the choices and acts of a man flow from only **ONE RULING CHOICE** of the heart or will. There cannot be **two opposing choices of the heart or will** at the same time. **You cannot serve TWO MASTERS**, self and God, but **can only serve ONE MASTER**. Two opposing masters cannot rule the life at the same time. One must be given up for the other. 'No man can serve *two masters*.' 'Ye cannot serve *God and mammon*.'

"All the following verses of the Bible teach the truth that all the deeds of a man can only flow from **ONE SINGLE RULING CHOICE** of the heart or will:

'The light of the body is the eye: if therefore **thine eye be single**, thy whole body shall be full of light. But if **thine eye** be evil, thy whole body shall be full of darkness. If therefore the light that is in thee be darkness, **how great is that darkness**! No man can serve two masters: for either he will hate the one, and love the other; or else he will hold to the one, and despise the other. Ye cannot serve God and mammon.' Matthew 6:22-24

'Either make the **tree good**, and his **fruit good**; or else make the **tree corrupt**, and his **fruit corrupt**...O generation of vipers, **how can ye, being evil, speak good things**? For out of the abundance of the heart the mouth speaketh. A good man out of the good treasure of the heart bringeth forth good things: and an evil man out of the evil treasure bringeth forth evil things.' Matthew 12:33-35

'Even so **every good tree bringeth forth good fruit**....A good tree **cannot bring forth evil fruit, neither can a corrupt tree bring forth good fruit**.' Matthew 7:17-18

'Doth a fountain send forth *at the same place sweet water and bitter*? Can the fig tree, by brethren, bear olive berries?...so can no fountain both yield salt water and fresh.' James 3:11-12

'He that is faithful in that which is least is faithful also in much: and *he that is unjust in the least is unjust in much*.' Luke 16:10

'For **whosoever shall keep the whole law, and yet offend in one point, he is guilty of all**. For he that said, Do not commit adultery, said also, Do not kill. Now if thou commit no adultery, yet if thou kill, thou art become a transgressor of the law.' James 2:10-11

"All sin flows from **one supreme and ultimate choice of the will**. And all virtue flows from **one supreme and ultimate choice of the will**. There cannot be two opposing choices ruling the life at the same time. There can only be one choice of the heart at a time. Either love to God rules, or selfishness rules. You deceive yourself if you believe that **God will accept a partial consecration** of your life to him. **God will accept nothing less than ALL THAT YOU HAVE**.

246

GOD'S JUDGEMENT ON BELIEVERS WHO BACKSLIDE

"Dear friends you are living in **willful sin and disobedience** here in CHRIST'S IMPUTED RIGHTEOUSNESS, POSITIONAL HOLINESS, AND PROGRESSIVE SANCTIFICATION. And God warns you that he will punish you for going back into sin and unbelief. Listen to what Hebrews says to the **believer who backslides**:

"First warning against sin and unbelief.

'For if the word spoken by angels was steadfast, and every transgression and disobedience received a just recompense of reward; how shall **WE** escape, if **WE** neglect so great salvation?' Hebrews 2:2-3

"Second warning against sin and unbelief.

'Take heed, **BRETHREN**, lest there be in any of you an evil heart of **unbelief**, in **departing from the living God**. But exhort one another daily, while it is called Today; lest any of you be hardened through the deceitfulness of sin. For we are made partakers of Christ, if we hold the beginning of our confidence steadfast unto the end.' Hebrews 3:12-14

"Third warning against backsliding into sin.

'For it is impossible for those who were once enlightened, and have tasted of the heavenly gift, and were made partakers of the Holy Ghost, and have tasted the good word of God, and the powers of the world to come, if they shall fall away, to renew them again unto repentance; seeing they crucify to themselves the Son of God afresh, and put him to an open shame....But that which beareth thorns and briers is rejected, and is nigh unto cursing; whose end is to be burned.' Hebrews 6:4-8

"Fourth warning against backsliding into sin.

'For if we **sin willfully** after that we have received the knowledge of the truth, there remaineth no more sacrifice for sins, but a certain fearful looking for of judgment and fiery indignation, which shall devour the adversaries.' Hebrews 10:26-27

"Fifth warning against backsliding in unbelief.

'He that despised Moses' law died without mercy under two or three witnesses: of how much sorer punishment, suppose ye, shall he be thought worthy, who hath trodden under foot the Son of God, and hath counted the blood of the covenant, wherewith he was sanctified, an unholy thing, and hath done despite unto the Spirit of grace? For we know him that hath said, Vengeance belongeth unto me, I will recompense, saith the Lord. And again, The Lord shall judge his people. It is a fearful thing to fall into the hands of the living God.' Hebrews 10:28-31

"Sixth warning against drawing back in unbelief.

'Now the just shall live by faith: but if any man draw back, my soul shall have no pleasure in him. But we are not of them that draw back unto perdition; but of them that believe unto the saving of the soul.' Hebrews 10:37-39

"Seventh warning against turning away from God and holiness.

'Follow peace with all men, and holiness, without which no man shall see the Lord: looking diligently lest any man fail of the grace of God....For if they escaped not who refused him that spake on earth, much more shall not we escape, if we turn away from him that speaketh from heaven....for **OUR GOD is a consuming fire**.' Hebrews 12:14-15, 25, 29

"Oh friends, do you know that **OUR GOD is a consuming fire**? Did you think that our God is only a God of mercy, who will never cast you into hell for your sins?

"Oh friends, have you never read II Thessalonians 1:7-9, which tells of the fiery vengeance of our Lord Jesus Christ? 'The Lord Jesus shall be revealed from heaven with his mighty angels, *in flaming fire taking vengeance* on them that *know not God*, and *obey not the gospel of our Lord Jesus Christ*. Who shall be punished with everlasting destruction from the presence of the Lord, and from the glory of his power.' II Thessalonians 1:7-9

"And Revelation also tells of God's fiery wrath upon sinners:

'The same shall drink of the wine of the *wrath of God*, which is poured out without mixture into the cup of his indignation. And he shall be ***tormented with fire and brimstone*** in the presence of the holy angels.' Revelation 14:10

'But the fearful, and unbelieving, and the abominable, and murderers, and whoremongers, and sorcerers, and idolaters, and all liars, ***shall have their part in the lake which burneth with fire and brimstone.*** ' Revelation 21:8

"Oh, friends, you have **lied about God**! You have said he created you with a nature that makes it impossible for you to obey him! You have **blamed God** for the nature he has given you! And all this, while God testifies in his holy Word that *he created you in his own image and likeness with a good nature*!

"Oh, sinners! Will you ever **believe** God's Word? *God created you in his own image and likeness*! The *law of God is written in your hearts*! And *God has given you a conscience* that directs you in the way you ought to go!

'For when the gentiles, which have not the law, **DO BY NATURE** the things contained in the law, these, having not the law, are a law unto themselves: which show the work of the **law written in their hearts**, their **conscience** also bearing witness, and their thoughts the meanwhile **accusing** or else **excusing** one another; in the day when *God shall **judge the secrets of men*** by Jesus Christ according to my gospel.' Romans 2:13-16

"Oh, my friends! Every time you commit a sin, you **go against** *the law of God written in you hearts*, and you **go against** the conscience God created you with. Yes, **you go against** the *good nature* God created you with!

'For this cause **God gave them up** unto vile affections: for even their women did **change the natural use** into that which is **AGAINST NATURE**: and likewise also the men, **LEAVING THE NATURAL USE OF THE WOMAN**, burned in their lust one toward another; men with men working that which is unseemly.' Romans 1:26-27

"And now, Jed Truly, moved by the Holy Ghost, pointed straight at two men standing in the crowd before him; and said, "See those two men standing there before you? See them? They are homosexuals! They openly declare their pride and arrogance against God by committing lewd acts—acts that God forbids. Acts that are **completely contrary to their nature**, and a **complete perversion of the nature** God gave them. Yet their motto is **gay pride**!

"But their pride, and the pride of every one of you who defy God by going on in your sin, will be swept away in a moment, when God comes in flaming fire to take vengeance on you for sinning **against the good nature God created you with**!

"Or, do you really think that you can go on sinning, and can still escape the judgment of God? Oh my friends, you cannot escape! Listen to what God's word says:

'And thinkest thou this...that thou shalt escape the judgment of God?....But...thy hardness and impenitent heart **treasurest up unto thyself wrath against the day of wrath and revelation of the righteous judgment of God**; who will render to every man according to his deeds...' Romans 2:3-6

"Oh, sinner, you cannot escape! If it were only a man, you might escape! But it is not a man! **It is God** against whom thou hast sinned! And it is impossible to escape God's wrath. 'For we know him that hath said, Vengeance belongeth unto me, I will recompense, saith the Lord. And again, **The Lord shall *judge his people*.** It is a *fearful thing to fall into the hands of the living God*.'" Hebrews 10:30-31

And, now, even as Jed spoke these last words, he saw that the people in the crowd were falling to their knees as if the sword of the Lord were cutting them down. Then Jed truly dropped to his knees and began to agonize in prayer for the lost souls before him. And then the Christians around Jed also began falling to their knees in prayer.

And suddenly, above the scattered cries of praying sinners and praying Christians could be heard the glad cry of Freed From Sin: "Annabellee! Annabellee! Annabellee! I've found you! I've found you at last!"

Then Freed From Sin's son saw his mother as she stood alone in the midst of the praying crowd. And, he cried out, "Mother! Mother! Oh, Mother!"

And together, Freed From Sin and his son ran to the one who had been lost to them for so many days.

Deacon Faith and Miracles stood at the pulpit and watched with joy, as the three, now together, came toward him. He viewed the great assembly, down on their knees, crying out to God; and his heart swelled and nearly burst with joy.

And suddenly he was conscious that the cold gusts of wind had vanished. And he felt the warmth of the sun, and looking up, he saw that the sun had broken through the fog and shone down in splendor upon them. "Praise God!" he exclaimed, as the three stepped up before him.

Chapter LVII
Heaven On Earth

It was a glorious day. Not a wisp of fog remained. The sun was shining brightly. Shouts of joy were heard all over the park.

The work in the hearts of the people had been complete in its sin-eradicating effects. Practically the whole settlement had been converted to God. Even the Elder, Pastor Nicolaitan, was converted; and afterward, in the baptismal tank he confessed the pride he had had in ruling over God's people. But it was when he confessed his hypocrisy in handling the Word of God that it so deeply touched the hearts of all those who heard his confession. For he was manifestly broken hearted and filled with sorrow for what he had done. He said, "I must confess, I have not been faithful with God's Word. I have misused God's Word to prove doctrines I had doubts about—doctrines I knew were contradicted by God's Word in other parts of the Bible.

"I know God's Word as well as most people here. But I have used God's Word deceitfully when wanting to prove my doctrine. I have resorted to knowingly taking Scriptures out of context, and knowingly twisting the meaning of Scriptures, to prove my doctrine. I have refused to think on and preach on some Scriptures, because I knew they were Scriptures that contradicted what I already believed. And I have avoided reading them or preaching from them in public, because I knew they showed my doctrine to be false. I have used arguments, which I knew were fallacious and deceitful, to prove doctrines I had doubts about.

"Please forgive me. Oh, please forgive me if you can." And here Elder Nicolaitan broke down and his whole body shook with sobs. And as he broke down, sobbing over his sins, others around him began to cry as well, for they knew they had done the same thing.

God worked signs and wonders that day. And God began by delivering Annabellee from demon possession.

But that was only the beginning of the marvelous works of God. God poured out the Holy Ghost upon all the believers who were kneeling and standing around the pulpit. Freed From Sin, upon witnessing the miraculous deliverance of his wife, was filled with the Holy Ghost. His son, standing beside him, was filled with the Holy Ghost. The old man, and the two young men who were converted with him, were filled with the Holy Ghost. Head Lighter Man was filled with the Holy Ghost.

And finally Little Alice was filled with the Holy Ghost. And with face lifted heavenward she praised God in an unknown tongue while tears of joy streamed down her face.

And, oh, how the Christians rejoiced when they saw the work of God done in the hearts of the people of the settlement! For it was a deep and genuine work. There had been genuine repentance and sorrow for sin, and a radical change in the hearts and lives of the people.

And the change in the hearts of the people was manifested immediately; Gladness and happiness and shouts of joy were heard in every corner of the settlement.

And there was a great outpouring of love toward one another (Romans 5:5), and a remarkable love toward the people who had brought the message of grace and deliverance to them. They prepared an evening meal for their visitors, and opened the door of hospitality to them to stay with them and rest that night before they continued on in their journey the next day. And these were graces they had never performed before.

But so great was the love of God in their hearts that they could not forbear sharing all that they had with their visitors. Their love for God, and the joy unspeakable and full of glory that they now had, made this settlement a place like heaven on earth!

Chapter LVIII
The Parable Of The Tares Of The Field

Early in the morning, when they had awakened from their sleep, they were treated to a breakfast of bacon and eggs with toast. And when they had finished their breakfast, the people begged them to stay for one more service and to let Deacon Faith and Miracles preach.

And although the five sojourners wanted with all theirs hearts to be on their way back home, they wanted even more to stay for the Christian fellowship in the morning service, and to hear Deacon Faith and Miracles preach. And after a brief conference among themselves they all agreed to stay.

And now Deacon Faith and Miracles stepped up to the pulpit and opened the big black Bible. He looked up at the people, who were gathered close around the pulpit, and smiled with joy. And filled with the Holy Ghost, he raised his hands and praised God over and over again, saying, "Glory, glory, glory to God. Glory, glory, glory to God."

And all over the congregation hands were lifted and voices were lifted in worship and praise to God. And hardly had the worship softened to a quiet whisper of holy reverence, when the voice of Deacon Faith and Miracles rose in prayer and supplication that God would empower him in preaching his word.

Then he began preaching: "Dearly Beloved, I want to talk to you about two persons who have a profound effect upon our lives. The one for good, and the other for evil. It is very difficult to talk about them together, for their characters are completely opposite. And to compare them, or talk about them together, seems almost to demean the one who is good, and to exalt the other who is evil. For the one is God: holy, loving, kind, and compassionate; filled with righteousness, goodness, mercy, grace and truth. The other is the devil: a hater of God and man; a hater of all that is good and holy; and filled with murder, lies, deceit, and wickedness.

"But since Jesus talks about them together in the parable of the tares of the field; I know that I also must talk to you about them—and the work that each one does in our lives. So, Dearly Beloved, open your Bibles to Matthew chapter thirteen, and we will read Matthew 13:24-30, along with its interpretation found in Matthew 13:36-43:

'Another parable put he forth unto them, saying, The kingdom of heaven is likened unto a man which sowed good seed in his field: but while men slept, **his enemy** came and **sowed tares** among the wheat, and went his way. But when the blade was sprung up, and brought forth fruit, then appeared the tares also. So the servants of the householder came and said unto him, Sir, didst not thou sow good seed in thy field? From whence then hath it tares? He said unto them, **An enemy hath done this**. The servants said unto him, Wilt thou then that we go and gather them up? But he said, Nay; lest while ye gather up the tares, ye root up also the wheat with them. Let both grow together until the harvest: and in the time of harvest I will say to the reapers, gather ye together first the tares, and bind them in bundles to burn them: but gather the wheat into my barn.' Matthew 13:24-30

"Now let's read the interpretation of this parable in Matt. 13:36-43:

'...His disciples came unto him, saying, Declare unto us the parable of the tares of the field. He answered and said unto them, He that soweth the Good seed is the **Son of man**; the **field** is the **world**; the **good seed** are the **children of the kingdom**; but the **tares** are the **children of the wicked one**; the **enemy that sowed them** is the **devil**; the **harvest** is the **end of the world**; and the **reapers** are the **angels**. As therefore the tares are gathered and burned in the fire; so shall it be in the end of this world. The *Son of man shall send forth his angels, and they shall gather out of his kingdom all things that offend, and them which do iniquity; and **shall cast them into a furnace of fire: there shall be wailing and gnashing of teeth**. Then **shall the righteous shine forth as the sun** in the kingdom of their Father.*' Matthew 13:36-43

"Jesus tells us that he sows *the good seed*. He makes men righteous and holy. He makes them children of God, and children of God's kingdom.

"And, Jesus tells us that the devil sows *the tares*. He makes men disobedient to God and wicked. He makes men his children, and members of his wicked kingdom—to be lost forever because of their sin and iniquity.

"But, stop and think, dearly beloved. We all know that neither God nor the devil can make us do anything against our will! God cannot make us holy unless we are willing to be holy. And the devil cannot make us wicked unless we are willing to be wicked.

"Adam and Eve were *made sinners* by the devil. But they were not made sinners against their will. They were not forced to sin! They were persuaded to sin! They *willingly* ate of the fruit of the tree that God had said, 'In the day that thou eatest thereof thou shalt surely die.' They *willingly* ate of the fruit, *were made sinners*, and *became the devil's children.*

THE DEVIL IS THE ENEMY OF GOD

"Dear Brothers and Sisters, the devil is the *enemy* of God! Matthew 13:25 says, '*His enemy* came and sowed tares among the wheat.' Because the devil is the enemy of God, he opposes the good work of God, and sows tares among the wheat.

"The devil began at the very beginning to oppose the work of God:

"He began by drawing a third of the angels into rebellion with him against God.

"And the devil continued to oppose God's work when God created Adam and Eve. He tempted them, and made them sin.

"Then when Jesus began his earthly ministry the devil tried to make Jesus sin. The Bible speaks much about the devil's repeated temptation of Jesus. Matthew 4:1-10, Mark 1:12, Luke 4:1-13, Hebrews 4:15

"Finally, Jesus tells us in the parable of the tares of the field that *the devil tempts ALL MEN*. And that he tempts them to *make them sin, make them his children, and make them members of his wicked kingdom*—so that they will finally be cast into the lake of fire and brimstone where they will suffer everlasting punishment for their sins.

THE DEVIL IS THE ENEMY OF BOTH GOD AND MAN

"Dearly beloved, we must not think that the devil is the enemy of God alone. He is our enemy also. And he is our enemy because we are made in the image and likeness of God, and belong to God.

"The devil is our *mortal enemy*. He is our *life-long enemy*. He hates us and wants to destroy us. He wants to turn us away from God. He wants to make us disobey God—like he made Adam and Eve disobey God. *He wants to make us sinners and send us down into hell.*

"So let's read some of the verses that talk about our wicked enemy who wants to deceive us, make us sin, and make us go down into hell.

'The tares are the *children of the wicked one….*the tares are *gathered and burned in the fire.*' Matthew 13:38, 40

'Those by the way side are they that hear; *then cometh the devil*, and taketh away the word out of their hearts; *lest they should believe and be saved.*' Luke 8:12

'When any one heareth the word of the kingdom…*then cometh the wicked one* (the devil), and *catcheth away that which was sown in his heart.*' Matthew 13:19

'The god of this world (the devil) *hath blinded the minds* of them which believe not, lest the light of the glorious gospel of Christ, who is the image of God, should shine unto them.' II Corinthians 4:4

THE DEVIL'S CHARACTER AND ORIGIN

"The Devil is a sinner. In fact the devil was the first sinner. The Bible says, 'The devil sinneth from the beginning.' I John 3:8

"The devil is a liar. The Bible says, 'He is a liar, and *the father of it.*' (John 8:44) He is the father of all men who tell lies. He conceived and brought into existence the first lie that ever existed: the lie that he was as glorious as God who had created him; and that he could rob God of what was God's alone—the worship of all his rational creatures. He was perfect when he was created. But he beheld his own glory, was lifted up with pride, and he said in his heart:

'**I will** ascend into heaven, **I will** exalt my throne above the stars of God: **I will** sit also upon the mount of the congregation, in the sides of the north: **I will** ascend above the heights of the clouds; **I will be like the most High**.' Isaiah 14:13-14

"The devil is a *thief and a robber*. He wants to rob God of what belongs to God alone. He wants to supplant God, and be worshipped as God. He wants the honor, glory, and worship that belong to God alone. See Matthew 4:8-10 and Revelation 13:2, 4

"The devil is a *murderer*. Not only is the devil a murderer, he is the father of all men who commit murder.

> 'But now ye seek to kill me...Ye do the deeds of your father...Ye are of your father the devil, and the lusts of your father ye will do. He was a murderer from the beginning, and abode not in the truth.' John 8:40-41, 44

> 'Cain...*was of that wicked one*, and *slew his brother*.' I John 3:12

"Dear Brothers and Sisters, the devil is a murderer. And he wants to murder you! Oh, dear Brothers and Sisters, did you know that the devil wants to destroy you, kill you, **MURDER YOU**?

"Dear Christian Brothers, I am not overstating the vicious hatred and murderous nature of our enemy. He is a murderer who is working to destroy every single human being that God has created upon the face of the earth. He wants to destroy all men, Christian and non-Christian. But, dear Christian, the devil has an even greater hatred of you who are Christians. For at one time he had you ensnared in sin. And now that Jesus has freed you from sin, he is doing all in his power to ensnare you again in sin, and take you down into hell. II Timothy 2:26

"The devil hates the saints of God, those whose eyes have been opened to the gospel of Jesus Christ, and are walking with God in obedience and godliness. But he is happy with the nominal Christian, who is walking in worldliness and sin.

NAMES OF THE DEVIL

"The devil is 'the great dragon,' 'that old serpent,' 'the devil,' and 'Satan.' The devil is 'the god of this world,' 'the prince of the devils,' 'The prince of this world,' 'the wicked one,' and 'the prince of the power of the air.' The devil is 'the spirit that now worketh in the children of disobedience.' And 'the deceiver who deceiveth the whole world.' Revelation 12:9-10, II Corinthians 4:4, Ephesians 2:2

258

"Four more names of the devil: He is the 'accuser of the brethren.' He has a special hatred of men who are Christians, so he 'accuses the brethren' before God day and night. (Revelation 12:10) He is 'the tempter.' (He tempts all men, all over the world, without exception. But is especially vicious in his temptation of the most godly of men. (See first two chapters of Job.) He is 'the mystery of iniquity.' He is the one who brought iniquity into the world. And, he works now and in the future to make all men members of his iniquitous kingdom!

"The devil **now works** to make men sinners. Matthew 13:39, II Thessalonians 2:7, Job chapters one and two, and Ephesians 2:2b

"And the devil **will work later** to make a man the antichrist, and give him a worldwide kingdom that is opposed to everything godly and holy in God's kingdom. II Thessalonians 2:3-9 and Revelation Chapter 13

'...In time past...ye walked according to the *prince of the power of the air,* the *spirit that now worketh* in the children of disobedience.' Ephesians 2:2

'For the *mystery of iniquity* doth already work: only he who now letteth will let, until he be taken out of the way. And *then* shall that *Wicked* (the antichrist) be revealed, whom the Lord shall consume with the spirit of his mouth, and shall destroy with the brightness of his coming: even him, whose coming is after the working of *Satan* with all power and signs and lying wonders.' II Thessalonians 2:7-9

'And the great *dragon* was cast out, that old *serpent*, called the *Devil*, and *Satan*, which deceiveth the whole world.' Revelation 12:9

'For the *accuser of our brethren* is cast down, *which accused them before our God day and night.*' Revelation 12:10

'And the *dragon* gave him his power, and his seat, and great authority....And they *worshipped the dragon* (Satan) which gave power unto the beast: and they *worshipped the beast.*' Revelation 13:2-4

'Again, *the devil* taketh him up into an exceeding high mountain, and showed him all the kingdoms of the world, and the glory of them; and saith unto him, All these things will I give thee, if thou wilt fall down and worship me.' Matthew 4:8-9

'He was in *all points tempted* (by the tempter) *like as we are*, yet without sin.' Hebrews 4:15

'And the *dragon* was wroth with the woman, and *went to make war* with the remnant of her seed, which keep the commandments of God, and have the testimony of Jesus Christ.' Rev. 12:17

'Put on the whole armor of God, that ye may be able to stand against the wiles of the devil. For we wrestle not against flesh and blood, but against principalities, against powers, against the rulers of the darkness of this world, against spiritual wickedness in high places.' Ephesians 6:11-12

'Be sober, be vigilant; because your *adversary the devil*, as a roaring lion, walketh about, seeking whom he may devour.' I Peter 5:8

"Dear saints, we must be sober! We must be vigilant! Peter warns us in I Peter 5:8 to be sober and vigilant. And it is necessary to repeat his warning, 'Be sober, be vigilant; because your *adversary the devil*, as a roaring lion, walketh about, **SEEKING WHOM HE MAY DEVOUR!**'

"God created the devil perfect and without sin. But his heart was lifted up with pride because of his great beauty and glory, and he rebelled against God.

"Ezekiel describes the perfection of the devil, before his heart was lifted up with pride:

'Thou hast been in Eden the garden of God; every precious stone was thy covering....Thou art the anointed cherub that covereth; and I have set thee so: thou wast upon the holy mountain of God; thou hast walked up and down in the midst of the stones of fire. **Thou wast perfect** in thy ways from the day that thou wast created, till iniquity was found in thee...therefore I will cast thee as profane out of the mountain of God: and I will destroy thee, O covering cherub, from the midst of the stones of fire. Thine heart was lifted up because of thy beauty, thou hast corrupted thy wisdom by reason of thy brightness: I will cast thee to the ground, I will lay thee before kings, that they may behold thee.' Ezekiel 28:13-17

'How art thou fallen from heaven, O **Lucifer**, son of the morning! How art thou cut down to the ground, which didst weaken the nations! For thou hast said in thine heart, **I will** ascend into heaven, **I will exalt my throne** above the stars of God: **I will** sit also upon the mount of the congregation, in the sides of the north: **I will** ascend above the heights of the clouds: **I will be like the most high**. Yet thou shalt be brought down to hell, to the sides of the pit.' Isaiah 14:12-15

'And there was **war in heaven**: Michael and his angels fought against the dragon; and the dragon fought and his angels, and prevailed not; neither was their place found any more in heaven. And the great dragon was cast out, that old serpent, called the devil, and Satan, which deceiveth the whole world: he was cast out into the earth, and his angels were cast out with him.' Rev. 12:7-9

THE DEVIL'S ANGELS

"Sin did not exist before the fall of Lucifer. When he fell he drew a third of the angels into rebellion with him. His kingdom includes 'his angels.' and 'his children' whom he has ensnared into sin:

'...that they may recover themselves out of the *snare of the devil*, who are taken captive by him at his will.' II Timothy 2:26

'And there appeared another wonder in heaven; and behold a great red dragon....And his tail drew the third part of the stars of heaven, and did cast them to the earth.' Rev. 12:3-4

'...But when the Pharisees heard it, they said, This fellow

doth not cast out devils, but by **Beelzebub** the *prince of the devils*....And Jesus knew their thoughts, and said unto them....And if Satan cast out Satan, he is divided against himself; how shall then *his kingdom stand*?' Matthew 12:22-26

'But the *prince of the kingdom of Persia* (a fallen angel) withstood me one and twenty days: but, lo, Michael, one of the *chief princes* (an archangel of God), came to help me....And *now will I return* to fight with the *prince of Persia*: and when I am gone forth, lo, the *prince of Grecia* (another fallen angel) shall come.' Daniel 10:13, 20

'For **we wrestle not against flesh and blood**, but against *principalities*, against *powers*, against *the rulers of the darkness of this world*, against *spiritual* **wickedness** *in high places*.' Ephesians 6:12

"Ephesians 6:12 speaks of the Christian's continual war with Satan and his fallen angels. The devil's angels are called devils in the Bible, for they, like the devil, are fallen angels. They are also called unclean spirits, and foul spirits, and wicked spirits. And they have these names because their names describe their wickedness and uncleanness. They are also called seducing spirits, for they, like the devil, seek to seduce men and make them sin. And like the devil, they work to bring sickness, destruction, and death upon man. Some of them are called *princes* who have *principalities*, because they hold wicked sway over nations or peoples. Finally, some of them enter into men, and dwell in them, to possess them. They bring desease, sickness, and physical infirmity upon men. They bring fear and confusion to men. They want to destroy men both spiritually and physically.

'Now the Spirit speaketh expressly, that in the latter times some shall depart from the faith, giving heed to **seducing spirits**, and **doctrines of devils**.' I Timothy 4:1

'When the unclean spirit is gone out of a man....Then he saith, I will return into my house from whence I came out; and when he is come, he findeth it empty, swept, and garnished. Then goeth he, and taketh with himself seven other spirits more wicked than himself, and they enter in and dwell there: and the last state of that man is worse than the first. Even so shall it be also unto this wicked generation.' Matthew 12:43-45

'And, behold, there was a woman which had a spirit of infirmity eighteen years, and was bowed together, and could in no wise lift up herself....And he laid his hands on her: and immediately she was made straight, and glorified God....And (Jesus said) ought not this woman, being a daughter of Abraham, whom *Satan hath bound*, lo, these eighteen years, be loosed from this bond on the sabbath day?' Luke 13:11, 13, 16

'My daughter is *grievously vexed with a devil.*' Matt. 15:22

'Then was brought unto him one possessed with a devil, blind, and dumb: and he healed him, insomuch that the blind and dumb both spake and saw.' Matthew 12:22

'And one of the multitude answered and said, Master, I have brought unto thee my son, which hath a dumb spirit; and wheresoever he taketh him, he teareth him: and he foameth, and gnasheth with his teeth, and pineth away: and I spake to thy disciples that they should cast him out; and they could not. He answereth him, and saith, O faithless generation, how long shall I be with you? How long shall I suffer you? Bring him unto me. And they brought him unto him: and when he saw him, straightway the spirit tare him; and he fell on the ground, and wallowed foaming. And he asked his father, How long is it ago since this came unto him? And he said, Of a child. And oftentimes *it hath cast him into the fire, and into the waters to destroy him.*' Mark 9:17-22

'And when he went forth to land, there met him out of the city a certain man, which had devils long time, and ware no clothes, neither abode in any house, but in the tombs....And he was kept bound with chains and in fetters; and he brake the bands, and was *driven of the devil* into the wilderness.' Luke 8:27, 29

'And when he was come out of the ship, immediately there

met him out of the tombs a man with an unclean spirit, who had his dwelling among the tombs; and no man could bind him, no, not with chains. Because that he had been often bound with fetters and chains, and the chains had been plucked asunder by him, and the fetters broken in pieces: neither could any man tame him. And always, night and day, he was in the mountains, and in the tombs, crying, and cutting himself with stones.' Mark 5:2-5

THE DEVIL'S CHILDREN

"We have seen the Scriptures which show that the devil was the first to rebel and sin against God. We have seen that he is the enemy of God and man, who stands against every righteous purpose of both God and man. We have seen that he is a liar who deceives the whole world. We have seen that he is the tempter who entices, and baits, and tempts men into sin. And we have seen the Scriptures that show that the devil's angels do the same evil works as Beelzebub their prince.

"What we haven't seen are the Scriptures which tell about the 'children of the devil.' We will now look at those Scriptures:

'Ye seek to kill me...Ye do the deeds of *your father*.' John 8:40-41

'Ye are of *your father* the devil, and the lusts of *your father* ye will do.' John 8:44

'He that committeth sin is *of the devil*; for the devil sinneth from the beginning. For this purpose the Son of God was manifested, that he might destroy the works of the devil.' I John 3:8

'In this the **children of God** are manifest, and the **children of the devil**: whosoever doeth not righteousness is not of God, neither he that loveth not his brother.' ·I John 3:10

'Then Saul, (who also is called Paul,) filled with the Holy Ghost, set his eyes on him, and said, O full of all subtlety and all mischief, thou **child of the devil**, thou **enemy of all righteousness**, wilt thou not cease to pervert the right ways of the Lord?' Acts 13:8-10

"The **devil's children** form a *vast network of tempters,* who *do the same evil work of tempting others, as their father the devil.*

"I remember back many years ago, when I was converted to God, that my former companions in sin, purposely offered me cigarettes *to tempt me to go back to smoking.* They purposely *used filthy language* and *told dirty jokes* while I was in their company, trying to bring me back into sinful fellowship with them. They were tempting me, trying to get me to go back into sin!

"And, oh, what a devilish work this is! Children of the devil, tempting others to go back with them to drugs, to cigarettes, to liquor; to filthy language and dirty jokes; to lie, steal, and rob; to commit adultery and fornication; to kill, commit crime, and rebel against God! What a **vast** *web and network of temptations* this makes! It exists in the most intimate of relations. It exists with both friends and enemies. The *work of temptation* by the devil's children fills this world, so that John said, 'The *whole world lieth in wickedness.*' I John 5:19

"Eve tempted her husband Adam. He yielded to temptation and sinned!

"Jesus was tempted by men, as well as by the devil! He was tempted by the religious and political rulers of his day. Herod the king tried to murder him while he was still a child. The religious rulers continually tempted him, trying to trap him in his words and get him to take positions that would make him worthy of death.

"It was one of his closest friends, the Apostle Peter, who tempted Jesus to disobey the will of his heavenly Father; so that Jesus had to rebuke him for his satanically inspired words:

> 'But he turned, and said unto Peter, Get thee behind me Satan: thou art an offence unto me: for thou savourest not the things that be of God, but those that be of men.' Matthew 16:23

"The wife of Job only added another cruel trial, and vexation of spirit, to the cruel trials and temptations of the devil, when she said to her husband, 'Dost thou still retain thine integrity? Curse God, and die.' Job 2:9

"The wife of Potiphar **tempted** Joseph to lie with her and commit adultery:

> 'And it came to pass after these things, that his master's wife cast her eyes upon Joseph; and she said, Lie with me. But he refused....And it came to pass, as she spoke to Joseph day by day, that he hearkened not unto her, to lie by her, or to be with her....And she caught him by his garment, saying, Lie with me: and he left his garment in her hand, and fled, and got him out.' Genesis 39:7-8, 10, 12

"Peter tells of **false teachers** in the church of Jesus Christ, who have 'eyes full of adultery, and that cannot cease from sin; **beguiling unstable souls**.' II Peter 2:14

"Paul warned of 'false apostles' and 'deceitful workers' who, he said, were **ministers of Satan**, and could **corrupt the simple faith in Christ** of the Corinthian church:

> 'But I fear, lest by any means, as the serpent beguiled Eve through his subtlety, so your minds should be corrupted from the simplicity that is in Christ....For such are **false apostles**, **deceitful workers**, transforming themselves into the apostles of Christ. And no marvel; for Satan himself is transformed into an angel of light. Therefore it is no great thing if **his ministers** also be transformed as the ministers of righteousness; whose end shall be according to their works.' II Corinthians 11:3, 13-15

"Sinners do the works of their father the devil, and **tempt other men to join with them in their sin**. Whether we call it beguiling, or corrupting, or baiting, or enticing, or some other synonym for tempting, sinners do the works of their father the devil, and tempt other men into sin. And the word of God warns us, 'Don't be **beguiled**. Don't be **corrupted**. Don't be **enticed** into sin. **Don't go in the way** of the sinner.'

> 'My son, **if sinners entice thee**, consent thou not. If they say, Come with us, let us lay wait for blood, let us lurk privily for the innocent without cause: let us swallow them up alive as the grave; and whole, as those that go down into the pit: we shall find all precious substance, we shall fill our houses

with spoil....My son, *walk not thou in the way with them*; refrain thy foot from their path.' Proverbs 1:10-13, 15

'And if a man *entice a maid*...and lie with her....' Exodus 22:16

'If thy brother, the son of thy mother, or thy son, or thy daughter, or the wife of thy bosom, or thy friend, which is as thine own soul, *entice thee secretly*, saying, Let us go and serve other gods....Thou shalt not consent unto him, nor hearken unto him...But thou shalt surely kill him....because he hath sought to thrust thee away from the Lord thy God.' Deuteronony 13:6, 8-10

"The devil's children do not love Christians. They **hate**, and **persecute**, and **murder** Christians.

'*Ye seek to kill me*...Ye do the deeds of your father.' John 8:40-41

'If the world hate you, ye know that it hated me before it hated you. If ye were of the world, the world would love his own: but because ye are not of the world, but I have chosen you out of the world, therefore the world hateth you.' John 15:18-19

'Then shall they deliver you up *to be afflicted*, and *shall kill you*: and ye shall be **hated of all nations** for my name's sake. And then shall many be offended, and shall betray one another, and shall hate one another. And many false prophets shall rise, and shall deceive many. And because iniquity shall abound, the love of many shall wax cold. But he that shall endure unto the end, the same shall be saved.' Matthew 24:9-13

'But beware of men: for they will deliver you up to the councils, and they will scourge you in their synagogues....And the brother shall deliver up the brother to death, and the father the child: and the children shall rise up against their parents, and cause them to be put to death. And ye shall be hated of all men for my name's sake: but he that endureth to the end shall be saved.' Matt. 10:17, 21-22

"This *vast web of temptations*, that is almost impossible to overcome, now exists because of the devil's children! But *temptation will be much more sever, and even more difficult to overcome under the vicious rule of the antichrist.*

THE ANTICHRIST AND TEMPTATION

"Sometime in the future, the devil will raise up a man of sin to rule over the whole earth. And that time will be a time of temptation unmatched by anything that exists today. Will any resist the temptation to submit himself to the rule of the antichrist, while beholding his miracles and lying signs and wonders; and having the knowledge that resistance to his rule will cost him his life?

'That day shall not come, except there come a falling away first, and that **man of sin** (the antichrist) be revealed, the son of perdition; who opposeth and exalteth himself above all that is called God, or that is worshiped; so that he as God sitteth in the temple of God, **showing himself that he is God.**' II Thessalonians 2:3-4

'Then shall that Wicked (the antichrist) be revealed, whom the Lord shall consume with the spirit of his mouth, and shall destroy with the brightness of his coming: even him, whose coming is **after the working of Satan** with **all power and signs and lying wonders.**' II Thessalonians 2:8-9

'And I stood upon the sand of the sea, and saw a **beast** (the antichrist) rise up out of the sea....And the **dragon** (the devil) **gave him his power, and his seat, and great authority**. And I saw one of his heads as it were wounded to death; and his deadly wound was healed: and all the world wondered after the beast. And they **worshipped the dragon** (the devil) which gave power unto the beast: and they **worshipped the beast**, saying, Who is like unto the beast? Who is able to make war with him? And there was given unto him a mouth speaking great things and blasphemies....And he opened his mouth in blasphemy against God, to blaspheme his name, and his tabernacle, and them that dwell in heaven. And it was given unto him to make war with the saints, and to overcome them: and power was given him over all kindreds, and tongues, and nations. And **all that dwell upon the earth**

shall worship him, whose names are not written in the book of life of the Lamb slain from the foundation of the world.' Revelation 13:1-8

'And he had power to give life unto the image of the beast, that the image of the beast should both speak, and **cause that as many as would not worship the image of the beast should be killed**. And *he caused all*, both small and great, rich and poor, free and bond, *to receive a mark in their right hand, or in their foreheads*. And that no man might buy or sell, save he that had the mark, or the name of the beast, or the number of his name.' Revelation 13:15-17

ALL SIN COMES THROUGH TEMPTATION

"The Bible teaches that **temptation is COMMON TO ALL MEN**. The Bible teaches that **temptation is the OCCASION OF ALL SIN**. The Bible teaches that the **DEVIL TEMPTS ALL MEN**.

'And when the **TEMPTER** came to him, he said, If thou be the Son of God, command that these stones be made bread.' Matthew 4:3

'For this cause, when I could no longer forbear, I sent to know your faith, lest by some means the **TEMPTER** have **tempted** you, and our labor be in vain.' I Thessalonians 3:5

'Jesus was **IN ALL POINTS TEMPTED LIKE AS WE ARE**, yet without sin.' Hebrews 4:15 (Note: James 1:13 says, '**God cannot be tempted** with evil.' Jesus did *not come as God*. He came 'in the flesh' as man, and was *in all points tempted like as we are*, yet without sin!) Hebrews 4:15

THE DEVIL DECEIVES THE WHOLE WORLD

'And the great dragon was cast out, that old serpent, called the Devil, and Satan, which **DECEIVETH THE WHOLE WORLD**: he was cast out into the earth, and his angels were cast out with him.' Revelation 12:9

'And the **devil that DECEIVED THEM** was cast into the lake of fire and brimstone, where the beast and the false prophet are, and shall be tormented day and night for ever and ever.' Revelation 20:10

"The devil began to deceive men, with Adam and Eve. He first **deceived Eve** into sin! Then, through Eve, the devil tempted Adam into sin! I Timothy 2:14

'And unto Adam [God] said, Because thou hast **hearkened unto the voice of thy wife**, and hast eaten of the tree, of which I commanded thee, saying, Thou shalt not eat of it: cursed is the ground for thy sake....' Genesis 3:17

THE DEVIL STANDS AGAINST GOD'S SERVANTS

"The devil **RESISTS AND STANDS AGAINST the servants of God.** He **RESISTS THEM, AFFLICTS THEM, and MAKES WAR WITH THEM**, to turn them away from God, and make them sin against God. The following are just a few of the servants of God that the devil **STOOD UP AGAINST** trying to turn them away from God:

'And he showed me Joshua the high priest standing before the angel of the Lord, and Satan standing at his right hand **TO RESIST HIM**. And the Lord said unto Satan, The Lord rebuke thee, O Satan; even the Lord that hath chosen Jerusalem rebuke thee.' Zechariah 3:1-2

'And Satan **STOOD UP AGAINST ISRAEL**, and **provoked David** to number Israel.' I Chronicles 21:1

'And the Lord said unto Satan, Hast thou considered **my servant Job**, that there is none like him in the earth, a perfect and an upright man, one that feareth God, and escheweth evil? Then Satan answered the Lord, and said, *Doth Job fear God for nought*?....But put forth thine hand now, and touch all that he hath, and **he will curse thee to thy face**.' (In one day the devil took away all the possessions of Job, and in the same day murdered his seven sons and three daughters—*yet Job did not curse God*. Instead he fell down and worshipped God.) Job 1:1-22

'And (again) the Lord said unto Satan, Hast thou considered my servant Job, that there is none like him in the earth, a perfect and an upright man, one that feareth God, and escheweth evil? and still he holdeth fast his integrity, although thou movest me against him, to destroy him without cause. And Satan answered the Lord, and said, Skin for skin, yea, all that a man hath will he give for his life. But put forth thine hand now, and touch his bone and his flesh, and **he will curse thee to thy face**. And the Lord said unto Satan, Behold, he is in thine hand; but save his life. So went Satan forth from the presence of the Lord, and smote Job with sore boils from the sole of his foot unto his crown. And he took him a potsherd to scrape himself withal; and he sat down among the ashes. Then said his wife unto him, Dost thou still retain thine integrity? Curse God, and die. But he said unto her, Thou speakest as one of the foolish women speaketh. What? shall we receive good at the hand of God, and shall we not receive evil? **IN ALL THIS DID NOT JOB SIN WITH HIS LIPS.**' Job 2:3-10

THE RIGHTEOUS, ALL OVER THE WORLD, SUFFER THE SAME AFFLICTIONS AS JOB

'Be sober, be vigilant; because your adversary the devil, as a roaring lion, walketh about, seeking whom **HE MAY DEVOUR**: whom resist stedfast in the faith, knowing that the **SAME AFFLICTIONS ARE ACCOMPLISHED IN YOUR BRETHREN THAT ARE IN THE WORLD.**' I Peter 5:8-9

'And the Lord said, Simon, Simon, behold, **Satan hath desired to have you, that he may SIFT YOU AS WHEAT**: But I have prayed for thee, that thy faith fail not: and when thou art converted, strengthen thy brethren.' Luke 22:31-32

'But Peter said, Ananias, **why hath SATAN FILLED THINE HEART to lie to the Holy Ghost**, and to keep back part of the price of the land?' Acts 5:3

''Then **ENTERED SATAN INTO JUDAS surnamed Iscariot**, being of the number of the twelve....' Luke 22:3-6

'...The **TEMPTER** came to him, (and) he said, If thou be the

the Son of God, command that these stones be made bread...'
Matthew 4:2-4

'The **DEVIL** taketh him up into the holy city, and setteth him on a pinnacle of the temple, and sayeth unto him, If thou be the Son of God, cast thyself down...' Matthew 4:5-7

'Again, **THE DEVIL** taketh him up into an exceeding high mountain, and showeth him all the kingdoms of the world, and the glory of them; and sayeth unto him, All these things will I give thee, if thou wilt fall down and worship me...' Matthew 4:8-10

'Jesus was **IN ALL POINTS TEMPTED LIKE AS WE ARE**, yet without sin,' Hebrews 4:15

Chapter LIX
Jesus Makes Men Children Of God

Deacon Faith and Miracles stopped speaking, and looked out over the crowd of Christian believers. He had preached a long time. And the attention of some of the people was beginning to flag.

"Brethren," he said, "I have preached a long time. But I still haven't finished. I need another 30 minutes to show you the Scriptures that tell us how we must overcome our adversary the devil if we are to enter into heaven. And even more important, I will preach now about Jesus, and his work to save us from our sins. Especially of the fact that Jesus Christ had to *'come in the flesh'* **with the same human nature as we**, in order to save us from our sins. Jesus is the Son of God. But he did not come as God. He came as man in order to be tempted as all other men are tempted, and in order to shed his blood and die for our sins—Jesus had to be a real man in order to die and atone for our sins! All of this is clearly taught in the book of Hebrews.

"But let's take about five minutes or so for a break, so that you can stretch, and walk about a bit, and just relax from the work of listening."

Having said this, Deacon Faith and Miracles turned from the pulpit and began 'walking about a bit' as he had called it. He soon returned, fell on his face, and began calling on the name of the Lord.

Meanwhile, most in the crowd hardly moved from the place where they stood. But, instead, were happy to stay where they were and make comments on the sermon. Over and over again the comments were heard, 'I didn't know that the Bible said so much about the devil,' and, 'I didn't know that the Bible said that the devil makes men sinners.'

Now Deacon Faith and Miracles stood to his feet, and said, "I want to read Matthew 13:36-43 again, where Jesus declares to his disciples the meaning of the parable of the tares of the field:

'...his disciples came unto him, saying, Declare unto us the parable of the tares of the field. He answered and said unto them, He that **soweth the good seed** is the **Son of man**; the **field** is **the world**; the **good seed** are the **children of the kingdom**; but the **tares** are the **children of the wicked one**;

the **ENEMY** that sowed them **is the devil**; the **harvest** is the **end of the world**; and the **reapers** are the **angels**. As therefore the tares are gathered and burned in the fire; so shall it be in the end of this world. The Son of man shall send forth his angels, and they shall gather out of his kingdom all **things that offend**, and **them which do iniquity**; and shall cast them into a furnace of fire: there shall be wailing and gnashing of teeth. **THEN SHALL THE RIGHTEOUS shine forth as the sun** in the kingdom of their Father. Who hath ears to hear, let him hear.' Matthew 13:36-43

"There is no escaping the truth of this parable! The truth is so plain that even a child can understand it. On the one hand the Son of man **makes sinful men righteous**, and members of his **righteous kingdom**; and in the end of this world, they will be eternally blessed of God, and will shine forth as the sun in the kingdom of their Father.

"And on the other hand, the devil makes men sinners and members of his wicked kingdom. And in the end of this world all the wicked will be cast into a furnace of fire where there will be wailing and gnashing of teeth.

"I told you earlier that the devil cannot make anyone a sinner who is not willing to be a sinner. Adam and Eve were not forced to sin. They were *persuaded or tempted to sin*.

"No one is made a sinner by physical force. No one is made a sinner against his will. All men are persuaded or tempted to sin! So a baby cannot be a sinner at birth! He must first *know right from wrong,* and reach the *age of accountability* before he can be *persuaded or tempted to sin*."

The Human Nature of Jesus Christ

"Jesus was a man, with the same human nature as other men. The Bible tells us that Jesus was the son of David, the son of Abraham. It also says (over 50 times) that he was the **Son of man**. When God sent his only begotten Son into the world, he sent him not as God, but as man, with the **same human frailties** that all other men are born with.

'For we have not an high priest which cannot be **touched with the feelings of our infirmities**; but was *IN ALL*

274

POINTS *TEMPTED LIKE AS WE ARE, yet without sin.'*
Hebrews 4:15

"Jesus **came in the flesh**. (I John 4:2-3 and II John 7-11) The Bible says, 'The **Word** was **made flesh**, and **dwelt among us.**' (John 1:14) This verse says that God was made a mortal man, and dwelt among us! My dear Christian Brothers, you need to know that it is just as serious an error to deny the true humanity of Christ, as it is to deny the true divinity of Christ. Just as you cannot be saved if you deny the true divinity of Christ, neither can you be saved if you deny the true humanity of Christ!

'Hereby know ye the Spirit of God: every spirit that **confesseth that Jesus Christ is come in the flesh is of God**. And every spirit that **confesseth not that Jesus Christ is come in the flesh is not of God**: and this is that spirit of antichrist....'
I John 4:2-3

'For many **deceivers** are entered into the world **who confess not that Jesus Christ is come in the flesh**. This is a deceiver, and an antichrist....**Whosoever transgresseth** and **abideth not in the doctrine of Christ, hath not God**. He that abideth in the doctrine of Christ, he hath both the Father and the Son. If there come any unto you, and bring not this doctrine, receive him not into your house, neither bid him God speed: for he that biddeth him God speed is partaker of his evil deeds.' II John 7-11

"Jesus Christ had to came in the flesh with our human nature; Otherwise he could not have been **tempted as we are tempted**, (Hebrews 4:15) nor could he have shed his blood and died for sinners.

"And had he not been tempted as we are tempted, and that, without sin, he could not have offered himself **without spot** to God as the sacrifice for our sins. (Hebrews 9:14-17 and I Timothy 2:5) Nor could he, without a sinless life, be our great high priest, make a righteous atonement for our sins, or be the righteous mediator between God and man. I Timothy 2:5

'Seeing then that we have a great high priest, that is passed into the heavens, Jesus the Son of God, let us hold fast our profession. For we have not an high priest which cannot be touched with the **feelings of our infirmities**; but was in **ALL POINTS TEMPTED LIKE AS WE ARE, yet without sin**.' Hebrews 4:15

'How much more shall the **blood of Christ**, who through the eternal Spirit **offered himself WITHOUT SPOT to God**, purge your conscience from dead works to serve the living God? And for this cause he is the **mediator of the NEW TESTAMENT**.' Hebrews 9:14-15

"Jesus Christ was a real man. He really was tempted like we are tempted. He really did shed his blood and die! He really was dead when they laid him in the tomb!

"The fact that Jesus was a real man, and tempted in all points like other men, is clearly and forcefully taught in Hebrews.

'But we see **JESUS**, who was **MADE A LITTLE LOWER THAN THE ANGELS** for the **SUFFERING OF DEATH**.' Hebrews 2:9

'**Both** he that sanctifieth and they who are sanctified **ARE ALL OF ONE**.' Hebrews 2:11

'Forasmuch then as the **children are partakers of flesh and blood, he also himself likewise TOOK PART OF THE SAME**; that **THROUGH DEATH** he might destroy him that had the power of death, that is, the devil.' Hebrews 2:14

'For verily he took not on him the nature of angels; **but he TOOK ON HIM THE SEED OF ABRAHAM**.' Heb. 2:16

'Wherefore **IN ALL THINGS it behooved him to be MADE LIKE UNTO HIS BRETHREN**, that he might be a merciful and faithful high priest in things pertaining to God, to make reconciliation for the sins of the people.' Heb. 2:17

'*For we have not an high priest which cannot be touched with the feelings of our infirmities; but was IN ALL POINTS TEMPTED LIKE AS WE ARE, yet without sin.*' Heb. 4:15

"All men are created in the image and likeness of God with a rational, moral nature like God. God created us as **free moral agents** with the **law of God written in our hearts** and with a **conscience**.

'For not the hearers of the law are just before God, but **THE DOERS OF THE LAW SHALL BE JUSTIFIED.** For when the Gentiles, which have not the law, **DO BY NATURE** the things contained in the law, these, having not the law, are a law unto themselves: Which show the work of the **law written in their hearts**, their **conscience** also bearing witness, and their thoughts the meanwhile **accusing** or else **excusing** one another.' Romans 2:13-16

"All men have this rational, moral nature; **which they will have for all eternity**!

"In hell, sinners will *forever be tormented by a guilty conscience— which springs from the law that God has written in their hearts*, and their guilty conscience will be with them *forever* and augment their *torments* throughout *all eternity*.

"But in heaven, **the** *smile of a good conscience and the approval of God's law written in their hearts*, will forever bless the saints and augment their joy for all eternity.

ALL SIN COMES THROUGH TEMPTATION

"The Bible teaches that *ALL SIN comes through temptation.* The Bible teaches that *temptation is common to ALL MEN.* And the Bible teaches that *temptation is the occasion of ALL SIN.*

"The devil, himself, must have fallen into sin **through temptation.** He certainly was not created a sinner!

"Adam and Eve fell into sin **through temptation.** They certainly were not created sinners!

"The Bible clearly teaches that the devil is '**the tempter**' who **TEMPTS ALL MEN to make them sinners.** Matthew 13:38b-42

"Jesus commanded his disciples to **watch and pray** that they **not enter into temptation.** And he taught them to pray, '**Lead us not into** temptation, but **deliver us from evil.**' And he exhorted his disciples repeatedly: 'Pray that ye enter not into temptation.' Mark 14:38 and Luke 22:40, 46

'There hath **no temptation** taken you but such as is **COMMON TO MAN.**' I Corinthians 10:13

'Be sober, be vigilant; because your adversary the devil, as a roaring lion, walketh about, seeking whom he may devour: whom resist steadfast in the faith, knowing that **THE SAME AFFLICTIONS ARE ACCOMPLISHED IN YOUR BRETHREN that are in the world.**' I Peter 5:8-9

'My brethren, count it all joy when ye fall into *diverse temptations*; knowing this, that the trying of your faith worketh patience.' James 1:2-3

'Blessed is the man that **ENDURETH TEMPTATION**: for when he is tried, he shall receive the crown of life, which the Lord hath promised to them that love God.' James 1:12

'Let no man say when he is tempted, I am tempted of God: for **God cannot be tempted** with evil, neither tempteth he any man. But **EVERY MAN IS TEMPTED**, when he is drawn away of his own lust and enticed. Then when lust hath conceived, it bringeth forth sin: and sin, when it is finished bringeth forth death.' James 1:13-15

'In all this (temptation) Job sinned not, nor charged God foolishly.' Job 1:22

'Jesus was *IN ALL POINTS TEMPTED LIKE AS WE ARE*, yet without sin.' Hebrews 4:15

"The verses I have just read, teach that temptation is *common to all men*. But not that temptation always results in sin.

"Jesus **did not sin** when he was tempted.   And he was *tempted in all points, just like we are tempted.* And we know that Job and Joseph and Daniel and Shadrach and Meshach and Abednego, and a host of godly men throughout the Bible, in both the Old and the New Testaments, were sorely tempted of the devil, **and did not sin.**"

278

GOD HAS PROMISED VICTORY OVER ALL TEMPTATION

'There hath *no temptation taken you but such as is COMMON TO MAN*: but God is faithful, who *will not suffer you to be tempted above that ye are able*; *but will with the temptation also make a way to escape, that ye may be able to bear it.*' I Corinthians 10:13

'The Lord knoweth how to *deliver the godly out of temptations*, and to reserve the unjust unto the day of judgment to be punished.' II Peter 2:9

WATCH AND PRAY THAT YE ENTER NOT INTO TEMPTATION

"Jesus tells us, that although he is with us to deliver us out of temptation, we must **WATCH AND PRAY** lest we enter into temptation.

'And he said unto them, Why sleep ye? Rise and pray, lest ye enter into temptation.' Luke 22:46

'Watch and pray, that ye enter not into temptation: the spirit indeed is willing, but the flesh is weak.' Matthew 26:41

'After this manner therefore pray ye: Our Father which art in heaven...Lead us not into temptation, but deliver us from evil.' Matthew 6:13

'Pray that ye enter not into temptation.' Luke 22:40, 46

'And the Lord said, Simon, Simon, behold, **Satan hath desired to have you**, that he may **sift you as wheat**: but I have prayed for thee, that thy faith fail not: and when thou art converted, strengthen thy brethren. And he (Peter) said unto him, Lord, I am ready to go with thee, both into prison, and to death. And he said, I tell thee, Peter, the cock shall not crow this day, before that thou shalt thrice deny that thou knowest me.' Luke 22:31-34

CHRISTIANS HAVE OVERCOME THE DEVIL

'I write unto you, young men, because ye have **overcome the wicked one**.' I John 2:13

'I have written unto you, young men, because ye are strong, and the word of God abideth in you, and ye have **overcome the wicked one**.' I John 2:14

'And we know that **whosoever is born of God sinneth not**; but he that is begotten of God keepeth himself, and **THAT WICKED ONE TOUCHETH HIM NOT**.' I John 5:18

'And **they overcame him** by the blood of the Lamb, and by the word of their testimony.' Revelation 12:11

"But we must **watch and pray**! For the devil is our lifelong enemy and adversary; who wants to turn us from our Savior and destroy us in hell. And we are exhorted to stand against the devil, to put on the whole armor of God, to fight against the devil, to resist the devil, and to never give place to the devil.

'Finally, my brethren, be strong in the Lord, and in the power of his might. Put on the whole armor of God, that ye may be able to **stand against the wiles of the devil**.' Ephesians 6:10-11

'And the dragon...went to **make war** with the remnant of her seed, which keep the commandments of God, and have the testimony of Jesus Christ.' Rev. 12:17

'Be sober, be vigilant; because your adversary the devil, as a roaring lion, walketh about, *Seeking whom he may devour: whom resist steadfast in the faith*, knowing that the *same afflictions are accomplished in your brethren that are in the world*.' I Peter 5:8-9

'Resist the devil, and he will flee from you.' James 4:7

'Neither give place to the devil.' Ephesians 4:27

ONLY OVERCOMERS WILL ENTER INTO HEAVEN

"Only those who overcome sin, the world, the flesh, and the devil will enter into heaven. The message to the seven churches of the Revelation was that they were to **OVERCOME** if they were to enter into heaven, and be with God.

'To **him that overcometh** will I give to eat of the tree of life, which is in the midst of the paradise of God.' Rev. 2:7

'Fear none of those things which thou shalt suffer: behold, the **devil shall cast some of you into prison**, that ye may be tried; and ye shall have tribulation ten days: be thou faithful unto death, and I will give thee a crown of life. He that hath an ear, let him hear what the Spirit saith unto the churches; **he that overcometh** shall not be hurt of the second death.' Revelation 2:10-11

'He that hath an ear, let him hear what the Spirit saith unto the churches; **To him that overcometh** will I give to eat of the hidden manna, and will give him a white stone, and in the stone a new name written, which no man knoweth saving he that receiveth it.' Revelation 2:17

'And **he that overcometh**, and keepeth my works unto the end, to him will I give power over the nations: and he shall rule them with a rod of iron....And I will give him the morning star. He that hath an ear, let him hear what the Spirit saith unto the churches.' Revelation 2:26-29

'**He that overcometh**, the same shall be clothed in white raiment; and I will not blot out his name out of the book of life.....He that hath an ear, let him hear what the Spirit saith unto the churches.' Revelation 3:5-6

"Behold, I come quickly: hold that fast which thou hast, that no man take thy crown. **Him that overcometh** will I make a pillar in the temple of my God, and he shall go no more out. And I will write upon him the name of my God, and the name of the city of my God, which is new Jerusalem....And I will write upon him my new name. He that hath an ear, let him hear what the Spirit saith unto the churches.' Revelation 3:11-13

'To **him that overcometh** will I grant to sit with me in my throne, even as I also overcame, and am set down with my Father in his throne. He that hath an ear, let him hear what the Spirit saith unto the churches.' Revelation 3:21-22

281

'And the great dragon was cast out, that old serpent, called the Devil, and Satan, which deceiveth the whole world....And they **OVERCAME HIM** by the **BLOOD OF THE LAMB**, and by the **WORD OF THEIR TESTIMONY**.' Revelation 12:9, 11

'**HE THAT OVERCOMETH** shall **inherit all things**; and I will be his God, and he shall be my son. But the fearful, and unbelieving, and the abominable, and murderers, and whoremongers, and sorcerers, and idolaters, and all liars, shall have their part in the lake which burneth with fire and brimstone: which is the second death.' Revelation 21:7-8

CONCLUSION

"Dearly beloved, I must make a few concluding remarks concerning what the Bible calls the 'mystery of iniquity' and the 'mystery of godliness.' The **mystery of iniquity** speaks of the devil and **his work in men to make them workers of sin and iniquity**. And the **mystery of godliness** speaks of the Savior and **his work in men to make them workers of righteousness and godliness**.

THE MYSTERY OF INIQUITY

"The **mystery of iniquity** speaks of the devil's work, **NOW**, to make men sinners. And it speaks of the devil's work, **AT A LATER TIME**, when he will raise up that **man of sin, the antichrist**. II Thessalonians 2:3-9, Revelation 13:1-18, Revelation 14:8-13, Revelation 16:10 through 19:21, and Revelation 20:10-15

'For the **mystery of iniquity DOTH ALREADY WORK**...' II Thessalonians. 2:7

'**AND THEN** shall that wicked (the antichrist) be revealed, whom the Lord shall consume with the spirit of his mouth.' II Thessalonians 2:7

"The phrase, **mystery of iniquity,** speaks of the devil's work, **both now and in the future**, to make men members of his iniquitous kingdom. (II Thessalonians 2:7-12) It speaks of the **devil's very same work of iniquity in men** as is spoken of in the parable of the tares of the field. Matthew 13:24-30 and Matthew 13:36-43

282

THE MYSTERY OF GODLINESS

"The **mystery of godliness** speaks of Jesus the Son of God—who came to save men, and **make them holy, righteous, and godly. The Son of God, who was manifested in the flesh, works godliness** in all those who **BELIEVE IN HIM**.

'And without controversy great is the **MYSTERY OF GODLINESS: God was manifest in the flesh, justified in the Spirit, seen of angels, preached unto the Gentiles, BELIEVED ON IN THE WORLD, received up into glory.**' I Timothy 3:16

"The phrase **mystery of godliness** describes **the very same good work of Jesus in men** that is spoken of in the parable of the tares of the field. Matthew 13:24-30, 36-43

"Dear Christian brothers, I have preached almost entirely about the devil and *his evil work in men*. And it was necessary. But now, I want to conclude by talking about Jesus, and *HIS GOOD WORK in men*.

ALL GOD'S WORKS ARE GOOD—GOD CANNOT DO ANYTHING EVIL OR UNJUST.

"All God's works are good. God is perfect in love and goodness and mercy and truth. He is perfect in righteousness, holiness, and justice. 'God is light, and in him is *no darkness at all.*' (I John 1:5) There is not in him even a shadow of turning from light to darkness!

"God is the **Father of lights**. Our Father in heaven begets children who are **lights**, like their Father. James 1:17

'Do not err, my beloved brethren. **EVERY GOOD GIFT and EVERY PERFECT GIFT** is from above, and cometh down from the **Father of lights**, with whom is no variableness, neither shadow of turning. Of his own will begat he us with the word of truth, that we should be a kind of **firstfruits of his creatures**.' James 1:16-18

"The **devil tempts men** in order to make them sin. But God does not tempt any man. He does not make any man a sinner. His only work, is to make men holy, righteous, and good.

"God is perfect in justice. So he cannot do anything evil or unjust. He will not judge or condemn any man for another man's sin. Nor will he make any man a sinner for another man's sin. Ezekiel 18:1-32, Genesis 18:25

"God is perfect in all his moral attributes. And his perfect moral attributes will not allow him to do anything evil or unjust.

'Let no man say when he is tempted, I am tempted of God: for **God cannot be tempted with evil, neither tempteth he any man**. But every man is tempted, when he is drawn away of his own lust and enticed. Then when lust hath conceived, it bringeth forth sin: and sin, when it is finished bringeth forth death.' James 1:13-15

"But let's repeat James 1:16-18:

'**Do not err**, by beloved brethren. **Every good gift and every perfect gift is from above, and cometh down from the Father of lights, with whom is no variableness, neither shadow of turning**. Of his own will begat he us with the word of truth, **that we should be a kind of firstfruits of his creatures**.' James 1:16-18

"Dear Christian Brothers, I want you to forever remember this truth about the God we serve: **all of God's gifts and works toward men are good and perfect**!

"James tells us so in James 1:13-18!

"Paul tells us so in I Timothy 3:16!

"And Jesus tells us so in Matthew 13:37-38!

'He that soweth the **GOOD SEED** is the Son of man. The **good seed** are the **children of the kingdom**. But the tares are the children of the wicked one.' Matthew 13:37-38

"The 'Son of man' sows good seed. He sows **godly children** who belong to God's heavenly kingdom. It is the devil who sows bad seed. He sows **wicked children**. And his only gift to those he begets is everlasting punishment in hell!

"But God is love, and all his gifts toward men are good and perfect gifts. His children will enter into heaven and shine in heaven as the brightness of the firmament.

'And many of them that sleep in the dust of the earth shall awake, some to **everlasting life**, and some to **shame and everlasting contempt**. And they that be wise shall *shine as the brightness of the firmament*; and *they that turn many to righteousness as the stars for ever and ever*.' Daniel 12:2-3

'Then shall the righteous *shine forth as the sun* in the kingdom of their Father.' Matthew 13:43

'Every good gift and every perfect gift is from above, and cometh down from the Father of lights, with whom is no variableness, neither shadow of turning. *Of his own will begat he us* with the word of truth, *that we should be a kind of firstfruits of his creatures*.' James 1:16-18

"God loves us. All his works toward us are works of love. 'God so loved the world that he gave his only begotten Son that whosoever believeth in him should not perish, but have everlasting life.' John 3:16

"Oh, how God loves you, my dear brothers and sisters! He has made you his own dear children. He has begotten you, and you are now a kind of '**FIRSTFRUITS OF HIS CREATURES.**'

Chapter LX
Teacher Of Tradition And Dogma Seeks Revenge

A small band of men made their way on the path that led to the settlement of Christ's Imputed Righteousness, Positional Holiness, And Progressive Sanctification. They had chafed bitterly, but silently, under the burdens they were forced to carry.

They carried weapons that could bring pain and death to their enemies. Some carried clubs in their hands. Others carried stones in their hands. And one was loaded down with a small bag of stones slung over his shoulder. He struggled behind the others, doing his best to keep up.

Teacher of Tradition and Dogma marched before them. He was consumed with a burning hatred for Freed From Sin. He would stone him to death!

He hated the preachers also. Especially the preacher who had put a curse on him and made him dumb for almost 12 hours.

But by now the preachers were back in the Bright Regions. He would stone them later, when they came back through the settlements.

Finally he went up the last rise, and started down into the settlement. And it was then that he encountered the sunlight. He groaned, closed his eyes, and covered them with both hands. The men who followed him dropped their weapons, sighed with relief on being freed from their burdens; then raised their hands to their eyes.

Then, they all saw, when they looked through carefully shaded eyes, a great assembly of people in the park. And as they looked, they saw that there was much excitement and movement in the crowd. And leaving their weapons where they lay, and keeping their eyes shaded, they drew nearer. And they saw that many of the people had tears in their eyes, and were weeping for joy and speaking of the goodness and love of God toward them. They saw that others had not a tear in their eyes, but were filled with a joy that was irrepressible. 'All God's gifts to us are good and perfect,' one man was saying with a joy he could not contain. 'God has made us his own dear children. We are a kind of firstfruits of his creatures. He that spared not his own Son, but delivered him up for us all, how shall he not with him also freely give us all things?' Romans 8:32

And they now observed that the crowd was made up of many small bands of people, who stood around everywhere talking excitedly about God and his wonderful works.

And it was to one of these bands of men that Teacher of Tradition and Dogma drew near. "We're looking for Enforcer of Tradition and Dogma," he said. "The preachers brought him here to be baptized in water. Enforcer of Tradition and Dogma also calls himself 'Freed From Sin.' He has a son with him who has epileptic fits. Are they here?"

"Freed From Sin?" asked one of the men. "Freed From Sin's not here right now! He will be here later on. He left just a minute or two ago with the preachers and some new Christians. He's going with them at least part of the way to Pastor Truelove's home. He might even stay with the Pastor until he comes back through here again tomorrow. He testified today that God has called him to preach, and the Pastor asked him to accompany him for instruction on the requirements of those who preach God's Word. For the requirements for preachers are very strict you know! I Timothy and Titus

"But his wife and son are here now! They were both delivered from demon possession! Praise the Lord! God's been working miracles here in our settlement."

"Well," said Teacher of Tradition and Dogma, ignoring what the man had said about demon possession, "where is Freed From Sin now? Tell me which way they went! I need to talk to him now!"

The man who had been speaking to him, turned and pointed, "See that group of people over there in the distance? That's them! They just left for the Bright Regions. And Freed From Sin is with them. Hurry if you want to catch them. They're in a hurry, and they're moving fast!"

Chapter LXI
The Caves

"All these caves we are passing are man made," said Pastor Truelove. "They are the work of men who have rejected God's Word, in order to live according to the lies of the devil. They hide their lies in the darkness of these caves.

"We have passed cave's dug by atheists, who, although they know God created them, reject the truth of the Creator, because **THEY DO NOT WANT GOD TO RULE OVER THEM**. So they gladly accept the devil's lie that the whole universe just popped into existence out of nothing, and life on earth just popped into existence out of lifeless matter.

"We have passed caves dug by idolaters, who know that the idols they worship were made with their own hands, and have no life. Yet, instead of worshipping the living God who made them, they worship the idols they have made with their own hands! Sadly, they believe the devil's lie that an idol they have fashioned with their own hands can hear and answer prayer!

"But sadder than those caves, are the three caves we just passed: caves dug by professing Christians, and dug to cover the darkness of the devil's greatest lie to the Christian: that he can live in disobedience to some of God's commandments, as long as he obeys most of them."

Having said this, Pastor Truelove went on to the last cave. And there he stopped and said, "And the saddest of all the caves, is this last one, before which I now stand! It houses mere youth, who say they are saved, but who brazenly disobey God's fifth commandment. They refuse to honor, and obey their parents. They hate the authority of their parents. They sass and talk back, they disobey, and even curse their parents. They believe the devil's lie that they can dishonor their parents, and worship God at the same time!

"But, we must hurry on. Our good friends here are on their way back home, and we must not delay them any longer."

Suddenly Deacon Faith and Miracles spoke up: "Pastor Truelove, there's a gang of men following us, and they're in a very great hurry to overtake us. And I think the one in the lead is Teacher of Tradition and Dogma."

At these words, Freed From Sin turned and looked behind him. "Yes," he said, "that man walks exactly like Teacher of Tradition and Dogma. We'd better get inside this cave. He may want to harm us. I think we should avoid a confrontation with him."

Pastor Truelove gave the OK to enter, and said, "Be careful, it's dark in there, and steep. You may have trouble standing up."

Head Lighter Man lit his torch and lifted it high above his head. They entered the cave, but the ground sloped so steeply downward, that even with the light of the torch it was hard for them to stand up.

But no sooner were they all in the cave than the cave began to level off and turned to the left. And immediately upon turning left, they entered into a large amphitheater with a huge merry-go-round alongside the left-hand wall. But several feet out from the merry-go-round, the ground fell away precipitously toward a huge opening in the earth far below. And from that huge opening, a great light shone, that was reflected upon the ceiling and walls above it—a reflection of flames dancing and leaping high into the air from within the bowels of the earth.

And, then the spectators heard, faintly, although very clearly, pitiful screams of anguish coming from within the great opening.

The children were moved to tears by the pitiful screams. And some of the men also were so moved that they began to weep.

"Stand back here on the level ground," warned Pastor Truelove, "and don't go near that merry-go-round! You might lose your balance and fall down the steep incline!"

Up to this time the merry-go-round was motionless: as were the youth stretched out upon it, for they were all sleeping. But the youth, now awakened by Pastor truelove's sharp warning to the group with him, began to grumble as they stretched lazily. "What's the idea coming in here and waking us up so early?" said the leader of the youth. "You're wasting your time preaching to us. We're Christians!

We're on the worship team. We lead the congregation in worship every Sunday morning.

"We've been practicing all week and we're ready for Sunday's praise and worship service!"

Here, the leader slung his electric guitar on, and motioned to others to sling theirs on as well. The drummer sat down before his battery of drums, and the leader said, "Extinguish that torch! We don't want any other light! We want the lights, here on the merry-go-round, to highlight us as we lead worship. Now we'll sing one of the choruses were going to sing on Sunday."

Immediately four young men began pushing from within the merry-go-round. Another youth, new to the group, and only 12 years old, began pushing on the outside of the merry-go-round. The merry-go-round began to move and pick up speed.

Lights flickered at first, and then stayed on. The electric guitars began to sound out. The microphones began to amplify the voices of the singers.

Faster and faster went the merry-go-round. The lights grew brighter and brighter, and then began to flash different colors.

The young man, pushing on the outside of the merry-go-round, was now in trouble. The outside of the merry-go-round was moving much too fast for his short legs to keep up. He cried out, "I can't keep up! Slow down! So I can get back on!"

Everybody heard him, but they were all insensitive to his cries. The four pushers continued to push, to increase the speed of the merry-go-round. The singers and players continued to sing and play to the honor and glory of God. And the drummer, when it was his time for a solo exhibition of his playing prowess, surpassed the performance of all the other performers, with his dazzling speed and dexterity, and his powerful, ear splitting performance.

Meanwhile the 12-year-old boy screamed twice more, "Please! Stop! Please! Stop!" Finally he stumbled, lost his grip, and was slung out to the steep descent that fed him down into the flames below.

In all this, the praise and worship leaders neither slowed nor halted their playing and singing. But continued to praise and worship God:

You're awesome God, God of mercy, grace, and love.
I love you God, God of mercy, grace, and love.

All I want to do, is praise and worship you.
All I want to do, is praise and worship you.

You're awesome God, high and lifted up, high and lifted up.
You're mighty God, high and lifted up, high and lifted up.

All I want to do, is praise and worship you.
All I want to do, is praise and worship you.

You're awesome God. I love you God, I love and worship you.

You're awesome God. I love you God, I love and worship you.

All I want to do, is praise and worship you.
All I want to do, is praise and worship you.
All I want to do, is praise and worship you.
All I want to do, is praise and worship you.
All I want to do, is praise and worship you, oh, yea-yeah!

Pastor Truelove was furious. "Let's get out of here," he said. "They're not leading anyone in praise and worship. All they're doing is exhibiting their talent while their audience listens. They don't even know the meaning of the words they're singing. They laud God's mercy, grace, and love; and then mercilessly sling one of their own into the flames below! Come on, let's get out of here!"

"Hey! What's the hurry?" said the leader. "You still haven't preached to us yet. You going to leave us without preaching to us?"

"No. We didn't come in here to preach this time. We came in because a gang of men is following us who want to do us harm. And they're probably waiting for us outside right now!"

"Well," said the leader, "we'll see about that. You're our preacher. And we're not going to let anybody hurt our preacher." Then he shouted in youthful abandonment to his fellow worshippers of God, "Pick up some rocks, men! Let's go out and run these men out of the country! Come on, let's go!"

Chapter LXII
The War Begins

Teacher of Tradition and Dogma, along with his followers, sat just inside the cave's mouth, next to the stones they had picked up before entering; and rested in the cool darkness.

They heard the singers sing the worship chorus. They heard the 12-year-old boy's screams. And then later, they heard the furious words of Pastor Truelove when he said, "Let's get out of here. They're not leading anyone in praise and worship…Come on, let's get out of here!"

And when they heard Pastor Truelove's words, they picked up the stones they had gathered earlier, and moved outside to either side of the cave's mouth. And, there, Teacher of Tradition and Dogma waited with deep satisfaction, expecting to surprise and kill at least one and maybe all his enemies.

But neither he nor his followers surprised any one. They were the ones surprised by a force twice their own size and much more adept. And they were quickly routed by the young praise singers, and fled, seriously wounded.

But, in spite of this, the praise singers could not 'run them out of the country.' For they kept coming back, trying to attack the Christian group from the side or rear—and to stone Freed From Sin or one of the hated preachers.

But the praise singers would not allow this, hedging them away from the Christians, and raining rocks upon them, so that they were forced away, to a safe distance, out to the left of the Christians.

Thus, both sides came to a stalemate, and they all continued at a safe distance, one from the other, and soon arrived at the great tunnel that would take the five Christians back home.

Chapter LXIII
They Enter The Great Tunnel

A mixed group of some 40 souls, led by Head Lighter Man and Pastor Truelove walked quickly down the tunnel toward the University of One Mile Circle.

The Holy Spirit had given a word of knowledge and wisdom (I Corinthians 12:8-11) to Pastor Truelove, and revealed to him that he was to accompany the five Christians into the tunnel. So he continued in the lead with Head Lighter Man and the other preachers and Christians.

In the rear, Teacher of Tradition and Dogma with his small band of men followed after them. For more than ever they wanted to kill Freed From Sin and the hated preachers—and held on to the stones with which to do so.

The praise singers insisted that Pastor Truelove and all the preachers with him, were 'their preachers,' and that they would not let anybody harm them. So they followed directly behind the Christians with rocks ready in their hands—ready to rain them on Teacher of Tradition and Dogma and his men, if they got too close and threatened the Christians.

But 'getting too close' was really no problem. For Teacher of Tradition and Dogma, and his men, seemed to fear the light much more than the praise singers, and willingly hung back further in the darkness.

And thus the 40 souls continued at a rapid pace until they made a final turn in the tunnel, and came in upon the checkpoint at the University of One Mile Circle.

The only light at the checkpoint was from two low-burning candles.

Two female students were there, 10 minutes late for their first class, and were waiting to be checked through by the guards.

As Head Lighter Man's torch was being carried closer to the final turn into the checkpoint, the two female students sensed the increasing light coming from behind them. And turning to see what it was, they were caught full in the face with the brightness of Head Lighter Man's torch as he burst into the dark checkpoint.

The two girls shrieked in pain and pressed their hands to their eyes. Then they quickly turned away from the bright light, and whimpering in pain, they pressed quickly past the guards, fleeing toward the safety of their class. At the same time, the two guards pressed their hands over their eyes, and turned their backs to the torch.

One of the guards then fell to his knees, with both hands still pressed over his eyes. He remained in that position for a few moments; then fell full on his face, groaning, and pressing hands and face hard against the earth.

The other guard, still standing, shrieked again and again, "Put out that light! Put out that light! Put out that light, or I'll have you...!" And then he realized he had no power to penalize anyone who did not obey his commands. So he spoke his thoughts out loud, "I never did like this job! At first, there was not enough light. And now, there's too much light. I'm going to the Dean of Education and put in my resignation."

And being a man slow to think but quick to act, he straightway made his way away from the bright light behind him, and marched over to the darkness of the Dean of Education's building.

Chapter LXIV
Ode To Theophilus

"Listen, O Theophilus! For I speak of the marvelous works of God!

"God is sovereign. He rules in all the affairs of men. Sinners as well as saints are in his hands. He raises up one ruler and takes down another according to his own good will and purpose. He elects one man to everlasting life, and reprobates another to everlasting damnation. But in all his works with men, in his sovereignty, in his predestination, and in his election and reprobation, *God never once violates a man's FREE MORAL AGENCY, or works an INJUSTICE TO HIM!*

"It may seem that God is unjust, but **God's election is an election of grace and mercy**; and **not of works**. *God OWES SALVATION TO NO MAN!* So **if he saved not a single soul** he would still be just. 'For all have sinned...being justified **freely by his grace through the redemption that is in Christ Jesus.**' God will save no one who does not come to the Father **by faith in his Son Jesus Christ, DEPENDING WHOLLY UPON GOD'S GRACE AND MERCY IN CHRIST JESUS for his salvation!** Romans 3:23-24, Romans 9:11-33, Romans 10:1-21, and Romans 11:5-36

"But if men were born sinners, *God would OWE SALVATION TO ALL MEN, especially to the heathen who have never once heard the gospel of Jesus Christ.* But men are not born sinners! Men are created in the **image and likeness of God**, and are born **free moral agents!**

"O Theophilus! It is **impossible** to be born a sinner! It is **impossible** to be guilty and blameworthy for the way we are born! It is **impossible** to be a sinner without having committed sin!

"God is perfect in holiness, righteousness, justice, mercy, grace, truth, and goodness. These perfect and immutable attributes of God make it **impossible** for him to create a sinner, or allow a man to be born a sinner. Could the God of **perfect righteousness, justice, and love** create a world of sinners, and then send them to hell for a nature they were created with, and which was imposed upon them by no choice of their own?

"And, if men are **created and born sinners**, they are not **FREE MORAL AGENTS!** But **all their acts are NECESSARY, because they sin by nature, and not by choice.**

"And **if they are born sinners**, then they are **BORN CHILDREN OF THE DEVIL.** For the Bible clearly teaches, '**He that committeth sin is of the devil.**' (I John 3:8-12) And, 'Ye are of your **FATHER THE DEVIL**, and the **LUSTS OF YOUR FATHER** ye will do.' John 8:44

"But God tells us on every page of the Bible that men are **ALWAYS FREE MORAL AGENTS.** They are alway free, and always able to choose between right and wrong, good and evil, and justice and injustice. The teaching of the Bible is that men are **always, at every moment, able to choose in the opposite way, rather than the way they actually have chosen.** Men are **ALWAYS FREE MORAL AGENTS!**

"God is sovereign. His sovereignty is absolute. No one is over him. He rules after the **counsel of his own will.** (Ephesians 1:1) For he **does not need man's counsel!** It would be **wicked for God to depend upon the counsel** of **FRAIL AND IMPERFECT MAN!**

"God is perfect in justice, righteousness, goodness, holiness, mercy, grace, love, and truth. He is the Eternal God. He is the Creator of the universe. He is immutable, omniscient, omnipresent, omnipotent, and all wise.

"The very fact of **man's free moral agency** makes a moral government over man a **NECESSITY!**

"And God's perfect natural and moral attributes make it **NECESSARY** that he alone be **SOVEREIGN RULER OVER MAN!**

"Man is a **free moral agent.** This means he is the **master of his own will.** But, although every man is the master of his own will, God will often **overrule** the **wicked choices** of sinners in order to fulfill his own good will and purpose. Ephesians 1:5, 11 and Romans 9:17-18

"The most notable example of God's **overruling the wicked choices of a sinner in order to fulfill his own good will and purpose** is that of the wicked Pharaoh, of Egypt, who stubbornly resisted God's will in order to keep the children of Israel in bondage. God overruled the Pharaoh's wicked purpose, and delivered his people from the bondage of Egypt.

"But God does **NOT ALWAYS OVERRULE the wicked designs of sinners**. See Romans 8:35-36 and Hebrews 11:35-38

"Now, most excellent Theophilus, I continue the account of the Christians, whose lives are imperiled by the wicked designs of the wicked."

Chapter LXV
Professor C. More Light

The two girls moved quickly through the open door to their seats at the back of the classroom. They were both sobbing audibly, but were hardly noticed; for a heated argument was going on between the Little Man and Professor C. More Light.

"This is not your class," shouted Professor C. More Light. "Dean Allotrope promoted me to your place as Head Professor of the Psychology Department almost three months ago, and nothing has changed since then."

"Yes, something has changed!" the Little Man shouted back. "I was with Dean Allotrope just day before yesterday; and he told me you're through! You're finished! You're dismissed from teaching anymore! And I'm to take your place!"

"I don't believe you," Professor C. More Light said. "Dean Allotrope has said nothing to me about this. And until he does, I'll certainly not leave my class because of what you say!"

*** *** ***

But lets back up in time to the beginning of what happened in that classroom on that particular day.

X. M. Plary was there in that classroom very early in the morning on that day; and he knew a lot about Professor Judas, who was now in a heated argument with Professor C. More Light. Judas had told X. M. Plary two days earlier of his plan to kill his enemies. Also Judas had told him two days earlier that Professor C. More Light was finished teaching, and that he, Judas, would be taking his place.

Then, one day later, X. M. Plary saw Judas buy a gun and ammunition from his very own father in the Bright Regions. And X. M. Plary followed Judas back into the tunnels hoping to keep Judas from using the gun to kill his enemies.

So, when X. M. plary walked into class after being absent for two days, he was surprised to see Professor C. More Light still there, ready to teach as usual.

Professor C. More Light stood behind the same low table upon which burned, not one, but two large candles. A copy of his book, Evidences of Design, lay on the table, and beside it lay an open Bible, just like before.

X. M. Plary walked down to his same front row seat, just a step or two to the left of Professor C. More Light and sat down. He was closer than any one else to the Professor, almost in front of him; and closer than any one else to the light from the two large candles. Many students now sat as far back as possible in the classroom to avoid the bright light from the two large candles. But X. M. Plary (along with some other students) loved the bright light from the two large candles.

And now X. M. Plary was thinking happily on the goodness of God in keeping Professor C. More Light in his same teaching position— when a noisy jerking open of the door occurred, followed by a louder than usual marching toward the front of the classroom. Everyone in the front of the classroom turned to see what was causing the disturbance.

When X. M. Plary turned to see the cause of the disturbance, his heart sank. It was Judas, striding purposefully toward Professor C. More Light with a look of hatred on his face!

The Little Man halted abruptly behind the front row of seats, and moved a few steps over to the left. He wanted to get closer, but the light from the candles was hurting his eyes. He held his hands stiffly at his side, restraining an overwhelming desire to lift them to his face and cover his eyes. "What are you doing here?" he roared. "You were told you were finished! You were told to leave! Why haven't you left? Why are you still here?"

Professor C. More Light was both perplexed and angered at the rude entrance and hateful outburst from his former colleague. "Professor Judas," he said, trying to restrain his anger. "Have you gone mad? What's the idea barging in here like this and disrupting my class? You don't belong here now. You had better get back to your work of engineering new tunnels!"

Now the Little Man was perplexed. And thought, "Didn't Professor C. More Light know that he was once again Head Professor of the Psychology Department?"

But now he saw the open Bible lying on the table, and cried out with contempt: "What are you doing with that Bible here at the University? It's a book of religious superstitions. It's a book for the gullible, the ignorant and the uneducated. And it's forbidden in government institutions of learning by the Constitution of the United States. The Constitution calls for the separation of Church and State. And you have brought that unlawful book into my classroom!"

"This is not your classroom!" shouted Professor C. More Light. I am the teacher here! And as for the Constitution of the United States, and its calling for the separation of Church and State—it does no such thing. It merely says, 'Congress shall make no law respecting an establishment of religion, or prohibiting the free exercise thereof.'

"Moreover, the Bible is not a book of superstition, as you say, that only the ignorant and the uneducated believe in. No, the teachings of the Bible are in such accord with every man's consciousness of his own innate convictions of reason and truth—that all reasonable men know it is true.

"There is no other book in the world that gives such a true and complete account of man's mind, reason, and free moral choices, as the Bible. It is impossible to know and teach the true psychology of man without the Bible! And, I teach psychology; so I also teach the Bible.

"Psychology is the study of man's mind, his thinking, his reasoning, his motives, his free will; and the moral conduct that necessarily follows from the choices of his free will.

"The Psychology of man has absolutely nothing to do with dogs, or mice, or chickens or geese or monkeys. *For animals are not moral agents*!

"Animals do not have a rational mind with free will as man does. And they are not moral creatures! They do not have a conscience. They do not know right from wrong. They do not have moral government over themselves as men do—with policemen and judges and courts of law—where lawbreakers are tried and sentenced for their evil conduct. They do not..."

The Little Man endured the words of C. More Light up to here, but no further. "Oh, come on now!" he said. "Quit your preaching! You're finished! You're through! You're dismissed from teaching anymore here at the University, and I've come to take your place. This is my class now!"

It was precisely at this moment that the two girls, who were late, quickly pushed through the open door to their seats at the back of the classroom. They were both sobbing audibly, but were hardly noticed because of the heated argument going on between the Little Man and professor C. More Light.

"This is not your class," shouted Professor C. More Light. "Dean Allotrope promoted me to your place as Head Professor of the Psychology Department almost three months ago, and nothing has changed since then."

"Yes, something has changed!" the Little Man shouted back. "I was with Dean Allotrope just day before yesterday; and he told me you're through! You're finished! You're dismissed from teaching anymore! And I'm to take your place!"

"I don't believe you," Professor C. More Light said. "Dean Allotrope has said nothing to me about this. And until he does, I'll certainly not leave my class because of what you say!"

"Well, you'd better leave, and leave right now," said the Little Man, "because Dean Allotrope says you're all through, and I'm taking your place."

Professor C. More Light said not another word; but stared steadily into the eyes of the Little Man. In the silence that followed everyone heard the sobbing catch in the voice of one of the girls, who was still sobbing intermittently.

"What's wrong? What are you crying about?" asked Professor C. More Light.

The girl lifted a tear-streaked face, and cried out, "The light! It was awful! It hurt so much! It was so bright! Like the Bright Regions! Only worse! Oh, it hurt my eyes! And they still hurt!" And having said this, the girl began sobbing again.

The Little Man, when he heard her tell of the bright light that hurt her eyes, became intensely interested. He thought of the bright light of John's flashlight, and he thought of the bright light of Head Lighter Man's torch.

He turned to face the girl, and said, "Tell us about the bright light. What was the light like that you saw? Where did you see it, and when did you see it?"

The girl lifted her tear streaked face again, and said, "I don't know. We were going through check-in and a light was coming toward us from behind. And we turned to see what it was. And suddenly it became bright. And it hurt. It hurt so much we turned away from it, and came here as fast as we could."

"What caused the bright light?" asked Judas.

"Was the bright light from a big torch? Was it from a flashlight?" asked Judas.

"I don't know." the girl answered. "It might've been a torch. But I don't know. It blinded me so that I don't know. But it might've been a torch...held up high."

Judas now took command. He turned to X. M. Plary, and said, "X. M., you're in charge of my class now. I'm going to find out who has brought the big torch into the University from the Bright Regions, and report it to the Dean of Education."

Then, Judas gave one quick pat to the place where he had concealed his pistol, and made his way out the open door.

Chapter LXVI
Armed Rebellion?

The Little Man hurried toward the checkpoint. He was deeply satisfied with himself. Very soon he would kill his enemies.

Not far behind the Little Man followed X. M. Plary, Professor C. More Light, and several of his students. X. M. Plary had informed Professor C. More Light, along with a few of his students, of Judas' purpose to kill some enemies with his gun. And they had all agreed to follow Judas and keep him from his evil purpose.

Only some 10 minutes before this the Dean of Education had hurried out the doors of the Hall of Education, followed by the guard, toward the checkpoint.

He did not have far to go. For the checkpoint was no more than a stone's throw from the Hall of Education.

But what he saw from the top of the steps made him pull up suddenly and stand frozen with fear. For the area everywhere below him was flooded with light from a large torch. And the large torch was advancing slowly toward the Hall of Education, the place where the Dean stood. But what struck fear to his heart, more than anything else, was the large assembly of people milling about, many with stones in their hands. And they were waving their fists, fists that were filled with stones, and shouting to one another!

"We've got to go down and talk to them." said Dean Allotrope, speaking to the guard. "Maybe we can appease them! Come on, let's go!"

But, as Dean Allotrope drew closer, the bright light dazzled him; and the pain became unbearable. So that he stopped some distance from Pastor Truelove and Head Lighter Man. And from there he called out with a shaky voice, "You sir, with the torch, will you please put it out? Why are you here with all these people, and why are your people armed with stones? Please, put your torch out, and let's talk this over! Please, don't do anything until we've had a chance to talk!"

Chapter LXVII
Head Lighter Man Explains His Mission

"Sir," responded Head Lighter Man. "I cannot put out my torch. For should I do so, there would be a bloodbath here. There are two warring factions among us, and the only thing that keeps them apart is this light that I hold above my head. Should I put it out, or even dampen it, they would do their best to stone one another to death. For, the one faction wants to murder all the preachers. The other faction has promised that they will kill the men who want to kill the preachers. This bright light is all that keeps them from the murder they have purposed in their hearts. Therefore, I cannot put it out!

"But you have no reason to fear us. We are not here to harm you! We are here only to take five Christians back to the place where they fell into the tunnels. For that is where they must go to get back home.

"And Dean Allotrope," he continued. "I know you, and you know me. I'm Head Lighter Man. You also know the five Christians here with me. We were all with you in the Education Department about three days ago. Professor Judas brought us before you with false charges, saying we were guilty of death.

"I didn't tell you then, but he tried to kill us that same day, before he brought us to you. He fired three rounds at us. But, thank God, he missed each time he fired at us.

"Then, after we left you, he fired at Jed Truly in Professor U. R. Matter's Biology class, and missed again.

"Then, the six of us went to the Bright Regions. And Professor Judas followed us there, still intending to kill us. And there, he stole a rifle and ammunition with which to do so. But, again, he failed in his purpose to kill us.

"Where he is now, I have no idea. He disappeared soon after we discovered he had stolen the rifle and ammunition."

Having said this, Head Lighter Man was poised to go past Dean Allotrope to take the five Christians to the new tunnel and back home. But as he looked ahead of him, he saw two things taking place at the same time.

First, he saw Professor Judas approaching at a run. He saw him stagger to a stop, a short distance away from him and the Dean of Education. And he saw him throw up both hands to cover his eyes, trying to alleviate the pain from the light of his torch.

Second, he saw a group of students, some distance behind Professor Judas, running full tilt toward him. And, following only a short distance behind them, he saw Professor C. More Light, struggling hard to keep up.

Chapter LXVIII
Judas Incites The Factions To War

But now, Judas lifted his voice, and cried out, from where he stood: "Dean Allotrope, command that Head Lighter Man extinguish his torch! He's got the five Christians here with him that preach the Bible. And he's got other preachers here that preach the Bible. They were all together, preaching lies, in the Foggy Bottoms! They should all die! Kill them! Let them die for preaching lies!"

Upon hearing these words, Teacher of Tradition and Dogma lifted his voice and cried out: "Kill the preachers." And he led his men in crying out: "Let them die! Let them die! Let them die for preaching lies!" Then he shrieked again, with all the bitter hatred of his heart, "Let them die! Let them die! Let them die!"

The Praise Singers then cried out in kind: "We'll kill anyone who touches our preachers! Death to those who touch our preachers! Death to those who touch our preachers! Death to those who touch our preachers!" Over and over again they repeated the threat to kill those who touched their preachers.

Then Dean Allotrope, hearing the shouting back and forth, and seeing hands raised with stones, and hands waving them in a threatening way—and Fearing he might soon have uncontrolled warfare on his hands, cried out in alarm, "Stop! Stop! Stop this foolishness! Nobody is going to die here at the University of One Mile Circle."

At this very moment X. M. Plary, along with a few students and Professor C. More Light, ran past Judas and came to a stop beside Dean Allotrope. They heard, and everyone else heard the words of Dean Allotrope.

They all heard him say, "Nobody is going to die here at the University of One Mile Circle."

X. M. Plary now spoke to Dean Allotrope: "Dean Allotrope, you just said, 'Nobody is going to die here at the University of One Mile Circle.' But Professor Judas has a pistol, hidden on him; which he bought in the Bright Regions. And he's planning to kill his enemies with it right now."

Dean Allotrope knew that what X. M. Plary said was true. Yet, because he and the Little Man were kindred spirits, he was willing to defend him. "How do you know that he has a gun that he bought in the Bright Regions?"

"I was there when he bought it." X. M. Plary answered quickly. "He bought it yesterday at my father's gun shop, in the Bright Regions."

"Well, there's nothing wrong with having a gun as long as you don't use it to kill someone!" And with that the Dean dismissed the charges against Judas.

But now Professor C. More Light spoke to the Dean: (And the Dean had feared this was coming! For he knew that he had been remiss in not notifying Professor C. More Light of his termination.) "Is it true, Dean Allotrope, that you told Professor Judas two days ago that I was terminated, without even bothering to tell me that I was terminated?"

The question hung in the air! What could he say? He could not tell the truth! For that's exactly what he had done.

"Well, not exactly," he finally answered. "You know how busy I am. I should probably have an assistant to help me with my overload of work. I meant to inform you of your termination the same day I made the decision. But with all my work I just wasn't able to do it.

"But I think what we'll do now is divide the Psychology Department into two heads. Professor Judas will head up General Psychology as we now teach it. And you will head up a special study in Psychology which we will call, 'The Question of Design in Evolution.'"

Professor C. More Light, knowing that he was being squeezed out, said nothing more.

And Judas, seeing that Dean Allotrope was conversing with Professor C. More Light. And knowing that he was being left out of all that was being said, drew near enough to hear the last words of Dean Allotrope to Professor C. More Light—"And you will head up a special study in Psychology which we will call, 'The Question of Design in Evolution.'

Judas, upon hearing these words, screamed out in a rage, "No! He's a preacher! He has a Bible in his classroom right now! And he preaches from that Bible! He deserves to die, like all the other preachers here! He's a preacher! Kill him too! Kill all the preachers! Let them all die!"

And Judas, in a frenzy, whipped out his pistol, and began to wave it around frantically. At this, Dean Allotrope threw up both hands, and hissed, "Stop that, Judas! Put away that gun!" Then he added in a very low whisper, "Put that gun away! Don't you dare use it to kill anyone as long as I am present with you."

And even as Dean Allotrope was frantically calling on the Little Man to put away his gun, and never to kill anyone while he was present, the two warring factions were again taking up their horrible threats to kill one another.

But this time the words of Judas were so inflammatory that it was like throwing gasoline onto an already raging fire. His words, "He's a preacher! Kill him too! Kill all the preachers! Let them all die!"— were lifted immediately in a frenzy of hatred by Teacher of Tradition and Dogma. And his men, carried away by the passion and frenzy of their leader, repeated the same words over and over again.

But, when the Praise Singers saw that their adversaries were at a grave disadvantage—for the light from the torch shone directly into the eyes of all those who wanted to kill the preachers—they immediately took advantage of this weakness and responded with deadly action.

First they cried out, "These are our preachers! We'll kill anyone who touches our preachers!"

Then they put action to their words and began to cast stones at their adversaries.

Not as they had done before, only raining stones upon them to keep them at a safe distance from the preachers. Now they cast stones with precision, and with intent to kill!

Teacher of Tradition and Dogma fell quickly at their feet, and expired under their stoning. And his followers were horribly bloodied, and fell at their feet also.

When Dean Allotrope heard the screams of pain he knew he had waited too long to intervene between the two warring factions. And he hurried with Professor Judas to put a stop to the warfare.

But when Dean allotrope finally arrived, and saw the bloodied body of Teacher of Tradition and Dogma, now dead; and his bloodied followers lying on the ground, he said, "This youth group, who committed this atrocity, and the men who brought them here, will pay for this crime."

He then pronounced the youth guilty of murder, and the preachers and Christians guilty for bringing them to the University of One Mile Circle—and called for a General Assembly in which to charge them all, and administer punishment for their crimes.

Chapter LXIX
The Rigged Trial

Although the assembly hall was large, it was filled to capacity. And although it was dark in the assembly hall, there was tolerable light where the prisoners were seated.

For, when Head Lighter Man stoutly refused to extinguish his torch and give it over into the hands of those who arrested him, they finally felt obliged to accept the compromise that Head Lighter Man proposed. He proposed that a few candles had to be placed throughout every part of the assembly hall, and that many more candles had to be used to light the place where the prisoners were seated—and that he would keep his unlighted torch as a guarantee.

Dean Allotrope and Judas took complete control of the proceedings. Dean Allotrope had agreed beforehand with Professor Judas exactly how they would proceed. They had agreed that the only way to maintain complete conformity to their teaching of cosmological and biological evolution was to eliminate all teaching that God created the heavens and the earth. That meant the elimination of all the men who believed and taught the Word of God! Although Dean Allotrope knew that what they purposed to do was unlawful and would have to be done in secret; he felt that the faculty and student-body would, almost to a man, agree with the steam-rolling tactics needed to bring it about.

Dean Allotrope took his place behind the podium and spoke awkwardly into the bright light where the prisoners were seated, "Dear faculty members and members of the student-body, as you can see by the light from the many candles...." (Head Lighter Man, seeing the Dean's expression of pain from the light, and his halting pauses because of it, jumped to his feet, lifted his torch, and was poised to light it if Dean Allotrope demanded that the number of candles be diminished.) "...As I was about to say," the Dean now continued. "We have seated before us a band of some 50 religious zealots who have invaded the University of One Mile Circle without being invited. Some of them are murderers—and they have this day slaughtered one man, right before our eyes, and left several others so bloodied that they are at the point of death!

"We are here to bring them to justice. They must pay for their crime of murder! And the preachers who brought them here must pay for the crime of invading the University of One Mile Circle and bringing others here, without any of them having an invitation to be here. In addition, they must pay for the crime of invading the University of One Mile Circle with the teachings of the Bible, especially the false teaching that there is a Creator who created the heavens and the earth.

"With this false teaching, they have violated the constitution of the United States, which commands the complete separation of Church and State.

"Professor Judas, who knows these men better than anyone else, will be their Judge, and will give verdict of their guilt or innocence. And now," Dean Allotrope concluded, "Court is in session, with the Honorable Professor Judas presiding as Judge."

Many people assembled in that hall, knew that Professor Judas was not honorable in any way, or in any way fit to judge others for their crimes.

Dean Allotrope himself knew that Professor Judas was not fit to judge others for their crimes. He knew all about Professor Judas! He knew that he had shot down Professor Blazer, the Head Astronomer at the University. He knew it was an accident. That Judas had been trying to kill the five Christians: and that the bullet meant for the Christians had missed its intended mark, and penetrated Professor Blazer's head. He knew also that Judas was fully aware that he had killed Professor Blazer; for he had to pass by the fallen Professor, to continue his pursuit of the five Christians.

Dean Allotrope knew also that he himself was no better than Professor Judas; for he had conspired with Professor Judas to railroad the preachers and Christians through to a sentence of death for their belief in God and the Bible. And he had done this, when he couldn't help but think that the murder of Teacher of Tradition and Dogma and the attempted murder of his followers were the only really serious crimes that had been committed.

Also, many others in the assembly knew that Judas was not an honorable man, and not fit in any way to judge others for their crimes. The five Christians, as well as Head Lighter Man, knew that Judas was not an honorable man. They knew there was nothing about him that was honorable or good. Three times he had attempted to murder them for being Christians. And now he was to be their judge.

Also, Professor U. R. Matter knew, and his class knew also, that Judas was not an honorable or decent man. For they had all witnessed a sham trial of the five Christians by Judas, and had also witnessed his failed attempt to murder Jed Truly. They knew there was nothing honorable about Professor Judas.

Also, Professor C. More Light and much of his class; the preachers from the Bright Regions; several of the Christians, and, of course, X. M. Plary, knew that Judas was in no way honorable or worthy to be a judge.

Nevertheless, Judas approached the podium, inflated and blind to his own smallness—thinking that he was perfectly acceptable as a judge.

But, as he approached the podium, the bright light hurt his eyes; and he had to look down at his notes on the podium to avoid the bright light coming up from the Christians:

"We will have no trial for the youth who killed Teacher of Tradition and Dogma, and bloodied his six co-workers. The youth are exonerated because of special circumstances.

"The special circumstances are these:

"One, that they are all mere youth and should not be tried as adults. Only two of the fifteen are past the age of eighteen, and none of them is past the age of twenty.

"Two, that they were incited to violence by fully grown men who knew better than to incite them to such violence.

"So, there will be no trial of the youth.

"Neither will there be a trial of the preachers and Christians who brought them here. I know practically every preacher and every Christian who is in this assembly. I encountered five of them in our new tunnel when they first invaded our University just three days ago. All they could talk about was God and the Bible.

"Then I followed them to the Bright Regions where I met more preachers and Christians. And they also spent all their time preaching about God and the Bible.

"And now the preachers who first invaded our University have brought these others back here with them. And one of them has brought a huge Bible with him, the largest I have ever seen—into this assembly—to spout his religious teachings from it."

And here, Judas shaded his eyes and pointed as best he could into the light where Pastor Truelove sat with his huge black Bible wide-open on his knees. Then Judas shouted with all the force in his tiny frame, "The Constitition of the United States of America commands the complete separation of church and state. And they have brought that huge Bible into our University in defiance of the Constitution of the United States of America!"

Bob Becker quickly rose to his feet and spoke so that all in the assembly could hear him, "Sir, I rise to a point of order! Sir, you must give these youth a trial, and that trial must be a trial by jury. Article III, Section 2 of the Constitution of the United States of America says, 'the trial of all crimes...shall be by jury.'

"These youth either have or have not committed the crime of murder. The Constitution of the United States of America promises them a trial, and it promises them a trial by jury. It not only promises a trial by jury to them; it promises a trial by jury to all the others here who are charged with criminal conduct.

"And the reason that the Constitution of the United States of America promises a trial by jury to all those accused of criminal conduct is to protect them from the tyranny of the powerful. That the **powerful not set the guilty free**, and that the **powerful not condemn the innocent for crimes they did not commit**.

"Sir, you have no right to rule arbitrarily on the guilt or innocence of these youth, or on the guilt or innocence of any of us who believe the Bible and preach the Word of God.

"We must each have a jury trial. The Constitution of the United States demands it! A jury must be impaneled of twelve of our peers to judge of the guilt or innocence of each one of us. And counsel must be allowed or provided, as the case may warrant, to defend all who are accused."

Judas endured Bob Becker up to here. Then he began to contend with him about trials, and juries, and counsel for the defense. He said that choosing jurors would take too much time, and that a good judge could rule more quickly and more efficiently than twelve jurors with all kinds of different viewpoints. And finally, he said that they didn't have to have a trial by jury just because the Constitution of the United States of America said so.

It was here that Bob became angry! "Why, you hypocrite!" He shouted. "You say that the Constitution of the United States of America requires the complete separation of Church and State. And that because of this no one can mention the Bible and its teachings in any State run school.

"But when the Constitution of the United States of America requires that all men accused of crimes be given a trial by jury you are quite ready to throw that requirement out of the Constitution. So that you can arbitrarily exonerate those you want to set free, and arbitrarily condemn those you want to condemn to death! You hypocrite!"

Judas was obliged to look down upon Bob Becker as Bob continued to heap scorn upon him. And the glaring light was hurting his eyes more and more. So that he closed them, pressed his hands over them, and cried out in frustration and pain, "All right! All right! We'll have a trial by jury!"

Chapter LXX
The Youth Stand Trial

Pastor Truelove was chosen as counsel for the defense. This was his counsel to the youth.

1. They would be tried together as one, for they had acted together as one.
2. They would plead guilty. For they were guilty.
3. They would not excuse their sin because of their youth (for they were churchgoers and fully cognizant of all God's commandments).
4. At the very beginning of the trial they would ask forgiveness of the men on whom they had inflicted such great pain and suffering.
5. If the court granted them mercy or clemency, they would express their gratitude, and confess that they knew they deserved to be punished with the full force of the law for the crimes they had committed.

And it was then that they all confessed to Pastor Truelove that they realized the awfulness of their crime, and repented of it. They went to their knees in contrition, and asked Pastor Truelove to pray for them.

And later, during the trial, they all pled guilty before the entire assembly and confessed that they had committed a horrible crime against those they had stoned. With tears in their eyes they each begged forgiveness of those who were yet alive. They asked for the mercy of the court, if it were possible. They stated that they knew they did not deserve mercy. But deserved punishment for killing Teacher of Tradition and Dogma, and for the awful pain and suffering they had inflicted on the others. They testified with a broken spirit that they knew God had forgiven them—but they knew that they had to be punished by the court for the crime they had committed.

And the court did grant them clemency—but with a sentence severe enough to make them, and all those who witnessed the trial, understand that the court could never justly exonerate the youth for their crime.

Their sentence: Five years in prison, with reduced time possible for good behavior. Sentence to be carried out in the Bright Regions with Pastor Truelove charged with taking them back for their sentence.

Chapter LXXI
Jed Truly Stands Trial

Next Jed Truly was put on trial. And Twelve new jurors were impaneled. He pled not guilty in a clear, strong voice.

Immediately Judas demanded that Jed stand trial for all the accused! Jed was seated next to his counselor, Pastor Truelove. But now he jumped to his feet and shouted, "No! We are not cattle to be herded together as one! We are human beings, made in God's image! And to have justice for each person, each person must have his own trial.

"And," he added, "if I were by some chance found not guilty, would you find everyone else not guilty as well?"

Judas hesitated to answer Jed's question just long enough that it was apparent to all that his design was to condemn all the Christians to death as one person. His response sounded lame, because it was lame: "But think of the time it will take if everyone has an individual trial! You pled, not guilty! And if everyone else pleads not guilty—we will never finish with the trials. Some thirty individuals to be tried, a new panel of jurors for each person, the time of the trial itself, then time for the jurors to deliberate and arrive at a verdict. We'll be here forever!"

"Wouldn't you," said Jed, "if you were being tried for a capital crime—with death the penalty if convicted—want the right to be tried by a jury of twelve of your peers? With the right to plead, not guilty if you knew you were not guilty; and with the right of an unhurried trial, so that you were able to fully present all the evidence in your defense? And wouldn't you want the jurors to have ample time to review all the evidence presented in your defense?

"Or is it true that a trial by twelve of your peers would be the worst thing in the world for you? That twelve of your peers would soon find you guilty and worthy of death? And that only someone as corrupt and worthy of death as you are, would introduce you, and say of you, 'Court is now in session with the Honorable Professor Judas presiding as Judge.'?

There was an almost silent gasp of amazement at this audacious remark; followed by a more audible titter of laughter that swept through some parts of the assembly.

But Jed was not finished, and he said, "Let's get on with the trial. I am here to defend my belief in God and the Bible. For that is the accusation brought against me, that I believe in God, the Creator of the heavens and the earth, and that I preach the message that God has given us in his Holy Book, the Bible.

"I am not accused of living in the sins of adultery or fornication. I am not accused of lying or stealing. I am not accused of hating my neighbor, or cursing him, or mistreating him in any way. And, finally, I am not accused of murder or attempted murder as I know you, sir, to be guilty of—and as many, right here in this assembly, know you to be guilty of."

Hatred exploded in Judas' heart at this sudden and unexpected uncovering of his true character; and he wanted to curse the man, rush upon him, and empty his gun into him. But it was impossible for him to so much as deny the charge; for the man had continued speaking without pausing for one moment:

"I am not accused of any evil or wickedness whatsoever. No! The only thing that I am accused of is believing in the one true God and his only begotten Son, the Lord and Savior Jesus Christ.

"Now isn't that strange? I am counted a criminal because I believe in God and preach the good news that God gave his Son Jesus Christ to die for our sins, so that we can be pardoned, and saved from a sinful life that is taking us down into hell! To me, that is strange indeed!"

Chapter LXXII
Judas Resists Jed's Right To Read The Bible

Now Jed Truly, bending over to his counselor, Pastor Truelove, asked to borrow his Bible. Then he picked up one of the long candles, and directing his words to Judas, said, "I am coming up where you are, sir, so that all who are here can see me as I make my defense. I will need a lectern or a pulpit on which to put the candle and the Bible, for I will be reading from this Holy Book, the Bible."

"No!" cried Judas. "You will never read the Bible here. It is strictly forbidden by the Constitution."

But Jed Truly walked forward, the Bible in one hand and the candle in the other.

"No!" screamed Judas. "Take that Bible out of here! I hate it! I hate it! I don't want you to read it here!"

Pastor Truelove, counsel for the defense, stood to his feet and spoke to Judas of his client's right to read from the Bible in his defense. "Your Honor I rise to speak for my client's right to read the Bible in his defense, since the only charges against him have to do with believing and teaching the truths that are found in the Bible. What is it in the Bible that you hate so much? Tell us exactly what offends you in the Bible. Tell us if you have read something in the Bible that should not be read! Your honor, have you read the Bible?"

Judas had read the Bible. He knew what it said. He had read it all the way through. And much of it, he had read many times. But if he told the truth, the whole truth, and nothing but the truth, he would reveal to all those present his former conversion to Christianity. So he lied. "No! I've never read the Bible. Why should I read the Bible? It's a book full of lies and superstitions. Only the gullible and superstitious would believe such a book!"

Pastor Truelove was stunned by the absence of science and logic in the mind of Judas. He was stunned and amazed by the pitiable irrationality of his words. An irrationality that bordered on utter stupidity!

How could Judas say, with a rational mind, that he hated the Bible when he had never read the Bible?

And how could he say that the Bible was full of lies and superstitions when he had never read it?

But it would not gain his client's rights, and would only offend Judas if he told him he was irrational to the point of stupidity. So Pastor Truelove said, "Your honor, since you have not read anything that is in the Bible, and do not know anything that the Bible says, you have no basis for saying what is, or what isn't in it. All of your ideas of what it teaches are null and void. For you simply do not know what it teaches. And all your characterizations of what it teaches are simply imaginations of your own mind, and can have no binding effect upon this court. So you must provide him with a pulpit or lectern on which to place his Bible. And you must let him use his Bible to make his defense. Otherwise you may be accused of willfully obstructing justice in his trial."

Chapter LXXIII
Jed Begins At The Beginning

Jed Truly was given a pulpit. He placed the Bible on the pulpit. And he placed the candle to the left side of the Bible. He was ready to read from Genesis, the first book of the Bible.

"The basic meaning of the word, Genesis," he said, "is **birth, beginning,** or **origin.** The book of Genesis, in effect tells us how all things had their **origin, beginning,** or **birth.** And the very first words of Genesis say, '**In the beginning** God created the heaven and the earth. And the earth was *without form,* and *void*; and *darkness was upon the face of the deep.*'" Genesis 1:1-2

Judas fumed in sullen disapproval. Finally he cried out bitterly against Jed's reading of the Bible. "We don't believe the Bible! Don't you understand that? You cannot use the Bible as evidence in your defense!"

"On the contrary!" Jed shot back. "The evidence given in the Bible, that the Bible is true, is so convincing that all men know it is true. But evil men harden their hearts against their convictions of the truth of the Bible because they do not want to serve God. Their reason and conscience agree with the Bible, but they resist the truth of the Bible because they do not want to submit to God's rule over them.

"And now Judas, I beg of you, even though you may have hardened your heart forever against God and his truth—there are others here who may open their hearts to God. So please allow me to read from the Scriptures, without interruption, and let me make my defense before these men who need to hear the Word of God and be saved."

Jed Truly paused for just a moment, and then continued. "Now, as I was about to say, God's work in the heaven and on the earth was not yet finished—the earth he had created still needed work—it was still **without form,** and **void**; and **darkness** was upon the face of the deep. So *God made light to shine out of darkness* on that same first day."

Jed paused for emphasis, and then continued. "*God made light to shine out of darkness. And God divided the light from the darkness* and *made day and night*—**all on that same first day**. And he did it **three days before he created the sun, the moon, and the stars**!

"God can do anything! Nothing is impossible with him.

"You need to know that! You need to know that God can do anything. That nothing is impossible with him. That he is omnipotent. That he works miracles, and that all his creative works are supernatural and miraculous. And that you are not trifling with a puny little man like yourself when you say, 'He does not exist.' But you are trifling with the Creator of the universe who will one day be your judge!

"So, you need to know that on the very first day of creation *God brought light out of darkness*—a supernatural feat that was naturally impossible. For the sun, moon, and stars did not yet exist.

"I repeat this because it destroys that ridiculous teaching of yours, called the 'Big Bang.' That is, the teaching that the universe has to be millions and even billions of years old. (12 to 20 billion years old by one account—15 to 18 billion years old by another account—and exactly 13.7 billion years old by another account!)

"The Bible account in Genesis of the miraculous creation of light upon the earth three days before any of the stars were created tells us that the billions of years for the light from some of the distant stars to reach earth, is not, and never was necessary!

"And anyone, with any intelligence at all, knows, that if God can create light on the earth three days before he has created the sun, moon, and stars, that he can create the light from the stars upon the earth at the same moment that he creates the stars! Or even three days before he creates the stars if he wants to! God didn't have to wait billions of years for the light from some of the stars to reach the earth. God created light on the earth, and day and night upon the earth three days before the sun, moon, and stars were even created!

"Every one of the works of God in the six days of Creation were supernatural works. And God has never discontinued his supernatural works. God is the same miracle worker today as he was when he created the heaven and the earth."

NEW TESTAMENT MIRACLES

"The Lord Jesus Christ fed a multitude with a boy's lunch of five barley loaves and two small fishes. John 6:9-14

"He walked on water. Matthew 14:22-33

"He turned water into wine. John 2:7-11

"He healed the sick, the lame, the infirm. The gospels

"He made the dumb to speak. He gave sight to the blind. The gospels

"He raised Lazarus from the dead. John, chapter eleven

"He died for our sins, and on the third day rose again from the dead. I Corinthians 15:3-4

"40 days after his resurrection, while his disciples beheld, he was taken up into heaven. This same Jesus who was taken up into heaven, will come again to reward his saints and punish the wicked. II Thessalonians 1:7-9

"He will destroy the **heavens** and the **earth**. II Peter 3:7, 10

"He will **create a new heaven and a new earth**. II Peter 3:13-14

"He will sit upon a great white throne to judge the world. The ungodly will be cast into the lake of fire and brimstone. And the godly will be taken up into heaven. Revelation 20:11-15

"What is heaven like? Not at all like the old heaven and earth.

'And I saw a **new heaven** and a **new earth**: for the first heaven and the first earth were passed away; and there was no more sea....And I heard a great voice out of heaven saying, Behold, the tabernacle of God is with men, and he will dwell with them, and they shall be his people, and God himself shall be with them, and be their God. And God shall wipe away all tears from their eyes; and there shall be **no more**

death, neither sorrow, nor crying, neither shall there be any more pain: for the former things are passed away….And I saw no temple therein: for the Lord God Almighty and the Lamb are the temple of it. And the city *had no need of the sun, neither of the moon, to shine in it*: for the **glory of God did lighten it**, and the **Lamb is the light thereof.**' Revelation 21:1, 3-4, 21-23

'And he showed me a pure river of water of life, clear as crystal, proceeding out of the throne of God and of the Lamb….and on either side of the river, was there the tree of life, which bare twelve manner of fruits, and yielded her fruit every month: and the leaves of the tree were for the healing of the nations. And there shall be no more curse: but the throne of God and of the Lamb shall be in it; and his servants shall serve him: and they shall see his face; and his name shall be in their foreheads. And there shall be no night there; and **they need no candle, neither light of the sun**; for the Lord God giveth them light: and they shall reign forever and ever.' Revelation 22:1-5

Chapter LXXIV
A Few Of God's First Miracles

GOD HAS ALWAYS WORKED MIRACLES

"God saved Enoch from the world of sin, wickedness and violence that filled the earth in his time. He **walked with God** for 300 years, and then **was translated bodily to heaven!** **Enoch never died!** Genesis 5:21-24, Hebrews 11:5, and Jude 14-15

"God sent a worldwide flood **to destroy every living thing on the earth** because of the sin, wickedness, and violence that filled the earth at that time. He commanded Noah, a **man who walked with God**, to build an ark for the salvation of himself and his immediate family. Genesis 6:1-22, II Peter 2:5

"God rained fire and brimstone upon Sodom and Gomorrah because of the wickedness of its inhabitants. Genesis 19:24-25

"God **spoke to Moses out of a burning bush**, worked **three miracles** before him, and then **sent Moses with these three miracles to deliver his people from slavery in Egypt.** Exodus 3:2-4

"God judged Egypt with **ten miraculous plagues** because Pharaoh would not let God's people go. Finally, Pharaoh did let the children of Israel go, **after the tenth plague**. But he later repented, and pursued them with his horses and chariots. He overtook them encamped by the Red Sea. With the Egyptians behind them, and the Red Sea before them, they needed a miracle. So God **parted the Red Sea and took his people through on DRY GROUND**—and destroyed all the Egyptians who followed them! Exodus 14:13-31

OTHER MIRACLES!

"God led his people in the wilderness with a pillar of fire by night, and with a pillar of cloud by day—**for forty years**!

"God gave Israel bread from heaven (mana) six days a week **for forty years** in the desert!

"He gave them water from a rock to quench their thirst, when there was no water in the desert!

Chapter LXXV
God Created Man In His Own Image And Likeness

"Jed was not concerned at all for the time he was taking in reading the Bible. He was not concerned that the panel of jurors might turn against him for reading from the Bible. He had no concern at all about his Bible reading; for he knew the power of the Word of God to convert the soul.

> 'For the word of God is quick, and powerful, and sharper than any two-edged sword, *piercing even to the dividing asunder of soul and spirit*, and of the joints and marrow, and is a *discerner of the thoughts and intents of the heart.*' Hebrews 4:12

"Now," said Jed, "let's go on with the creation account in Genesis. And we will look especially at the sixth day, in which **God created man** *in his own image and likeness*.

"For if it can be shown (and it can) that all men have the *image and likeness of God in them*, and that *none of the animals do*. Then this will prove beyond a shadow of a doubt that the evolution account of man is false, and that the Bible account of man is true!

"Now, let's look quickly through days two, three, four, five and six of creation:

"On day two, God did works of creation both in **heaven** and on **earth**. He created a firmament in the midst of the waters that were upon the earth, and divided the waters which were under the firmament from the waters which were above the firmament and called the firmament Heaven. Genesis 1:6-8

"On day three, God gathered the waters under the **heaven** together into one place, so that the **dry land appeared**. And God called the dry land Earth, and the gathering together of waters God called Seas. And, then, on the same day God created the first life upon the earth—all the plant life—the grasses, and herbs, and fruit trees. And God said that there was **no evolution** from one species of plant life to a different species of plant life, and **no evolution** from any species of plant life into a bird or a fish or an animal. But that every species of plant life would bring forth only after its own kind. Genesis 1:9-13

"On day four, God created the sun, moon, and stars. Gen. 1:14-19

"On day five, God created the fishes, and great whales, and all the living things that swim in the seas, and all the winged fowl that fly above the earth, which *all bring forth after their own kind*. Again, we see that there was no evolution! Each species brought forth after its own kind! A bird could only bring forth a bird, and nothing else! A fish could only bring forth a fish, and nothing else. Genesis 1:20-23

"On day six, God created the animals, *which all brought forth after their own kind*! And they all still bring forth after their own kind today! A hippopotamus always brings forth a hippopotamus! Always! A zebra always brings forth a zebra! An ape always brings forth an ape! Always! An ape never brings forth a man! It is impossible for an ape to bring forth a man.

"For man is **fundamentally different** from all the animals. As different as a clump of **grass** is different from a **cow**. And as different as a grove of **trees** is different from **birds and bees**.

"The *difference between a man, and any of the animals, is so fundamental*, that it is foolishness, nay, it is insanity, to speak of man descending from the apes!

"For after God had created all the animals, he said:

'Let us make man **IN OUR OWN IMAGE, AFTER OUR LIKENESS**: and let them have dominion over the fish of the sea, and over the fowl of the air, and over the cattle, and over all the earth, and over every creeping thing that creepeth upon the earth. So **GOD CREATED MAN IN HIS OWN IMAGE, IN THE IMAGE OF GOD CREATED HE HIM; MALE AND FEMALE CREATED HE THEM.** And God blessed them, and God said unto them, Be fruitful, and multiply, and replenish the earth, and subdue it: and have dominion over the fish of the sea, and over the fowl of the air, and over every living thing that moveth upon the earth.' Genesis 1:26-28

"Men, please listen to me! All of you who hear my voice today!

WE KNOW THAT THE BIBLE IS THE WORD OF GOD because man is created completely different from the animals. Man is created in the very image and likeness of God. He is endowed by his Creator with a rational, moral nature like God. He is able to think and reason and know. He is able to create, like his Creator. The history of man's creative genius on the earth is a history of ever more astounding inventions and creations!

"He is able to know God, and walk with God, and have fellowship with God. For he is created in the image of God, with the law of God written in his heart, and with a conscience that directs him in the path of righteousness.

"And we are all conscious of the fact that man alone rules over all the members of the animal kingdom, and has dominion over all the animals upon the earth—just as God commanded him to do. What greater evidence could there be that the Bible is the Word of God!

"None of the plants have ever ruled over man! Not one tomato plant, not one peanut plant, not one tree has ever ruled over man! The elephant, the hippopotamus, the zebra, the giraffe, and the monkey have never ruled over man. We shut them up in our zoos so our children can see some of the animals God has created. Not a creature in all of creation has ever ruled over man!

"Man is created completely different from all the animals! None of the animals are created **in the image and likeness of God!**

Chapter LXXVI
Rhetorical Questions

"A few rhetorical questions to all of you who are here!

"Do you know any **rational** animals? Animals that have a **rational mind** like man? Animals that can think and reason like man?

"Do you know any animals with a **conscience** like man? Animals that have the **law of God written in their hearts** so that they **know right from wrong, good from evil, and justice from injustice?**

"Do you know any animals that can **talk** or **read** or **write** like man?

"Do you know any animals that can **write a book,** or **publish a newspaper,** or **broadcast around the world on radio or television?**

"Do you know any animals that can **think** and **reason** and **argue** and **preach** as I am doing right now?

And again, do you know any animals that can **argue,** and **reason** and **speak** and **teach** as **YOU DO** here at the University of One Mile Circle? If not, why not? Is it not because they are animals only; and not men as you are, **created in the image and likeness of God?**

"Do you know any **animals that can create?** Animals that can create pins, and needles, and zippers, and saws, and hammers, and nails, and homes, and skyscrapers, and factories, and tractors, and farming equipment, and cars, and trucks, and trains, and ships, and submarines! Do you know any animals that can create alphabets, and talk and read and write, and study languages, and write books? And compose music, and teach music, and create musical instruments, and play them? Do you know any animals that can make a computer? Do you know any animals that can generate electricity, and make light bulbs, and candles, and matches? Do you know any animals that can create medicines and drugs? Animals that can build X-ray, CAT scan, and MRI machines? Do you know any animals that can make fuels, and make the vehicles that use those fuels? Animals that can make airplanes, and space vehicles; and animals that can 'man' those same space vehicles?

"Do you know any animals that can study and discover the physical laws of the universe? Do you know any animals that can study law and government? Do you know any animals that become Judges, and Prosecutors, and Defense Lawyers? Do you know any animals that know God, talk with God, walk with God, and have fellowship with God?

"No! Of course not! Because none of the animals are created in the image and likeness of God!

"Man, created in God's image, is a free moral agent. When God created man, he endowed him with a rational mind, with free moral agency—something that none of the animals have!

"Man, created in the image of God, is **free**! He has a **conscience**! The **law of God** is written in his heart. None of the animals have a conscience! None of the animals have the law of God written in their heart! None of the animals are moral agents. None of the animals are free. Everything they do, they do by instinct.

"Man, created in the image of God, is **responsible and accountable**. He is **free to do as he wills**, but is **responsible and accountable** for how he uses the freedom God has given him! None of the animals are responsible and accountable! When they kill another animal for food, they are not murderers. They have no feelings of remorse for what they have done. They have no compunctions of conscience as man has. Everything they do, they do by instinct.

"Man, created in the image of God, has a **sensibility like God**. He has **feelings**.

"**Plants have no feelings at all**. Men can chop down a tree, and the tree feels nothing, sees nothing, hears nothing, and knows nothing.

"Some of the animals have limited sensibilities: such as slugs, snails, and worms. But many animals have a full range of sensibilities—they can see, hear, smell, touch, and taste.

"But only man, created in the image and likeness of God, has a sensibility exactly like God! Man has a **sixth sense**, a **moral sense**, A SENSE THAT ONLY MORAL BEINGS HAVE! This **moral sense** makes men feel intense pain or hurt when someone says or does something hateful or mean to them.

"The moral pain or hurt given in man's moral sensibility can be felt without him even being touched by the person who hurts him! Just a hateful word or a hateful look can be so devastating that it will drive the person hated to commit suicide! Have you never heard of the divorce case in which the **husband or the wife commits suicide because of the cruel hatred and rejection of the other**?

"On the other hand **man's moral sensibility** can bring inexpressible joy to his heart as well. Have you never heard of (or experienced) the inexpressible joy and gladness that comes to your heart, when the girl you love tells you she loves you and will be your wife?

"**Man knows** he is not like the dumb beasts of the field. He knows that the gulf between the non-rational, non-moral, brute beasts; and rational, moral man is so vast, it could never be bridged by a silly thing called evolution.

"The theory that man evolved from a non-rational, non-moral, non-free, non-responsible, brute beast into a free and responsible, rational, moral man is so obviously impossible that it is ridiculous and laughable on the face of it.

"The very fact that men are **free moral agents**, and **have moral government over themselves**—and the **beast of the field do not**—is irrefutable proof of the fact that there exists a vast gulf between man and the animals that could never be bridged by evolution.

"Now let's look at a few verses of Scripture in Genesis that speak of the man that God had created in his own image:

'So God created man in his own image, in the image of God created he him; male and female created he them. And God blessed them, and **God said unto them**, be fruitful, and multiply, and replenish the earth, and subdue it: and have dominion over the fish of the sea, and over the fowl of the air, and over every living thing that moveth upon the earth.' Genesis 1:27-28

"Men, did you hear what I just read? **God spoke to the man and the woman** just as if they could understand him! I know he never spoke to an ape, a monkey, an elephant, or a zebra and expected them to understand his words!

"But let's read some more:

'And the Lord God took the man, and put him in the Garden of Eden to dress it and to keep it.' Genesis 2:15

"Men, did you hear that? God took the man, and put him in the Garden of Eden to dress it and to keep it! I don't have to guess why he didn't put an animal in the garden to dress it and keep it! I know why! None of the animals were either **physically** or **rationally** equipped to take care of a garden! Only man has both the **physical and rational endowments** to do the work of a horticulturist.

1. "The hands of man, with **opposable thumbs**, are **physical marvels**. They exactly meet all the needs of his rational mind, equipping him to create and make everything his rational mind requires of them.

2. "The **whole body** of man, with **perfect erect stance**, and two **amazing feet**, that enable him to stand **perfectly balanced**, yet bend over, turn, twist, walk, run, climb, swim, etc.—Is so fashioned by God that he is able to do practically any work he wants to do. For man can twist, turn, and manipulate his body into almost any shape he wants to, to do his work. But what could a man do, if he had four hooves for hands and feet, as the horses have? His rational mind would be wasted on a body that could do nothing.

"But as we read further, we find that man did several other things that distinguish him from the animals. **He talked!** He talked with God, and he talked with other men! He **created** musical instruments and he **played them!** And he **taught** others his arts and crafts. He **mined** and **smelted** ore! He **invented** implements to till the earth! He **farmed!** He **raised sheep and cattle!** He **used horses and other animals** to work the ground. He **built cities**. Genesis chapters two and three

"But the God-given faculty that enables man to talk and express his

thinking and reasoning through **rational speech**, is the God-given faculty that distinguish man from the animals more than any other!

WHAT IS MAN?

"Man is the **image** and **likeness of God**, with sensibility, intellect,
reason, conscience, and free will. Man is endowed with all the faculties
and powers of moral agency. He knows right from wrong. The law of
God is written in his heart. He is free and knows himself to be free.
His conscience approves his right conduct and condemns his wrong
conduct.

"All men, everywhere, have these same moral faculties and powers.
A heathen man may be ignorant and primitive in many ways, but he has
a **conscience** and the **law of God is written in his heart**. His
conscience approves his right conduct and condemns his wrong
conduct. He has the same moral consciousness of right and wrong that
any man who knows the Bible has. The Bible says:

> 'For when the Gentiles, which have not the law (have not the
> written law or the Bible), **do by nature** the things contained
> in the law, these, having not the law, are a law unto
> themselves: which show the work of the **law written in their
> hearts**, their **conscience also bearing witness**, and **their
> thoughts** the meanwhile **accusing or else excusing one
> another**; in the day when God shall judge the secrets of men
> by Jesus Christ according to my gospel.' Romans 2:14-16

"Nevertheless, wicked men still deny that right and wrong are the
innate revelations of their nature. They claim that they are merely
learned convictions acquired through Bible reading, or through the
influence of the civilized society they live in.

"But in spite of what wicked men may say, the fact remains that **all
men know** right from wrong, good from evil, and justice from injustice
without the influences of society or the teachings of the Bible. They
know them by the **innate revelation of their God-given nature**; and
they know them **without the Bible**.

"Let me illustrate:

- "Suppose I come down to one of you right now and punch you in the nose! Would you need to be acquainted with the Bible to know I had wronged you? I think not! For you have a **conscience** that tells you without the Bible that I have wronged you! What man ever needed the Bible to know that murder, and rape are wrong? Do you need the Bible to know it is wrong for a person to insult you, lie about you, or abuse you in some other way? Could any society convince itself through education that it is really right to hate, lie, steal, rape, and murder—or that it is wrong to love your neighbor and do good to him? To maintain that hatred, murder, lying, stealing, and every other kind of meanness and injustice are wrong only in the eyes of those who have been taught to frown upon them is sublimely ridiculous.

- "This is because right and wrong are **first truths of reason**. They **are self-evident truths** derived or given to us from our nature and relations as moral beings, and not from the philosophy, teaching, or arbitrary will of society. Right and wrong do not even come from the arbitrary will of God. For if the arbitrary will of God made law right, then God could command any law to be right. He could command: 'Thou shalt hate, lie, and steal. Thou shalt be selfish, and seek the misery and unhappiness of thy neighbor.' And upon the supposition that God's arbitrary will made law right, it would be right to lie, steal, hate, and do everything possible to make mankind miserable and unhappy. But **God's law is declaratory**. He has **declared** to us the **law of our nature**. He has **declared** to us the same law he has written in our hearts.

- "Jesus recognized that all men have the **law of God written in their hearts**, when he gave the Golden Rule: 'And whatsoever ye would that men should do to you, do ye even so to them: for this is the law and the prophets.' Matthew 7:12 If men did not have a common knowledge of right and wrong revealed to them **in their nature**, they could not obey the Golden Rule; because obedience to the Golden Rule depends upon an innate knowledge, common to all men, of right conduct toward others.

- "The claim that morality is only a changing thing, which is established by the particular society in existence, has missed the point. For what a man will do, and the convictions of his conscience are two different things. For instance, a man may be a thief and a liar. But if someone steals from him will he say, 'I just love it when people steal from me.' Or what liar would ever say, 'I'm so happy when people tell lies about me.' And what murderer would ever say, 'There's nothing wrong with murder. If someone tried to murder me, I would put up no resistance at all.'

- "If there were no common standard of right and wrong revealed to man in his nature, moral government over man could not exist. In fact, moral government over man would be ridiculous, were it not for man's moral nature: as ridiculous as a moral government over animals. The very fact that men do have moral government over themselves shows that men know themselves to be moral agents and responsible. It shows that they have innate convictions of right and wrong, and that they have a conscious knowledge of responsibility and accountability.

- "It is a known fact that human government is judged to be unjust, if it legislates arbitrarily and imposes unjust penalties. This fact shows that there is an ultimate standard of right and wrong, a law revealed in our nature, which all men know and appeal to. For instance, let a judge decide that he wants to sentence a convicted murderer to one day in jail, and see if society does not rise up as one man to denounce the injustice of the sentence! But what does society appeal to in pronouncing the sentence unjust? Of course, it appeals to that self-evident standard of right and wrong, which is revealed to all men in their nature.

- "Or suppose that a new government comes into power, and all the laws of the land are repealed overnight, and are replaced by new laws such as the following: "It is a felony, punishable by life imprisonment, to do anything good for your neighbor. Therefore, all citizens are required by law to seek the misery and hurt of others. Those who resist this new law, appealing to the Golden Rule given by Jesus, will suffer the death penalty. For there is no such thing as an absolute standard of right and wrong, but all men's convictions of right and wrong are merely the result of education and environment, and can be changed at will. Therefore all citizens who are imprisoned for past crimes will now be set free, and all citizens who will devote their lives to selfishness and seeking the misery of others will have the favor of this government. Now this supposition is **ludicrous**. But it would not seem ludicrous at all were it not for the innate convictions of right and wrong in all men which makes them see it as ludicrous. The very fact that it is so **obviously ludicrous to everyone** shows that everyone has the same innate convictions of right and wrong.

- "Language shows that all men have the same innate ideas of justice, right and wrong, and accountability. Words such as sin, wickedness, justice, injustice, right, wrong, good, evil, obligation, accountability, innocence, and guilt, are just a few of the words which men use to express innate moral concepts that all men have. Man's language is a mirror of his rational moral nature!

- "Novelists know that all men have the same standard of right and wrong revealed to them in their nature. They do not write different novels for the wicked than they do for the righteous. The reason is that both wicked men and good men have the same standard of right and wrong revealed to them in their nature. It is not necessary for a novelist to write two versions of his novel, one for good men and another for bad men. For to write a novel in which the hero is evil and unjust would offend the conscience of both wicked and good men. The hero of the novel is never described as an evil man. He is always described as a good man, a just man, and a courageous man. And when the reader (even the reader who is wicked and unjust) sees that the hero is just and fights against evil, he will identify with him and experience satisfaction when he finally triumphs. Wicked men do not identify with the villain, because their irresistible convictions of justice, by a law of necessity cause them to take sides with righteousness, justice, and goodness. The truth is that all men, whatever their character, have a common awareness of right and wrong. God has written his law in the hearts of all men!

- "The fact that men will deny the wrong they have done shows that they recognize an absolute standard of right and wrong. For instance, a man is accused of lying, cheating, and stealing. If the accusation is true, why does he deny it? It can only be that he knows that what he has done is wrong, He would have no reason to deny it, if he did not know it to be wrong.

- "The fact that all men blame other men for their wrongdoing shows that all men have the law of God written in their hearts. All men resent unjust treatment. If anyone abuses then with degrading or filthy language, they will be offended and blame the one who has abused them. And they will blame the one who has wronged them even if they know that they themselves are guilty of the same wrongdoing. A man may be a liar, a thief, and a cheat himself, but he still judges those attributes as wrong in others that do wrong to him.

- "Man's whole system of **human government**, with its law and its penalty for the broken law, is **founded and built upon the common awareness of right and wrong written in the heart of every man**. Without this common awareness, human government would not and could not exist. Human government, with its laws, penalties, police forces, courts, judges, etc., gives mute testimony to the fact that all men know themselves to be moral agents and fully responsible and accountable for all their deeds.

"Man is created as more than one of the dumb beasts of the field. Man is an intelligent rational spirit. He is able to know God, commune with God and have fellowship with God. How noble is the nature that God has given man! How glorious are his powers and faculties as a moral being, created in the image and likeness of God! How lofty is his position by creation; but how criminally low he has fallen! He has fallen from the glorious position of a child of God to the perverted position of a devil. Man is a child of God by creation, but a child of the devil by choice! 'We are **God's offspring**.' Acts 17:29 '**Ye are gods**; and all of you are the **children of the most High.** But ye shall die like men (because of your sins), and fall like one of the princes.' Psalm 82:6-7

"The Bible represents man to be just exactly what he **knows himself to be**, and that is why **man cannot escape the conviction that the Bible is the Word of God**!

"The Bible represents man as being endowed by God with faculties and powers that enable him to know and do right, but who has sinned against the truth revealed to him in his nature. It represents him as having resisted reason, trampled on conscience, and abused free moral agency. And, it represents man as being under God's **JUST WRATH** for resisting, abusing, and perverting the good nature God created him with.

"I will read from the Bible now where it tells of the **wrath and judgment of God** against men who resist the truth of God revealed to them in their nature.

'For the **wrath of God** is revealed from heaven against all ungodliness and unrighteousness of men, who hold (hold back, suppress, restrain) the truth in unrighteousness; because that which may be known of God is manifest in them; for **God hath showed it unto them.** For **the invisible things of him from the creation of the world are clearly seen**, being understood by the things that are made, even his eternal power and Godhead; **so that they are without excuse.**' Romans 1:18-20

"Man's nature (his reason) **reveals to him that there is a Creator!** And man's nature (his conscience) **reveals to him that he has sinned, and is accountable and guilty for his sins.**

'WHEN THEY KNEW GOD, they glorified him not as God, neither were thankful; but became vain in their imaginations, and their foolish heart was darkened....And even as they **DID NOT LIKE TO RETAIN GOD IN THEIR KNOWLEDGE**, God gave them over to a **REPROBATE MIND**, to do those things which are not convenient; being filled with all unrighteousness, fornication, wickedness, covetousness, maliciousness; full of envy, murder, debate, deceit, malignity; whisperers, backbiters, **HATERS OF GOD**, despiteful, proud, boasters, inventors of evil things, disobedient to parents, without understanding, covenant-breakers, without natural affection, implacable, unmerciful: **WHO KNOWING THE JUDGMENT OF GOD**, that they which do such things are worthy of death, not only do the same, but have pleasure in them that do them.' Rom. 1:21-32

"Sinners, who are **abandoned by God** and **given up to a REPROBATE MIND** (verse 28), go on in their sins, and take pleasure in others who do the same!

'WHO KNOWING THE JUDGMENT OF GOD, that they which commit such things are worthy of death, not only do the same, but have pleasure in them that do them.' Romans 1:32

"Then Paul **singles out the Jews**, who had the additional revelation of the law of God, given by Moses, and were not keeping it. Telling them that they also would fall under the wrath of God for their sins:

'And **thinketh thou this**, O man…**that thou shalt escape the judgment of God?**….But after thy hardness and impenitent heart **treasurest up unto thyself wrath** against the **day of wrath** and revelation of the righteous judgment of God; who will render to every man according to his deeds: to them who by patient continuance in well-doing seek for glory and honor and immortality, eternal life: but unto them that are contentious, and do not obey the truth, but obey unrighteousness, indignation and wrath, tribulation and anguish, upon every soul of man that doeth evil, of the **JEW FIRST**, and **ALSO OF THE GENTILE.**' Romans 2:2-9

"And Paul concludes, declaring **both Jews and Gentiles** guilty and accountable for their sins.

'For as many as have sinned **without law** (the Gentiles) shall also perish without law. And as many as have sinned in the law (the Jews) shall be judged by the law; (for not the **hearers** of the law are just before God, but the **doers** of the law shall be justified. For when the **Gentiles**, which have not the law, **do by nature** the things contained in the law, these, having not the law, are a law unto themselves. Which show the work of the *law written in their hearts*, their *conscience* also bearing witness, and *their thoughts* the meanwhile *accusing* or else *excusing* one another;) in the day *when God shall judge the secrets of men* by Jesus Christ according to my gospel.' Romans 2:12-16

"God will judge the **secrets of all men** on the judgment day. He will judge the secrets of men who have had only the revelation of God given in their nature. And God will judge the **secrets of men** who have had both the revelation of God, in their nature, and the additional revelation of God given in the Bible.

"Thank God for the additional revelation God has given to us in the Bible. **For all of us have sinned against God and are condemned to everlasting punishment in hell for our sins!** But the Bible tells us that **God gave his only begotten Son Jesus Christ to suffer and die on the cross, for our sins, to make an atonement for us.**

'For God so loved the world, that **he gave his only begotten Son**, that whosoever believeth in him should not perish, but have everlasting life.' John 3:16

"Oh, dear friends, do you know that the heathen, who have never heard the gospel of salvation through Jesus Christ, will be punished with a punishment much more tolerable than yours? For the heathen have no knowledge of salvation! They have only the revelation of nature. They know nothing about the Savior. But you do know about the Savior!

"And if you reject Jesus Christ, the Savior, you have not only trampled under foot the law of God written in your heart! You have also trampled under foot the Savior, who suffered and died on the cross to save you from your sins!

340

Chapter LXXVII
"The Work Of Justice Must Go On."

Jed was finished! He picked up the Bible, and was about to pick up the candle and take it back with him, when he realized that the whole assembly had come alive with unrestrained talk. Jed paused a moment, wondering about such conduct being allowed in a court of law—then, picking up the candle, he made his way down to where his counsel sat.

He leaned over and whispered to Pastor Truelove, "Pastor, I am finished with my defense."

"Sit down," replied Pastor Truelove. "Something is wrong. Something is terribly wrong, and I don't know what to do."

The Pastor's words and grave demeanor, and the fact that the talk going on throughout the whole assembly was continuing to increase in volume and was now wholly unrestrained, alerted Jed to the fact that something very serious had happened that he was not aware of.

Pastor Truelove now turned to Jed, and, raising his voice, said, "Did you know that Professor Judas and Dean Allotrope are not with us any more? Did you know that they have both vacated their places, and have been gone now for some thirty or forty minutes?"

Pastor Truelove did not wait for Jed's answer, but continued to speak, "But I believe God, brother Truly. Let us pray for God to give us favor with the people here at the University of One Mile Circle. Pray with me brother Truly, and I will appeal to them to act rationally and judiciously according to the circumstances that have been thrust upon us."

Jed Truly agreed to pray with Pastor Truelove; and they both went to their knees and began to call upon God. Their prayer was not prolonged, and the assembly, taking note that they were praying, quickly quieted down and became silent.

Then Pastor Truelove stood up and began to address them: "Men and brethren," he said, "the work of justice must go on even though Professor Judas and Dean Allotrope are no longer here. They seem to have abdicated their responsibilities as officers of this court. For they are no longer here, and they have been gone now for some forty minutes!

"This is highly irregular!

"In fact, all the proceedings of this court have been irregular from the very beginning!

"ARTICLE 1, Section 9 of the CONSTITUTION OF THE UNITED STATES says, 'No ex post facto Law shall be passed.' But all we Christians and preachers were charged by Dean Allotrope with criminal conduct just for being here without an invitation. But is there a law that makes it a capital crime to be here without an invitation? If there is such a law, we have a right to see the legal document produced here in court that affirms it!

"Again, ARTICLE 1, Section 9 of the CONSTITUTION OF THE UNITED STATES says, 'The Privilege of the Writ of Habeas Corpus shall not be suspended.' But, brethren, it has been suspended in this court from the very beginning! Dean Allotrope has never brought charges against any of the accused here in open court. He brought no charges in open court against the youth. And he has brought no charges in open court against my client, Jed Truly. Since no charges have been made against my client, he should be set free immediately! For we have the privilege and the right of Habeas Corpus according to ARTICLE 1, Section 9 of the Constitution. And for the same reason, all those who are yet to be tried should be set free immediately—for the officer who arrested them is not here in court to charge them with the crime for which they are being held.

"But the greatest irregularity of all was the illegal appointment by Dean Allotrope of Professor Judas to this court as Judge—making him, in effect, both Prosecutor and Judge! This appointment makes a mock of justice, and shows clearly that there was collusion between Dean Allotrope and Professor Judas to convict innocent preachers and believers simply because they believe the truths of the Bible.

"For these four reasons—and for two reasons more that I will soon set before you—my client, Jed Truly, and the other defendants in this court should all be set free immediately.

"But, we have a problem! A grave problem, which we did not bring upon ourselves! It was thrust upon us by Dean Allotrope and Professor Judas!

"The problem is this: Now that Dean Allotrope and Professor Judas have abdicated their responsibilities as officers of this court, do we just let justice come to a halt? Or do we go forward soberly and judiciously, yet expeditiously to arrive at a just verdict in the trials of Jed Truly and the rest of my clients?

"Men and brethren, we cannot do the former; and, we must do the latter!

"For Amendment VI, of the AMENDMENTS TO THE CONSTI-TUTION OF THE UNITED STATES OF AMERICA, demands it and guarantees it. Amendment VI says: 'In **all criminal prosecutions**, the accused shall enjoy the right to a **speedy** and **public trial**, by an **impartial jury** of the **State and district** wherein the crime shall have been committed;…to **be informed of the nature and cause of the accusation**; to **be confronted with the witnesses against him**; to have **compulsory process for obtaining witnesses in his favor**, and to have the assistance of **counsel for his defense.**'

"You see," men and brethren, "Why you must not let this trial languish and come to a halt. The accused has a right to a **speedy** and **public** trial!

"The accused also has a right to a **public trial** by an **impartial jury** of the **State and district** wherein the crime shall have been committed. But this trial is not a public trial! It is a secret trial! The State and the district wherein this crime was alleged to have been committed have not even been notified, and they know nothing of what is going on here. If they did know, they would put an end to it, and prosecute those who are responsible!

"This **secret trial** is also far from a **public trial** with an **impartial jury** guaranteed by the Sixth Amendment. For Professor Judas was made both Prosecutor and Judge **by the mere fiat** of Dean Allotrope. And then Professor Judas attempted to declare the guilty, innocent, and the innocent, guilty **by mere fiat**—until an eighth grader pointed out that it was unlawful under the Constitution for him to do so.

"The only right that has been allowed to my client, is the right of counsel for his defense.

"But, finally, the Fifth Amendment gives two important guarantees to every person accused of a **capital crime**. The first guarantee is that no person accused of a capital crime can be prosecuted for his crime unless he is indicted by a Grand Jury. (And you know there has been no Grand Jury indictment of any of my clients.) The second guarantee in the Fifth Amendment is the right of 'due process.' It says, 'Nor shall any person ...be deprived of life, liberty, or property without **due process** of law.' This simply means that the court cannot suspend or take away any of the rights given in the Constitution to those accused of crimes!

"Now, " men and brethren, "what will you do?

"I have made my case. I have outlined to the best of my ability why my client Jed truly, and all my other clients, who have not yet been tried, should be detained no longer; but should be set free immediately.

"Will you do it? I appeal to you—you who are the twelve members of this jury. Set us free! We have committed no crime. Will you do justice by us?

"I thank God that justice has been done up until now!

"The youth who committed the terrible crime of murder pled guilty, and asked for mercy—if possible. And you saw fit to grant them clemency—but with a sentence severe enough to make them, and all those who witnessed the trial, understand that this court could never justly exonerate them for their crime. Their sentence was justice mixed with mercy. And I thank God for the sentence you handed down. And I have pledged myself to carry it out in the Bright Regions according to the wishes of this court.

"Now, let justice continue. For we have committed no crime. Set us free, I beg of you who are the twelve jurors in this trial, set us free, and we will be on our way back to the Bright Regions, after we take these five Christians home!

Will you? Will you set us free?

Chapter LXXVIII
Judas Attempts To Murder Jed Truly

Professor Judas stood with his eyes closed against the light of the single candle where Jed Truly stood preaching. He groaned as Jed Truly launched his series of rhetorical questions. He continued to groan, and groaned more deeply and bitterly as Jed continued the rhetorical questions, and began the many proofs that man is created completely different from the animals.

Finally, he could no longer endure the bitterness of soul that the compelling arguments of Jed Truly caused him. Slowly he backed away from his lectern. He reached for his gun, pulled it out, and pointed it directly at the broad back of Jed truly. "At this distance, I can't miss," he thought.

Dean Allotrope was seated just a step behind Judas. He saw the gun pointed at Jed Truly's back, and sprang to Judas's side. "What are you doing with that gun?" he demanded in a whisper that was barely audible. He caught Judas's arm and forced it strait up into the air. Then the two of them stood, locked in their positions, straining against each other, and glaring into each other's eyes.

Finally, Dean Allotrope spoke in a rasping voice, "I've told you again and again, don't ever kill anyone when I'm with you."

"Let's go outside." responded Judas in a voice that was just above a whisper.

Outside, Dean Allotrope spoke to Judas with unrestrained anger. "What in the world do you think you are you doing? Have you gone mad? You can't shoot a man just because you don't like what he preaches."

"Yes, I can. I'm going to kill that preacher. He'll never be convicted. He's too good a debater. I've never heard anyone speak like him." And waving his gun around, Judas said, "I'm going to kill him!"

"Judas, give me that gun. I've told you not to use it when I'm with you."

"I've got it! And I'm going to keep it!"

"Judas, you're not going back in there! I'll stay right here to keep you out. Judas, just go on to the new tunnel, and wait for them there? They have to go back there to go home."

Judas glared at Dean Allotrope in silence, and they both sat down, carefully watching one another.

Presently Judas said, "I don't believe their story that they fell into the new tunnel from some place up above. I think they came into the tunnels from the Bright Regions."

"Well, why don't you go out to the Bright Regions and wait for them there?"

"Because I want to be here where I know they are; where I know I have a chance to kill them."

"If you don't leave right now, I'll warn them that you are waiting here to kill them! I will not allow you to kill anyone as long as we are together."

The two sat there in anger. One at the door to give warning to those within, and the other only a few steps away from the door, to shoot down the first preacher or Christian to come out.

Chapter LXXIX

The Verdict: Not Guilty

The twelve jurors did not seclude themselves. They stood in a circle, right where they were, and reached a unanimous verdict within five minutes.

The jury's verdict was: not guilty by reason of illegalities.

All were declared not guilty for the same reason—their rights under the Constitution of the United States of America had been denied, and their trial was illegal.

When the verdict was given, there was silence for a brief moment, and then a shout of jubilation erupted in the assembly hall.

Then, as the shouting died down, the door to the assembly hall opened, and the voice of Dean Allotrope cried out in warning: "Judas is out here with a gun! Watch out for him! He wants to kill the preachers and Christians! I don't know where he is right now. Watch out for him!"

Chapter LXXX
The Entire Underworld Escorts The Five Christians

Head Lighter Man held his torch high over his head as he walked cautiously down the tunnel toward the place where he had first laid eyes on the five Christians.

On his right walked Pastor Truelove, his eyes sweeping the area on either side of them.

Ahead of them walked the great mass of students and teachers from the assembly hall who had come to escort the five Christians safely home.

Ahead of them walked the twelve jurors, who had volunteered to go first, to escort the five Christians safely home.

Dean Allotrope had volunteered to go with the twelve jurors. Not because his heart was in it! (He wanted to be far away from the killings he expected.) But to protect his image, he gave in to the wishes of the jurors, and went with them.

And immediately behind Head Lighter Man and Pastor Truelove, came the five Christians who were on their way back home.

Behind the five Christians came the rest of the preachers and Christians who were with Pastor Truelove.

Finally, in the very rear, came the youth with the men they had nearly stoned to death. Some of these were crippled, and needed help. And the youth were helping them make their way down the tunnel.

Then, behind them, lurking in the shadows of the fourth and last turn in the tunnel, crouched Judas—with his gun drawn and pointed at the backs of those walking past him.

Judas stepped out of the shadows. But Judas was not a man to step lightly and carefully. And he made a noise; and was seen. The youth leader saw him, and quickly said to his companions, "Judas is right behind us with his gun drawn! Block his way if you can. I'm going ahead to warn the others."

Quickly he warned the preachers and Christians. And as they dispersed to either side, he stepped ahead to the five Christians—and warned them. Quickly he stepped from the five Christians to Head Lighter man and Pastor Truelove, and warned them.

Immediately, Pastor Truelove went into action. He turned to the five Christians who were still behind him and shouted angrily, "Didn't you hear what the youth leader said? Move! Move! Move, now! God doesn't want you to stay here and die like brave martyrs! Run through that mass of students and teachers up ahead and save yourselves! Go! Go! Run! Flee! Escape for your lives!"

And they did! Quickly they pushed their way through the mass of humanity that was before them, and were helped on their way, for the teachers and students saw that the five Christians were being pursued by Judas, who had his gun pointed in their direction.

But Judas was able to stay close behind the Christians. For many of those who opened the way for the Christians to pass through, only fled in fear of the gun in Judas' hand, and did nothing to obstruct his passage.

But, finally, the Christians—Jed Truly, Bob and Bill Becker, little Alice Becker, and John Frank—came to the end of the tunnel.

They looked up! There hung the buffer, just as it had hung some three days earlier. The words of the Holy Spirit now went through the mind of John Frank, "You know the way back home. Go back the way you came."

But now, Judas stepped quickly past the Dean of Education. He moved silently, until he stood close behind the five Christians. A smile of satisfaction crossed his face. All five of the Christians stood in a bunch before him. He had them now where he could easily kill them, one by one. He played the gun over their backs and began to gloat, so that all those who were close by could hear him: "I'm in no hurry. I've got plenty of time and plenty of ammunition. When my gun is empty, I have more bullets in my pocket." Then Judas spoke to Dean Allotrope, "Dean Allotrope, you told me not to kill anyone as long as you were around. But you're here. Why did you come?"

Dean Allotrope took one step toward Judas, but stopped when he saw the pistol pointed at him.

The jurors, and those close by wondered why the five Christians did not break and run at this opportune time. Instead, the Christians had their backs to Judas, and were not even paying attention to what he was saying.

The twins, one on each side of John Frank, had lifted him some four feet off the ground; (They wondered at the fact that they were able to lift him as if he were weightless) so that John Frank now had his hands on the handles of the buffer.

Next, Jed Truly wrapped his arms around John Frank's torso. Then little Alice crawled onto Jed Truly's back, and wrapped her arms around his neck. (She wondered at the fact that she had crawled up his back as if she were weightless.)

Suddenly the buffer came alive, and began to whir. But this was not what took them up!

What took them up, both them and the buffer, was a blinding, roaring, whirlwind of fire! And all those who were there saw it!

Christians shouted for joy when they saw and heard the blinding, roaring, whirlwind of fire take the five Christians up! And all the unbelievers cried out in awe when they saw the five Christians go up in the blinding, roaring, whirlwind of fire!

But Judas and Dean Allotrope did not! They cried out with an anguished scream of agony. For the same blinding, roaring, whirlwind of fire that had taken the five Christians up, descended upon them both, and burned them alive. They fell where they were; an example, to all those who witnessed their burning, of God's judgment upon stubborn, obstinate, intractable sinners.

Chapter LXXXI
Giddy With Gladness

Up, up, up they were carried by the blinding, roaring, whirlwind of fire. Until they and the buffer were deposited on the dining room floor on the very same spot from which they had been taken three days earlier.

They were entangled, but immediately rolled apart into separate entities. They got to a sitting position and looked about them.

The lights were still on.

The tables were still standing over to one side, piled high with chairs.

The buffer on which they had returned was there on the floor before them.

They were home!

They were giddy with gladness.

They jumped to their feet, and began to shout and dance for joy.

"How did you get in here?" a man shouted angrily. How did you sneak past me? And how did you get that buffer in here?"

A policeman stood at the foot of the stairs. He was angry. And he was angry because the intruders had gotten past him. And he knew it was impossible for intruders to get past him! What had happened? Ghosts might have gotten past him—but with a buffer, and in broad daylight?

He grabbed his radio transmitter. "Five intruders have gotten past me! They brought in a buffer! Send a force to arrest them!"

"Five intruders?"

"Yes, five intruders!"

"Are they armed?"

"I don't think so!"

"How could they get past you without arms, and without using force?"

"I don't know! Surreptitiously, furtively, stealth! But send a force to arrest them. They have brought in a big buffer and corrupted the evidence!

Jed Truly took all this in, and could see they would soon be in jail. "Sir," he said, "have you been looking for this buffer right here, that mysteriously disappeared some three days ago; and have you been looking for five people who just as mysteriously disappeared from off the face of the earth just three days ago?

"If you have, you need look no further. We are all standing right here before you."

The officer walked the dozen or so steps to stand before the five Christians. He saw a small girl., two big boys, and two grown men. He also saw the buffer. And he remembered that there had been a buffer that had disappeared. Now he looked again at the cord, still plugged in and taut, that ran to the center of the spotlessly polished floor and disappeared into the solid concrete floor. Next, he looked about twenty inches to the right and saw the very same cord emerge from the same solid concrete floor, to run up to the motor of the big buffer.

After observing this new evidence with some amazement, the officer looked up at little Alice. "What's your name," he asked.

"Alice," she replied.

"Do you go to school?" asked the officer.

"Yes. I go right here. I'm in the first grade." Alice replied brightly.

"Where have you been the last three days? Your mom and dad's been looking for you since last Thursday."

"Mom and Dad? Where are they? Are they here?"

"Yes, I think they are. They're probably in the prayer meeting. But I asked you a question, first. Where have you been the last three days?"

"I've been down there," Alice pointed down, "down there in the dark world!"

Now the officer switched his attention to the two boys. "What is your name?" He asked Bob.

"My name's Bob, and that's my brother, Bill. We're the Becker twins. And we're eighth graders here at the same school our sister goes to. And we've been in the Underworld, the Bright Regions, and the Foggy Bottoms.

"We've been there for about three days. God just now brought us up out of the Underworld in a whirlwind of fire, and set us down here where we now stand."

Now the officer looked over at John. "And you, who are you?"

"I'm John Frank, the maintenance man here at this school."

"Well, where have you been, and what have you been doing for the last three days?"

"I've been in the Underworld. Also in the Foggy Bottoms—preaching and testifying. All five of us have been preaching and testifying for the last three days!"

The officer just stared at John for a few moments, then finally shifted his attention to Jed. "And you, what is your name and where do you work?"

"My name is Jed Truly, and I teach Bible and Science here at Lynwood Christian Elementary School."

Suddenly, the wail of sirens split the afternoon stillness, and two squad cars pulled up a short distance from the basement, dining hall. Then a loud voice from a police bullhorn penetrated the dining hall area, "Throw down your weapons, and come out with your hands up!

You have three minutes to throw down your weapons, and come out with your hands up!"

"Stay here! Do not move!" said the officer. "I'm going out to tell them that they need not arrest you—that everything is OK. But you might have to answer more questions—if there are charges of criminal conduct against you by anyone from the Church or School." And the officer turned and fled up the stairs.

Chapter LXXXII
The Glad Reunion

The Pastor; the parents of Bob, Bill, and Alice; the wife and children of John Frank; and the wife and children of Jed Truly all poured down the stairs into the basement dining hall.

The Pastor led the way.

He had repented for his bitter attitude toward Jed Truly and John Frank. In the last business meeting of the Church, Jed Truly and John Frank had led the opposition to his proposal that the NIV be used as the preaching and teaching Bible of the Church instead of the KJV. And they had been successful in keeping his proposal from passing. He had taken it personally and had been bitter against them.

He now knew he had been wrong in his bitter attitude toward them. He saw now that his bitterness toward them amounted to hating them.

Now the Pastor literally ran to the five and embraced them one by one! Then he said, "I'm so glad to see you! But where have you been for the last three days?"

Then, before anyone could answer him, the wife and family of Jed Truly swept down upon him; John Frank's wife and children ran to him; and the mother and father of the Becker children ran to them. And, oh, what a glorious reunion they had! There was gladness, and joy in seeing each other again! And praise and thanksgiving to God— until the wives and parents and children began to ask the question, "Where have you been for the last three days?"

Alice pointed down to the floor, and said, "We've been down there in the dark world!"

Jed Truly said, "We've been in the Underworld, preaching the Word of God. We also went to the Foggy Bottoms to preach. We preached in two settlements there. Today we were back again in the Underworld, preaching there. And about 30 minutes ago God brought us back up here on this buffer, in a roaring whirlwind of fire."

John Frank saw the unbelief on the faces of all those present, and thought, "Unbelief is not unusual when it comes to the miraculous workings of God—Even the Christians who were praying for Peter, said to Rhoda, 'thou art mad' when she told them Peter was out of prison and standing at the gate—and I probably wouldn't believe Jed myself, if I hadn't been there with him!"

Then John Frank gave his own account: "Where have we been for the last three days? We've been in The Underworld. We've also been in the Foggy Bottoms—preaching and testifying. All five of us have been preaching and testifying in the Foggy Bottoms and in The Underworld!"

Bob Becker saw the unbelief also, and said, "For three days we've been in either The Underworld, the Bright Regions, or the Foggy Bottoms. We've preached and testified in both the Underworld and the Foggy Bottoms. My brother Bill and my sister Alice have preached and testified there also. We are not boasting; for we know it was God who took us there. And we know it was God who brought us up out of the Underworld in a roaring whirlwind of fire, and has set both us, and this buffer down right here where we now stand."

Bill Becker, who didn't always want to speak after his brother, wanted to speak now! He said, "It's true! Everything Brother Truly, Brother John, and my brother have said is true. And my little sister seems to have a powerful way with words. She knows when and how to speak for God. But she also knows when and how to act! Did you know that she kept Jed Truly from being murdered? She tackled the Little Man, who had his pistol aimed at Jed Truly, and she knocked him to the floor. Otherwise Jed Truly would not be with us today!"

Now all eyes were turned on Little Alice. But when Alice spoke she did not speak of what she had done in the Underworld. Her mind was on God, and she spoke of God's works in the Underworld.

Very slowly and solemnly she said, "God did miracles in the Foggy Bottoms—especially in the last settlement. And then, when we got back to the dark world, God did the greatest miracle of all. He brought us all back home in a great big whirlwind of fire." Alice paused for several moments; then said, "Mom, I want to be baptized in water! Jesus commanded us to be baptized in water as soon as we are saved. And I want to obey his command, and be baptized."

Alice's mother turned, with a questioning look to her Pastor.

He responded in a quiet, matter of fact voice, "Alice, I don't think we can baptize you now. We have a rule that we don't baptize children until they are at least twelve years old."

The Pastor had been looking with awe at the buffer and the taut cord going into the solid concrete floor, to come out again about twenty inches away and go up to the motor of the big buffer. The evidence was too great to look any longer with unbelief on the words the five Christians had spoken! Especially the simple, unaffected words of a seven year old child!

Now Jed truly spoke, "Pastor, don't you think that when a child is mature enough in the Lord to ask for water baptism, and to give the biblical reason why she ought to be baptized—that she is quite old enough to be baptized?"

The Pastor took one last look at the buffer. Then he looked up at Jed Truly and said, "You know Brother Truly, I think you're right. Alice is old enough! She knows she must be baptized because Christ commanded her to be baptized!" And turning with a smile to Alice, he said, "Alice, be ready. Because after the preaching tonight, I will baptize you as our Lord Jesus Christ commanded!"

www.ingramcontent.com/pod-product-compliance
Lightning Source LLC
Chambersburg PA
CBHW070012110426
42741CB00034B/1202